# PHILANTHROCAPITALISM

**ALSO BY MATTHEW BISHOP**

*Essential Economics*

# PHILANTHRO-CAPITALISM

## HOW THE RICH CAN SAVE THE WORLD

MATTHEW BISHOP & MICHAEL GREEN

BLOOMSBURY PRESS

*To our parents, Don and Dorothy, George and Esmé.*

Published by Bloomsbury Press, New York

Michael Green taught economics at Warsaw University in the early 1990s under a Soros-funded program. The views or opinions in this book are entirely his own and do not represent those of DFID, where he has worked for several years.

All papers used by Bloomsbury Press are natural, recyclable products made from wood grown in well-managed forests. The manufacturing processes conform to the environmental regulations of the country of origin.

LIBRARY OF CONGRESS CATALOGING-IN-PUBLICATION DATA

Bishop, Matthew, 1964–
Philanthrocapitalism : how the rich can save the world / Matthew Bishop and Michael F. Green.
    p.   cm.
ISBN-13: 978-1-59691-374-5
ISBN-10: 1-59691-374-6
1. Social responsibility of business.   2. Businesspeople—Conduct of life.
3. Philanthropists.   4. Humanitarianism.   I. Green, Michael F.   II. Title.

HD60.B52 2008
361.7—dc22
2008017880

First U.S. Edition 2008

1   3   5   7   9   10   8   6   4   2

Typeset by Westchester Book Group
Printed in the United States of America by Quebecor World Fairfield

# Contents

## CHAPTER 1

# The Age of Philanthrocapitalism

SHORTLY BEFORE LUNCHTIME ON JUNE 26, 2006, the then second-richest man in the world stepped onto a stage in the New York Public Library to be greeted by a standing ovation from several hundred of the wealthiest and most powerful people in the city. After saying a few words, Warren Buffett, whose record of brilliant investment decisions had earned him the nickname "Sage of Omaha," reached into his jacket pocket, took out a pen, and with a flourish began to sign five letters, each one promising a part of his fortune. "The first three letters are easy to sign. I just sign Dad," he joked, before handing a billion-dollar letter starting "Dear Suze" to his only daughter. The next letter he gave to his elder son; the third, to his second son; the fourth, to a representative of his late wife, Susan, who had died two years earlier.

So far, these letters had promised to give away a combined $6 billion or so. Finally, he held only the fifth letter, alone worth an estimated $31 billion. He signed it and handed it to the wife of the only man on the planet who was then richer than himself, Bill Gates, the cofounder of Microsoft, the world's biggest software firm. Then the two tycoons smiled and shook hands as the crowd cheered wildly.

Not one of these gifts was for the personal benefit of those accepting the letters. Buffett had long made it clear that his children should expect to receive far smaller sums for themselves in his will. Rather, each gift was for the charitable foundation that the grateful recipient had established. At a combined total estimated at $37 billion, Buffett's philanthropic donation was the largest ever. It beat even the $31 billion that

Gates had by then given to the foundation that bears his name and that of his wife (although Gates had already said that most of his remaining fortune—estimated at over $50 billion—would go the same beneficent way). By 2009, the Bill & Melinda Gates Foundation plans to give away over $3 billion of that endowment every year, unprecedented in the history of philanthropy.

Buffett and Gates are leading a revival and reinvention of an old tradition that has the potential to solve many of the biggest problems facing humanity today. Making the announcement in the New York Public Library was a deliberate nod to that tradition. The striking marble beaux arts building had been paid for more than a century before by a previous generation of great American philanthropists. But modern philanthropy was invented several centuries before that, in Europe, at the same time as the emergence of what we now call capitalism. The Buffetts and Gateses of this first golden age of philanthropy were the merchants of Tudor England and Renaissance Europe, who helped the poor in growing trading cities like London, Florence, and Bruges. Next, in the eighteenth century, philanthropy was embraced by the inventors of the joint stock company and the original hedge-fund-like speculators such as Thomas Guy, who sold at the top of the South Sea Bubble and used his profits to found Guy's Hospital in London. This was also the age of the enlightened financiers who backed crusading activists such as William Wilberforce, destroyer of the slave trade. In the nineteenth century, philanthropy became a way of life for Britain's newly wealthy Victorians, as reflected in the novels of Charles Dickens.

But the fortunes that Buffett and Gates are giving away dwarf those of the leading philanthropists of golden ages past, even those of Andrew Carnegie and John D. Rockefeller a century ago. Nor are Buffett and Gates, the leading examples of a fast-growing army of new philanthropists, merely doing the same old thing. The new philanthropists believe they are improving philanthropy, equipping it to tackle the new set of problems facing today's changing world; and to be blunt, it needs improvement—much philanthropy over the centuries has been ineffective. They think they can do a better job than their predecessors. The past couple of decades have been a golden age for capitalism, and today's new philanthropists are trying to apply the secrets behind that money-making success to their giving. That is why we call them philanthrocapitalists.

TODAY'S PHILANTHROCAPITALISTS SEE a world full of big problems that they, and perhaps only they, can and must put right. Surely, they say, we can save the lives of millions of children who die each year in poor countries from poverty or diseases that have been eradicated in the rich world. And back home in the United States or Europe, it is we who must find ways to make our education systems work for every child, instead of failing so many students. And if these children are to have a decent life when they grow older, we must find a solution to climate change and the underlying causes of terrorism. And so on.

As evidence of the seriousness of his philanthropy, Bill Gates had made a big announcement of his own a few days before Buffett handed out his letters. At the end of June 2008, he would leave his day job at Microsoft, which he had cofounded in 1975, and start working full time at his foundation—a significant career change for a man aged only fifty-two, still at the peak of his powers, and proof that when it comes to philanthropy, he means business.

Sitting in his huge office in Microsoft's Seattle headquarters in September 2007, Bill Gates rocks back and forth in his chair as he gets excited about what he is saying. "You know, if you picked the five most interesting and important things that have happened in my time frame, I think that these two would be in the top five, if not at the top," he says, now tapping his pen to the rhythm. "The personal computer, which I got a chance to participate in, has had this amazing, almost unbelievably great impact on billions of lives, so I'm very proud to be involved in that." But now he is looking to have at least as great an impact on at least as many lives through his philanthropy as he takes on some of the world's deadliest diseases. "Now I get to put more into what is sort of a new frontier—more like Microsoft at age three than at age thirty-three."

In business, the philanthrocapitalists are used to achieving success on a grand scale, to thinking big and going for it. If that approach works in making money, they reason, why wouldn't it work when it comes to giving the stuff away?

In the United States, Gates wants to transform the entire

government-funded public school system. Already, his money is starting to make a difference, and Gates believes this is just the beginning. In New York City, for example, Gates has provided money to start dozens of small schools, such as the Bronx Lab. One of four new schools sharing the former campus of the Evander Childs High School in one of New York's poorest areas, which was closed due to its persistently low levels of educational achievement, the Bronx Lab opened its doors in 2004. After three years, a remarkable 90 percent of its first class of students was on track to graduate in 2008, compared with a typical graduation rate of under 31 percent at Evander Childs. Gates thinks this sort of success can be repeated throughout the education system, in New York and nationwide.

But what gets Gates rocking and tapping even more excitedly are the things his philanthropy could achieve outside America by ending disease and reducing poverty. More than one million people die from malaria every year, most of them children in poor countries. That is the equivalent of losing every student in the New York public school system in one year. "We're sort of crazy enough to say, 'Let's eliminate malaria,'" says Gates. And it is not just malaria that is on his hit list. His foundation also wants to dramatically reduce deaths from other diseases that annually kill millions of people in the developing world, such as acute diarrhea, pneumonia, tuberculosis, and HIV/AIDS. And it is funding research into fourteen "grand challenges in global health," ranging from creating new vaccines to finding economically efficient ways to measure public health.

Gates is also giving hundreds of millions of dollars a year to accelerate economic development in poor countries. In 2006, he announced a partnership with one of the foundations created during an earlier golden age of philanthropy, the Rockefeller Foundation, to increase the productivity (and thus, income) of poor farmers in Africa. The Alliance for a Green Revolution in Africa aims to build on what many people believe is philanthropy's greatest ever success: the first "green revolution." Over many years the Rockefeller Foundation, guided by Norman Borlaug, funded research into how to increase crop yields in poor countries, which is reckoned to have saved over one billion lives since the 1940s. But most of those lives were in Asia, not Africa. As global food prices soar increasingly beyond the reach of the poor, Gates believes something just as dramatic can now be done about that.

None of this will be easy. Buffett admits that his gift amounts to only "one dollar each per year for the poorest half of the world population" and describes philanthropy as a "tougher game" than business. Gates concedes that "given the scale of the problems of global development, education, we will only be a small part of the solution." But there is no doubting their determination. Nor is it just the two richest men on the planet who are thinking such world-changing thoughts. The massive commitment of Gates and Buffett to philanthropy is the most dramatic evidence so far of a movement—philanthrocapitalism—that is growing hand in hand with the rise in the number of very rich people on the planet. Since the early 1980s, the world has enjoyed a remarkable period of prosperity that, whilst spread quite broadly, has benefited the people at the top of the pyramid considerably more than the rest of the population. According to *Forbes* magazine, in 2008 the world had a record 1,125 billionaires, up from a mere 140 in 1986, as well as thousands of multimillionaires.

Buffett and Gates were relatively slow to join the movement. In 1997, Ted Turner, the founder of the CNN cable news channel, made headlines by giving $1 billion to support the United Nations and criticizing his fellow tycoons for being tightfisted. He called specifically on Gates and Buffett—and other people "awash in money"—to "give the money away that you have no idea what you're going to do with."

It remains to be seen how many of today's newly wealthy will become serious philanthrocapitalists, but the omens seem good—not least because Buffett, Gates, and others are challenging the rest of the rich to join their movement. "There is a great question of all the wealth that has been created in this era," says Gates. As he throws down the philanthropic gauntlet to his fellow tycoons, he is optimistic. "This is a momentum thing; the more people that are involved, the more it draws other people in." "But what proportion of the new rich will ultimately start to give back? I think it'll be a high percentage," says Gates, "more like seventy percent than fifteen percent."

The annual Capgemini/Merrill Lynch *World Wealth Report* noted a 20 percent surge in giving by the rich in North America in 2006. This trend is not confined to America. "Led by the ranks of the ultra-wealthy, [high-net-worth individuals] are increasing the financial resources, time and thought they donate to philanthropic causes," concluded the report, which found that those wealthy individuals who engaged in philanthropy typically gave away around 7 percent of their wealth, far more than did the average citizen. "Veteran fund raisers say the outlook for giving is the most upbeat in a generation," reported the house journal of the American giving business, the *Chronicle of Philanthropy*, in 2006.

This impressive picture is reinforced by various rankings of philanthropists. Since 1997, online magazine Slate has been publishing its Slate 60 ranking of the largest philanthropic donations of the year. This was inspired by Turner's complaint that the rich are always measured in terms of what they own rather than what they give. ("I think that the culture towards philanthropy has changed," says Turner. "Why? Because we drew attention to it. We should have lists of givers, which is why I came up with the Slate 60. That is why rich people own sports teams—wealthy people like to get their name in the paper.") Since it began, the minimum gift needed to get on the list has tripled to $30 million.

A similar picture emerges from the fast-growing number of charitable foundations in America and abroad. New bequests, combined with strong investment returns on the endowments of older foundations, drove a doubling in real terms of American foundation giving from $13.8 billion in 1996 to $31.6 billion in 2006.

As THEY APPLY their business methods to philanthropy, philanthrocapitalists are developing a new (if familiar-sounding) language to describe their businesslike approach. Their philanthropy is "strategic," "market conscious," "impact oriented," "knowledge based," often "high engagement," and always driven by the goal of maximizing the "leverage" of the donor's money. Seeing themselves as social investors, not traditional donors, some of them engage in "venture philanthropy." As entrepreneurial "philanthropreneurs," they love to back social entrepreneurs who offer innovative solutions to society's problems. (Inevitably, some charity traditionalists dismiss all this as empty jargon.)

As well as seeking better ways to work with charitable nonprofit, nongovernmental organizations (NGOs), philanthrocapitalists are increasingly trying to find ways of harnessing the profit motive to achieve social good. This is controversial, to say the least: isn't philanthropy supposed to be about giving away money, not making more of it? But as the philanthrocapitalists see it, if they can use their donations to create a profitable solution to a social problem, it will attract far more capital, far faster, and thus achieve a far bigger impact, far sooner, than would a solution based entirely on giving money away. Thus, their money can lever, in a good cause, some of the trillions of dollars in the for-profit business world.

At the same time as individual philanthropists are embracing the profit motive, a growing number of big for-profit businesses are catching the philanthrocapitalism bug and getting into giving—or at least trying to do good. Gates sees this as potentially the start of a "system innovation" in how business operates, which he calls "creative capitalism."

This is very different from traditional corporate philanthropy, which has often been ineffective: giving away small sums of money typically to generate positive publicity rather than change the world. Nor is it like old-fashioned corporate social responsibility, which is too often nothing more than a cynical exercise in public relations. Indeed, the ineffectiveness of both these traditional approaches is one reason why many people view with skepticism the notion that large companies can be a force for good.

To prove the skeptics wrong, some of the world's biggest firms are now making advancing the good of society an integral part of their business strategy. Wal-Mart, for instance, is championing environmentalism, seeing it as a profit opportunity because it will both cut costs (of packaging, for example) and allow the retailer to sell new products (long-lasting low-energy lightbulbs). Oil giant Shell is redeeming its reputation by helping to develop small businesses in Africa on the basis that job creation is the only sustainable strategy for ending poverty.

Arguably the most innovative firm of all is Google. When the Internet search and advertising company first sold shares to the public in 2004, it promised to give 1 percent of its shares, 1 percent of its profits, and 1 percent of its employees' time to Google.org, which the firm's thirtysomething founders, Sergey Brin and Larry Page, hope will one day "eclipse Google itself in overall world impact by ambitiously applying innovation and significant resources to the largest of the world's problems." Given the impact achieved already by Google.com, that would be something to behold.

The test of these fine words will be whether rich philanthropists and companies can walk the walk as well as they talk the talk. The road to hell is paved with good intentions. And the problems they are addressing are highly complex. Will they have the humility to listen to others who have been grappling with these problems for far longer? Will they be willing to learn from their mistakes? Will they stick at it when the going gets tough, as it surely will?

A FEW MILES from the proliferating skyscrapers of Bangalore, the center of India's booming high-tech business-process outsourcing industry, is a camp.of metal huts housing the families of laborers who have come from far-off villages to work on the city's many construction sites. A bright yellow bus stops in the dirt square, and immediately it is surrounded by about thirty children, aged four to ten. Once on board, they sit—three per screen—by computers where specially developed software teaches them language and mathematical skills. The children are clearly comfortable with the computers, absorbed in their learning.

The bus is provided by the Azim Premji Foundation, which is headquartered next to the modern campus of the Indian tech firm Wipro. The company's boss, who established the eponymous foundation in 2001, was the sixtieth-richest person on earth in 2008, according to *Forbes*, with an estimated fortune of $12.7 billion. "A more educated child is very critical for democracy," Premji says, worrying that India's population is growing dangerously fast. "If a girl is educated up to level five or six, she is aware of the need for a smaller family. A little basic education improves knowledge of primary health care."

Just as globalization has been one of the driving forces of the current golden age of capitalism, so the idea that the wealthy winners should engage seriously in philanthropy has gone global. Even ten years ago it was easy to regard large-scale philanthropy as a U.S. exception to the global consensus that the state, not private giving, offers the best solutions to society's biggest problems. Today philanthropy is booming everywhere there is entrepreneurial wealth creation. In 2007, the then third-richest man in the world announced he would give away $10 billion through his foundation. He was not from the United States, but from Mexico: telecommunications boss Carlos Slim Helú.

SHAKIRA'S HIPS DON'T lie—and Bill Clinton can't keep his eyes off them. Nor, to be fair, can most of the audience, a strange mix of students, social activists, and billionaires, in the legendary Apollo Theater in Harlem. This particular evening, in September 2007, the Colombian pop star is singing her latest hit, "Hips Don't Lie," at a debate-cum-party, screened live on MTV, at the end of the annual meeting of the Clinton Global Initiative (CGI). Since the former president, now as much a celebrity as a politician, first held this annual giving fest in 2005, it has become a must-attend event for philanthrocapitalists eager for recognition at what the *Economist* has christened "the Philanthropy Oscars."

At least since the Live Aid concert in 1985, celebrities and philanthropy have become ever more entwined. Now, movie and rock star "celanthropists" are serious partners with the superrich. Rock star and activist Bono and Bill Gates—who, with Melinda Gates were named *Time* magazine's "People of the Year" in 2005—have "had a common cause" ever since their first meeting in New York in 2002, says Gates: "He's been great." Some celebrities are even superrich philanthropists in their own right. Oprah Winfrey, for example, the billionaire television host and producer, has paid for a school in Africa and also works in partnership with the Gates Foundation.

This makes some people uneasy. What does a rock star really know about the poor in Africa? Yet just as celebrities are now an integral part of capitalism, due to their ability to touch and influence the mass market, so too they are becoming a key ingredient of philanthrocapitalism, particularly on issues in which mobilizing public opinion is crucial.

WHEN RICH PEOPLE get involved in what are essentially political issues, it is easy for everyone else to fear the worst. Today's democratic freedoms have been hard-won; voters do not want to trade their rights for plutocracy. "For traditional-minded Americans, George Soros is public enemy number one," thunders TV pundit Bill O'Reilly in *Culture Warrior*, his 2006 bestseller. "We ignore him at our peril." A financier who has given away billions to promote democracy around the world, Soros has provoked conservatives like O'Reilly by backing liberal causes in America. Yet, even for those who would support Soros's goals, his philanthropy can raise troubling questions, such as why should the rich determine society's priorities?

Many people are also suspicious of how the rich made their money, and mistrust them accordingly. Gates and Soros have both been accused of exploitation, whether through monopoly or financial market manipulation. Questions about the source of wealth can seem even more pertinent when the philanthropist is, say, a Russian oligarch who stands accused of stealing assets from the public.

If philanthrocapitalists are to be a legitimate part of the solution to the world's problems, a new "social contract" is needed to spell out what it means to be a good billionaire, in terms of how much is given and in what way, how much tax is paid, whether the money has been made in a legitimate way, and what the rich can expect from everyone else in return. Soros, for one, believes the public should hold philanthropists to account. "I always tell people who question my motives that they are right to do so. When I claim to be disinterested, the burden of proof is on me." He says that it is "very important to have transparency as the basis on which a judgment can be made." The onus in the social contract should be on the rich to be transparent and accountable. If not, they run the risk of being forced to do so by government regulation.

Given the difficulties presented by the rise of philanthrocapitalism, wouldn't it be better to simply tax the rich more heavily and let governments solve the world's problems? For much of history, it has been possible to see the state and philanthropy as alternatives. The previous golden ages of philanthropy each ended with the state significantly increasing its role in areas where philanthropists had tried to find solutions, such as educating the poor. In some cases, the state stepped in with alternative approaches; in others, the state took successful philanthropic ideas to a much larger scale.

But it is the state that has been retreating over the past thirty years. Today, it looks unlikely that big government will return. A government's ability to raise taxes is constrained, not least by the need to generate economic growth, which means attracting investment and wealthy residents who are increasingly globally mobile. In rich countries, aging populations are likely to only intensify the pressures on the state. In poorer countries, governments are struggling to meet the challenges of accelerating economic development and of public health, not least diseases such as malaria and HIV/AIDS. At the same time, genuinely new global challenges have emerged, from climate change to international nonstate terrorism, that existing multilateral governance organizations, such as the United Nations, struggle to address. In these circumstances, no wonder governments, of both right and left, seem increasingly keen for wealthy individuals to give them a helping hand. Even so, if the rich do not take on this responsibility, they risk provoking the public into a political backlash against the economic system that allowed them to become so wealthy.

---

## HOW TO GIVE MONEY AWAY

Most people, when their philanthropy goes beyond dropping some coins in a collection tin or sponsoring a friend to run the London marathon dressed as Daffy Duck, make a cash donation to their chosen charity (on a regular basis please, the charity hopes). In America, most donors will claim a tax benefit for that gift in their annual income tax return.

The impact of such giving might be increased by joining a "giving circle." These allow money to be pooled and donors to work in partnership, give larger amounts, and so have a greater say in how the organization uses the money.

For those with a large sum to give away, there are other options that can maximize the tax benefits (which vary significantly from country to country), and more important, the value of the gift. Putting philanthropic capital into what is called a foundation in the United States, and a charitable trust in the United Kingdom, earns a tax benefit for the whole donation. Some people give to the foundation as its need for the money arises, others endow the foundation up front with a large sum of money that can be given away over many years. Investment income earned on the endowment in future years is also typically exempt from tax.

For the seriously wealthy, a foundation can be run out of a family office, along with their other financial affairs, or independently staffed with philanthropy professionals (so-called philanthropoids or philanthrocrats). Most foundations limit themselves to giving out money to support the work of other organizations (charities and other NGOs, hospitals, and so forth), and in the best cases, monitoring how the money is used. But a few choose to run their own projects and programs. These are known as operating foundations.

Running a foundation costs money (someone has to select the recipients and manage the grants). One cut-price way of getting the tax advantages of a foundation in America is to give to a donor-advised fund, typically managed by a financial services company.

An alternative is to give to a community foundation. These were first created in America in 1914 to provide an easy way for donors to give to good causes, typically in the area where they live or grew up. There are now around 1,400 worldwide, around half of them outside America.

In short, a new division of labor is needed between governments, businesses, charitable NGOs, and philanthropists. Philanthrocapitalists can play a key role in this—certainly a far greater role than their relatively limited financial resources might suggest. (Even the billions that Gates is giving away pale in comparison to most government budgets.) This is not to underplay the importance of the changes taking place within governments, businesses, or NGOs, nor the role that every individual citizen can play. Bono may be right to claim that "as great as some of the philanthropists in your book are, the real change comes through social movements." Yet when he wanted to start DATA, a professional organization to drive forward a social movement to reduce the debt burden and increase aid and trade to help some of the poorest people on the planet, it was to philanthropists such as Gates and Soros that he turned for money and advice. Nor is Bono's experience particularly unusual. Over the centuries, behind many a great social movement there has been a wealthy philanthropist.

Philanthrocapitalists are "hyperagents" who have the capacity to do some essential things far better than anyone else. They do not face elections every few years, like politicians, or suffer the tyranny of shareholder demands for ever-increasing quarterly profits, like CEOs of most public companies. Nor do they have to devote vast amounts of time and resources to raising money, like most heads of NGOs. That frees them to think long-term, to go against conventional wisdom, to take up ideas too risky for government, to deploy substantial resources quickly when the situation demands it—above all, to try something new. The big question is, will they be able to achieve their potential?

## CHAPTER 2

# Carnegie's Children

"THE PROBLEM OF OUR AGE IS THE proper administration of wealth, that the ties of brotherhood may still bind together the rich and poor in harmonious relationship." So wrote Andrew Carnegie in his essay "Wealth," which first appeared in the *North American Review* in 1889. Published today as the book *The Gospel of Wealth*, it is practically holy scripture for many of today's philanthrocapitalists. Long before Warren Buffett gave his money to Bill Gates, he gave Gates a copy of Carnegie's text, and so helped inspire him to become a philanthropist. Scottish investor Sir Tom Hunter, who is leading the philanthropy revival in Britain, was similarly inspired. Chuck Feeney, an Irish American billionaire known as the "anonymous donor" because of his highly secretive philanthropy, presented copies of Carnegie's essay to his children to explain why he had decided to give away most of their inheritance.

In the early twenty-first century, as inequality widens, social and environmental challenges proliferate, and friction grows between rich and poor, the proper administration of wealth is again the problem of the age. Carnegie's approach to that problem is hugely appealing to the successful entrepreneurs who are embracing philanthropy today: that the solution is in their hands.

Carnegie proposed a third way for the rich to dispose of their surplus wealth, as an alternative to leaving it to their descendants or bequeathing it to the state for public works. A better option, he said, is to give it away during their lives. Leaving one's fortune to one's children was often a mistake, with bad consequences for the inheritors: witness the dysfunctional landed classes of old Europe. And leaving the money to the state meant missing the opportunity to put one's own superior talents to work for the public good. Besides, it could lead people to suppose that the bequest came from the sort of man "who would not have left it at all, had they been able to take it with them." Carnegie favored heavy death taxes as a mark of the state's "condemnation of the selfish millionaire's unworthy life."

In common with many of today's philanthrocapitalists, Carnegie was anything but a bleeding-heart do-gooder: he believed that 95 percent of charity was "unwisely spent" and "indiscriminate," encouraging "the slothful, the drunken, the unworthy." That was because the givers were too often driven by gratifying their own feelings or avoiding annoyance. Instead, the rich who had prospered as a result of their organizational and managerial talents should deploy these abilities with the primary goal being "to help those who will help themselves." The philanthropist, Carnegie said, should "assist, but rarely or never do all." That is music to the ears of today's philanthrocapitalists, who are determined to apply their business talents to their giving, convinced wealth creation offers the best route out of poverty, skeptical about the value of much traditional charity, and keen to provide the needy, as they like to put it, with "a hand up not a handout."

Like today's entrepreneurs, Carnegie reveled in the "inventions of this scientific age," which, in his case, enabled him to become the leading producer of low-cost steel for the railroad and build what was then the largest, most profitable company on earth. The pace of innovation in his day was so rapid that within a generation, he wrote, "luxuries have become the necessaries of life." This had benefited everybody, but, he conceded, the rich a great deal more, and sooner, than the masses.

The inequality, he argued, was the inevitable result of the laws of accumulation and distribution. These rewarded a "talent for organization and management" rare among men with "more revenue than can be judiciously expended upon themselves." This view—though probably not his enthusiasm for philanthropy—derived from his social Darwinism. Carnegie was heavily influenced by the English thinker Herbert Spencer, who coined the phrase "survival of the fittest," and he believed that inequality was the unavoidable price of the rapid economic growth that benefited everyone. Today, Carnegie would be called a believer in trickledown economics. As he argued, it is "much better this great irregularity than universal squalor."

Carnegie saw philanthropy as an answer to the social problems created by a spurt in wealth creation, but he also regarded that boom in wealth as an unambiguous blessing. Popular political alternatives to capitalism such as socialism or anarchy, he thought, would be "disastrous" for everyone, "attacking the foundation upon which civilization itself rests." Instead, the rich should regard their surplus wealth "as the property of the many" and themselves as trustees whose duty is to administer it "for the common good." The rich, he argued, "have it in their power during their lives to busy themselves in organizing benefactions from which the masses of their fellows will derive lasting advantage—and thus dignify their own lives." This is a rallying cry to which a growing number of today's newly wealthy are responding with enthusiasm.

IN THE PAST quarter century, the global economy has enjoyed a similar, perhaps greater period of wealth creation than that in which Carnegie made his fortune. Since the early 1980s, capitalism has been extraordinarily productive. Average incomes almost everywhere have reached record levels, and the quality and range of goods and services that people can afford to buy with that income are also far greater

The value of shares in the world's stock markets—one of the main sources of wealth, and for many of us, future retirement income—has soared since 1982, even after the occasional crash along the way. According to Morgan Stanley Capital International, the total value of publicly traded shares worldwide at the end of 2007 was $32.2 trillion, up from $13.2 trillion in 1997 and $4.1 trillion in 1987. The American economy, the world's largest, has experienced a so-called productivity miracle, whilst the spread and deepening of globalization has turned once poor countries into economic tigers. Since 1995, developing countries, led by China and India, have grown faster than at any time since the 1960s, lifting hundreds of millions of people out of poverty. This is truly a golden age of global economic growth—and one that, despite the capital market crash of 2007 and its economic aftermath, could continue for many years.

As Carnegie might not be surprised to learn, this strong economic growth has come at a price. Whilst, overall, financial innovation has driven faster growth, some of the inevitable failures that accompany it have hit the people least able to cope. For instance, in 2007, new financial products related to subprime mortgages in America suffered huge losses, paralyzing the global financial system and causing problems for millions of home owners.

For several decades in the mid-twentieth century, inequality between individuals and between nations seemed in inevitable decline. Today, the gap between rich and poor is, in some respects, widening again, even as the great majority of the world's population is becoming better off. This is particularly true at the very top of the wealth ladder, as a new generation of successful entrepreneurs profits from a remarkable array of new opportunities for wealth creation.

The acceleration of globalization since the Second World War, as trade barriers have been gradually (often controversially) dismantled, has affected most industries, enabling more efficient companies to increase their growth rate—offering their goods and services to, say, billions of customers rather than mere hundreds of millions. (Global trade as a proportion of global gross domestic product has risen from 24 percent in 1960 to over 50 percent in 2007.) If a company can reach global scale, and fast, so can the fortunes of its owners. Sectors such as information technology and financial services have grown far faster than the economy as a whole, driven by waves of innovation that have made a group of entrepreneurial businesspeople fabulously rich.

Vibrant stock markets have made it easier for founders of companies to turn their paper fortunes into hard cash at an early age by selling shares; this is how Bill Gates and Google founders Sergey Brin and Larry Page became billionaires in their early thirties. Earlier generations of tycoons took far longer to accumulate vast fortunes. Carnegie eventually cashed out by selling his biggest business, U.S. Steel, to John Pierpont Morgan—but that was in 1901, when he was sixty-six years old.

The emergence of genuinely global firms has brought with it equally large-scale share-based remuneration for those hired to run them. As Robert F. Frank and Philip Cook observe in their 1996 book, *The Winner-Take-All Society*, new technology, globalization, and market economics have changed the structure of many industries in such a way that their star performers now earn vastly more than the average performer. As they explain, these are markets where "the value of what gets produced in them often depends on the efforts of only a small number of top performers, who are paid accordingly."

A booming world economy combined with winner-take-all markets has resulted in an increase in the number of billionaires that might have shocked even Carnegie. In 2008, *Forbes* magazine's annual survey of the richest people in the world listed 1,125 billionaires, up from 946 a year earlier—and more than twice the total in 2003. When *Forbes* first entered the rich-list business in 1982 with an annual ranking of America's 400 wealthiest families, the threshold for inclusion was a net worth of $90 million. In 2006, for the first time, all 400 on the list were billionaires.

If anything, the *Forbes* lists understate the pace of change. Shifting to mere millionaires, in 2007 the annual Capgemini/Merrill Lynch *World Wealth Report* found that the number of ultrarich people, with at least $30 million in financial assets, had risen to a record 94,970 worldwide, up from around 70,000 in 2003. As Robert Frank (no relation to *The Winner-Take-All Society* co-author) writes in *Richistan*, his 2007 book about America's new wealthy, for several decades before the late 1980s "new fortunes were rare." But since then, thousands of people have built fortunes of $100 million or more. "Most made their money by starting their own companies and selling them," concludes Frank, before noting that "CEOs and money managers (especially hedge funders) are rapidly joining the ranks."

This pattern is now being mirrored outside America. Across the pond, for example, "the scales of wealth today . . . simply dwarf the levels found in the past by the probate statistics, even allowing for inflation," says William D. Rubinstein, author of *Men of Property*, the definitive study of wealth in Britain over the past two hundred years. Looking at a shorter time frame, Philip Beresford, who has produced Britain's *Sunday Times* Rich List since 1989, reported in 2007 that the past decade had been "a golden age for the rich, rarely seen in modern British history."

The number of billionaires on Beresford's list has shot up in recent years, in part because he includes noncitizens who live in the U.K. In 2007, the two richest "Britons" were the Indian steel magnate Lakshmi Mittal (£19.25 billion) and the Russian oligarch and Chelsea soccer club owner Roman Abramovich (£10.8 billion). This reflects not just the quality of life (and favorable tax treatment) in London but also the rise of the billionaire from emerging markets.

The table shows the number and percentage of billionaires on the *Forbes* list from a selection of countries. The United States dominates, but Russia has overtaken Germany as the billionaire factory of Europe,

## *Forbes* List Billionaires by Country in 2008

| COUNTRY | NUMBER OF BILLIONAIRES (2008) | PERCENTAGE OF FORBES BILLIONAIRES |
|---|---|---|
| United States | 444 | 39.5 |
| Russia | 87 | 7.7 |
| Germany | 59 | 5.2 |
| India | 53 | 4.7 |
| China | 42 | 3.7 |
| U.K. | 35 | 3.1 |
| Turkey | 35 | 3.1 |
| Canada | 25 | 2.2 |
| Japan | 24 | 2.1 |
| France | 14 | 1.2 |
| South Korea | 12 | 1.1 |

SOURCE: *Forbes*; authors' calculations.

and India and China have overtaken Japan in Asia. Among the emerging economies, Turkey now has as many billionaires as the U.K. and the superrich in South Korea are fast catching up with the French.

THE GAP BETWEEN the superrich and average people is certainly widening. For instance, since 1980, the top 1 percent of U.S. earners have doubled their share of all income, the top 0.1 percent have tripled their share, and the top 0.01 percent have quadrupled their share—the richer you are, the richer you get. Put another way, the share of national income going to the top 0.01 percent of households, some 270,000 people, rose from 0.7 percent in 1980 to almost 3 percent in 2000—the same as it was in 1929. It has continued to increase since. The same trends are occurring in the distribution of wealth. From 1979 to 2004, the percentage of America's wealth controlled by the top 1 percent of earners increased from 20 to 34 percent.

Even those who believe that globalization delivers huge benefits to rich and poor countries alike increasingly worry that it may be brought down by inequality. An article in the July-August 2007 *Foreign Affairs* titled "A New Deal for Globalization," argues for a reform that "links engagement with the global economy to a substantial redistribution of income." Proposing that America should adopt a "fundamentally more progressive federal tax system," the article claims that the "notion of more aggressively redistributing income may sound radical, but ensuring that most American workers are benefiting is the best way of saving globalization from a protectionist backlash."

These proposals are not the work of rabid big-government lefties. One of the article's authors, Matthew J. Slaughter, had just stepped down from President George W. Bush's Council of Economic Advisers. Many of the superrich themselves share these fears. Witness the tycoons, including Buffett, Turner, and Soros, who in 2001 joined the unsuccessful campaign against President Bush's plan to scrap estate taxes (or "death taxes," as the Republicans called them), which would overwhelmingly benefit the rich. This included a petition claiming that "repeal of the estate tax would be bad for our democracy, our economy and our society." Carnegie, the original rich advocate of estate taxes, would have approved.

Fears about rising inequality are also high on the agenda in the developing world, where the political system may be less well equipped to ease the tensions, and so the absolute difference between the lives of the starving, the uneducated poor, and the superrich may mean that inequality is more politically dangerous. President Hu Jintao of China has been stressing the need for a "harmonious society," which will require a focus on tackling inequality and bringing citizens closer together.

In May 2007, India's prime minister, Manmohan Singh, gave a speech urging business leaders to adopt a ten-point "social charter" to ensure that economic growth "is more equitable and empowers the most deprived of our citizens." The electronic media, said Singh, "carries the lifestyles of the rich and famous into every village and every slum. Media often highlights the vulgar display of their wealth. An area of great concern is the level of ostentatious expenditure on weddings and other family events. Such vulgarity insults the poverty of the less privileged. It is socially wasteful and it plants seeds of resentment in the minds of the have-nots."

Journalist Matt Miller claims, controversially, that concerns about inequality are not primarily about rich and poor—the tension may be most intense at the top of the wealth ladder. "America's income gap is arguably less likely to spark a retro fight between proletarians and capitalists than a war between what I call the 'lower upper class' and the ultrarich," he wrote in *Fortune* in October 2006. "Economic resentment at the bottom of the top 1 percent of America's income distribution is the new wild card in public life. Ordinary workers won't rise up against ultras because they take it as given that "the rich get richer." But the hopes and dreams of today's educated class are based on the idea that market capitalism is a meritocracy. The unreachable success of the superrich shreds those dreams."

"Richistan"—which is itself divided into upper, middle, and lower Richistan—is Robert Frank's name for the separate country that he believes the rich are building (especially in America, but also elsewhere), with its own health, education, and shopping and leisure infrastructure, entirely divorced from the masses; Carnegie would certainly have recognized this lack of interaction between rich and poor.

In his 2008 bestseller, *Superclass*, David Rothkopf argues that the growing distance between a global elite and everyone else is not sustainable. "History is the story of a negotiation between the rich and powerful and the less fortunate but still dangerous: a bargaining over the price that must be paid for stability." He offers no solutions, just questions. "Who will make the first moves for change this time? What form will they take?" The leading beneficiaries of the winner-take-all society worry increasingly about the political risks inherent in growing inequality. They, like Carnegie before them, are concluding that philanthropy may be one of the best ways to manage those risks.

THE REVIVAL OF interest in Carnegie's ideas reflects the dramatic social and economic changes of the past thirty years. By the middle of the twentieth century, the world had come to see the state, not the generosity of the rich, as the means to solve the biggest problems facing society; *The Gospel of Wealth* seemed obsolete, and philanthropy an anachronism. Even in America, where there was the least enthusiasm for big government, the 1932 election of Franklin Delano Roosevelt, whose New Deal marked the creation of the U.S. welfare state, meant that state aid for the unemployed should be provided "not as a matter of charity, but as a matter of social duty." Henceforth, philanthropy was to be relegated to an important but secondary role, mostly in education, research, and the arts. Elsewhere, the rejection of philanthropy was even more extreme. By 1948, as the postwar British Labour government took control of much of what had been in the domain of philanthropy, it was reported that 90 percent of the population thought there was no longer any need for charity.

Taking the long view, however, it is the mid-twentieth-century disdain for philanthropy that is the exception to the historical rule. Since the birth of modern capitalism in Europe during the Middle Ages, rich businesspeople have consistently played a leading role in solving the big social problems of their day, often adapting the innovations of capitalism to make their philanthropy more effective. Indeed, to go further, it seems to be a feature of capitalism that golden ages of wealth creation give rise to golden ages of giving. Today's generation of philanthrocapitalists are heirs to a long tradition. Many people, especially in America, regard Carnegie's time as *the* golden age of philanthropy. In fact, there have been four golden ages, the first three in Europe. It is the fifth golden age that is now dawning.

Each past boom in giving was associated with massive wealth creation linked to innovation in business, and also to social upheaval that left big problems to solve. Often this was accompanied by political unrest that seemed to threaten capitalism, adding urgency to the need for a philanthropic response. Whilst it was not every newly rich person who engaged in philanthropy, many of those who had driven and benefited from the surge in wealth creation felt a responsibility to use some of their resources to address the big social problems of the day. Just as in business their success was often the fruit of an entrepreneurial talent for "thinking outside the box" and seeing the potential of applying new ideas, so in their philanthropy they brought a fresh, sometimes controversial approach.

Even in ancient societies, the rich were expected to give (see "Ancient Philanthropy" box), but the first flowering of the sort of modern philanthropy that thoughtfully seeks lasting solutions to social problems, rather than merely eases their symptoms, came with the birth of capitalism during the Renaissance. In merchant cities, traders and business families began to expand their fortunes and free themselves from interference from kings and princes on the one hand and the church authorities on the other.

Into these cities flooded the poor, the product of a surge in population as Europe finally recovered from the Black Death, a pandemic that from 1347 to 1450 killed around one third of the population of Europe. In England, the problem was made worse as peasants were driven from their traditional land and out of the welfare protection of their feudal lords. The newly rich merchants responded with a dramatic outpouring of generosity. In London alone, the resources devoted to charity soared by 50 percent in real terms between 1573 and 1597.

It was not only the scale of the giving by these merchants that was remarkable but also the way they gave. Renaissance philanthropists abandoned the medieval giving of alms to the poor and engaged instead in giving that sought to genuinely change lives. Inspired by humanist thinkers such as the social reformer Juan Luis Vives, a Spanish follower of Erasmus, they started looking for solutions to social problems, not

---

## ANCIENT PHILANTHROPY

The history of philanthropy would be a short one indeed had all philanthropists been rewarded like the first, Prometheus. According to Greek mythology, the titan was chained to a mountain and his liver was eaten by an eagle, as punishment from Zeus for his *philanthrōpos* of stealing fire from the gods on Mount Olympus to give to mankind.

While *philanthrōpos* (love for humanity) is the root of the term "philanthropy," the purpose of ancient philanthropy was very different from that of today. Aristotle saw philanthropy as the way that the rich should serve the state, not humanity. Slaves, indeed anyone who was not a citizen, were not the intended beneficiaries of the generosity of the haves in the ancient world, although they were probably the group in the most need. Instead, giving was focused on things such as sponsoring sporting and artistic events that would bring glory on the donor and benefit to citizenry.

Take the Roman general Marcus Vipsanius Agrippa, for example. As Cullen Murphy describes in his 2007 book *Are We Rome?*, "In a single year, [he] repaired many of the public buildings in Rome, put statues in the public baths, distributed salt and olive oil to the masses, paid barbers to give everyone haircuts, and after cleaning out Rome's great sewers sailed a small boat through their main channel, the Cloaca Maxima, and out into the Tiber." Giving was an integral part of Greek and Roman society, but donors in the ancient world would have been mystified by

palliatives: social housing, education, working capital for apprentices to start businesses. They also began the practice of endowing a foundation, or charitable trust, with enough capital to provide a stream of income to spend on good causes in perpetuity.

Such was the vibrancy of this philanthropy that, throughout the sixteenth century, private giving in England remained the main source of relief for the poor; so important had charity become that in 1601 the English Parliament passed the world's first legislation to regulate giving, the Charitable Uses Act, which remains the core of British charity law. But the speed of demographic and economic change meant that social problems grew faster than the donors could cope with, and in the same year, Parliament created the world's first national welfare scheme, paid for through taxation, known as the Poor Law.

Carnegie's talk of "brotherhood" between rich and poor as the basis of social harmony.

Christianity shook up this Greco-Roman civic view of philanthropy, basing its approach instead on a universal value of "charity" or "love" (agapē in Greek). Like the Good Samaritan, a Christian was obliged to provide help to any person in need, not just a fellow citizen. Philanthropy was evolving from munificence to beneficence. With the adoption of Christianity by the Roman Empire, the church established itself as the primary channel for assistance to the poor. As early as the Council of Nicea in 325, the church agreed that bishops should take responsibility for running hospitals in every cathedral city of the empire.

Whatever the ideals of the early church, philanthropy in the Middle Ages was almost as far removed from Carnegie's vision as was that in the ancient world. "The Christian doctrine of poverty had little to do with social reality" says Bronislaw Geremek, a medieval historian. "Poverty was treated as a purely spiritual value." Gifts to the church by the rich during this period were usually bequests to pay for prayers for the deceased to ease their way into the next world, not to alleviate the suffering of the poor on earth.

It was only with the rise of secular power in the hands of the new capitalist classes that philanthropy became a question of the administration of wealth.

Yet it was not competition from the state that brought the first golden age of philanthropy to an end. Rather, it was the series of religious and civil wars that devastated Europe in the seventeenth century that set back the development of capitalism, and with it, philanthropy.

The second golden age of philanthropy followed the return of peace, stability, and economic growth at the start of the eighteenth century. The merchant classes could get back to making money. In the coffeehouses of London, a new financial capitalism blossomed, with increasingly sophisticated trading of securities and a big idea: the invention of the joint stock company.

Not only did the success of the joint stock company make many people wealthier, so increasing the capital available for philanthropy, it also inspired a new way of giving, in which philanthropists pooled their resources to meet urgent social needs. The most popular object of this "joint stock philanthropy" was the collection of subscriptions to fund hospitals. Westminster (1719), St. George's (1733), Winchester (1736), London (1740), and Middlesex (1746) were each funded by subscriptions—typically large sums of money that could be afforded only by the seriously rich. Later in the century, subscriptions were used by Evangelical Christians to finance William Wilberforce's campaign against the slave trade.

As well as being a time of religious revival, this was also one of humanity's greatest periods of intellectual endeavor, as men looked to reason in order to explore their world, including the study of the causes of social problems. The "British Enlightenment" was, according to the historian Gertrude Himmelfarb, an inspiration for this "age of benevolence." But British empiricism also helped foster a growing skepticism about philanthropy. The economist David Ricardo argued that handouts to the poor pushed up the wages at which people were willing to work, and so increased unemployment. By saving today's poor from hunger, charity was only perpetuating or worsening the problem by ensuring there would be more mouths to feed tomorrow, argued the Reverend Thomas Malthus in his 1798 "Essay on the Principle of Population," in which he predicted that demand for food would outstrip supply as the population continued to grow.

Although neither critique stood the test of time particularly well, Malthus and Ricardo shook the confidence of philanthropists in the rectitude of what they were doing, helping to bring the second golden age of philanthropy to an end with a whimper.

It is perhaps surprising, then, that philanthropy recovered so quickly in the Victorian era. A major impetus for the third golden age of philanthropy was the social upheaval caused by industrialization on a scale unprecedented in the history of capitalism. The small workshops that had been the driving force of the early industrial revolution were now replaced by massive factories in burgeoning new cities in the north of England, which became centers of so much death and disease that the *Cambridge Urban History of Britain* describes the 1830s and 1840s as probably the "worst ever decades for life expectancy since the Black Death." In 1842 the average age at death of a laborer in Bethnal Green in East London was just sixteen years.

The demand for action was immense, and a new generation of philanthropists stepped forward to meet it from a new class of wealthy men. While landowners were to retain a firm foothold on the nineteenth-century "rich list," by 1840 about 40 percent of the millionaires in England had made their money from industry rather than land. Philanthropy boomed among these entrepreneurs. By the mid-1880s, the *Times* of London claimed that the income of the city's charities was greater than the governments of some European countries, "exceeding the revenue of Sweden, Denmark and Portugal, and double that of the Swiss confederation."

Charles Dickens, who worked as an adviser on philanthropy to one of the wealthiest donors of his day, produced probably the best descriptions of the complexity and contradictions of Victorian philanthropy. His novels should be required reading for today's rich. Anyone tempted to dismiss philanthropy with a "Bah! Humbug!" should probably start with *A Christmas Carol*. Others should turn to his more complicated tales of an age in which enormous need produced a response from many rich people that, whilst determined and sometimes effective, was often inadequate.

Some of Dickens's characters play a positive role, such as Mr. Brownlow, who adopts Oliver Twist, and the Cheeryble brothers, who give Nicholas Nickleby a job. But philanthropists also come in for some caustic ridicule in his later works. Mrs. Jellyby and Mrs. Pardiggle in *Bleak House* are, respectively, guilty of "telescopic philanthropy" and "rapacious benevolence," neither of them helping to save the life of the child Jo, who dies of pneumonia. In his final, unfinished novel, *The Mystery of Edwin Drood*, Dickens ridiculed a selfish, paternalist attitude to philanthropy that, even today, colors our perception of the Victorians, taking a direct swipe at the leading philanthropic body of the time, the Charity Organisation Society (COS)—or as critics of its judgmental approach to the poor dubbed it, "Cringe or Starve."

No group of rich people has given more, proportionately, to improve the lot of their fellow humans than the Victorians. (Continental Europe also had a philanthropy boom, from the last decades of the nineteenth century until the First World War.) Yet they found themselves increasingly swamped by the scale of the social problems. For example, the Ragged Schools movement, which provided free education to the poor, at its zenith numbered only 192 schools, not nearly enough to educate millions of future voters and workers. New reformers made the economic and social case for the state to provide universal welfare, although many Victorian charities resisted. The COS, in particular, fought to keep the government out of the business of helping the poor, which it argued was best done by philanthropy.

Yet government was increasingly persuaded that poverty and inequality posed a threat and that state-led universal welfare was the only way of buying off the working classes to defeat the revolutionary appeal of the growing socialist movement. Following in the footsteps of Germany's autocratic leader Otto von Bismarck, who had piloted social insurance in the 1880s, Britain opted in the 1909 "People's Budget" for state welfare funded by higher taxation.

Philanthropy in Britain was squeezed ideologically and fiscally, bringing the third golden age to an end. By the 1930s, taxes on the rich had increased dramatically, and most Britons believed that the state had all the answers to society's biggest problems.

Yet, as the Victorian era of philanthropy began to fade, so a fourth golden age was dawning on the other side of the Atlantic. At the start of the twentieth century, America reinvented what it meant to be wealthy. In 1907, the first Baron Allendale, a landowner, died, leaving one of the largest estates in Britain of that era: £3.2 million. That same year, in America, John D. Rockefeller became the world's first billionaire. Even allowing for the fact that there were almost five dollars to the pound, Rockefeller was by far the wealthier man.

Rockefeller was not alone in acquiring massive wealth, as American industrialists profited from the rapidly expanding U.S. economy. They built huge companies that dominated new industries such as oil (Rockefeller), steel (Carnegie), aluminum, railways, automobiles, and so on. Scale was the order of the day, so it was perhaps inevitable that Carnegie and Rockefeller, two of the greatest industrialists of the age, should make the leap to become the world's first mega-philanthropists.

Although some historians attribute Carnegie's philanthropy to guilt at how he made his money, and especially the deadly suppression of a strike at his firm's Homestead, Pennsylvania, site in 1891, it seems clear that he had decided long before that to give away most of his fortune (his essay "Wealth" was published in 1889). Among other things, he endowed over three thousand public libraries in America, Scotland, and elsewhere. Integral to his philanthropic strategy was the requirement that recipients make matching contributions. As he said, "I do not wish to be remembered for what I have given, but for what I have persuaded others to give." Those towns that would not pay their share of construction and operating costs got no library.

He also created the Carnegie Institute of Technology in Pittsburgh, established a Hero Fund in several countries to reward acts of heroism, and even offered $20 million to the people of the Philippines in 1898 to help them buy their independence from Spain and spare themselves American imperialism. Although this last initiative ultimately failed, it was a good reflection of his radicalism. President William Taft dismissed him as a "peace crank," but no world leader could afford to ignore letters sent from the diminutive philanthropist's lavish castle at Skibo in Scotland.

That American philanthropy boomed at the very moment Europe and Britain were putting their faith in government reflects in part the fact that Europe's embrace of state welfare was an explicit response to the threat of Communism, which was far greater there, and the aftermath of war. Without such a political impetus in early-twentieth-century America, government held back from the welfare state model.

Even the Great Depression that followed the Wall Street Crash of 1929 was initially treated by President Herbert Hoover as a problem to be solved by charity. He handed responsibility for the economic recovery and relief effort to the President's Emergency Committee for Employment, headed by Arthur Woods of the Rockefeller Foundation. The committee worked with the charitable and philanthropic community on programs to address unemployment. But the economy was in free-fall. In 1932 Hoover was convincingly defeated by FDR, who was soon dramatically expanding the role of the state. This never reached the scale it did in Europe, but from the 1930s onwards, America was moving in the same big-government, high-tax direction.

Philanthropy does not exist in a vacuum. Throughout history, wealthy philanthropists have had to define their role in relationship to the state. Each of the past philanthropic golden ages ended with the state ratcheting up its role in society, crowding out some of the philanthropists. In part, it is the recent attempt in many countries to roll back the borders of the state through privatization, deregulation, tax cutting, and attrition that has made space for the philanthrocapitalists of the fifth golden age.

THERE ARE STILL many rich people who are not involved in philanthropy, yet. Among the thirty richest people in the world in 2008 according to *Forbes*, only half have come out as active philanthropists. Of the twenty-nine British citizens who have made it onto the *Forbes* billionaire list, only two (Lord David Sainsbury and Sir Tom Hunter) can claim membership in the billion-dollar philanthropy club. The *World Wealth Report* finds much the same. Although on average the wealthy are more generous than the population at large, most of them do not give at all. According to the report, the pool of philanthropists is narrow but deep: only 11 percent of the global rich gave to philanthropic causes. The ultrarich were slightly more likely to be givers, with 17 percent making charitable donations.

But this may be only the beginning. Many of the world's rich are now reaching the end of their wealth-creating years and entering, with varying degrees of enthusiasm and activism, their wealth-disbursement years. According to some forecasts, $10 trillion to $40 trillion could pass from the Depression-era generation to baby boomers over the next quarter of a century. The prospect of having to make this transfer may prompt superrich people in later life to consider engaging in philanthropy while they are alive—or at least to allocate in their will a decent chunk of their wealth to charity. According to Paul Schervish of the Center on Wealth and Philanthropy at Boston College, there is a clear trend of rising charitable gifts in wills, including relative to the total value of estates. He also expects one third of inherited wealth to go to just 1 percent of baby boomers, many of whom will surely consider much of the money surplus to their requirements.

Moreover, some of the new ways in which today's philanthrocapitalists are attempting to use their wealth to achieve philanthropic goals do not show up in giving figures. One example is ethical investing (buying securities issued by businesses that are seen to do good, or at least do no harm). And as well as contributing money, the rich increasingly donate significant human capital to their philanthropy, in both time and ideas. Compared with the past, the ranks of the rich are increasingly dominated by entrepreneurs who have made, rather than inherited, their fortunes. Among these are some of the world's most successful problem-solvers. The fact that it is impossible to put a price on these contributions of talent should not detract from what could be achieved if what Carnegie called a "talent for organization and management" is applied to the world's big social problems.

Former President Bill Clinton, now an evangelist for giving, believes that philanthropy is already booming but will eventually be far bigger than it is today. "I think this is very real, and I think it will continue. I just think that wealth has concentrated more quickly than philanthropy has grown," he says. For all the people with good stories, Clinton says, "there are, for every one of them, fifty or sixty people that aren't as famous that have a ton of money that haven't done anything like this." Well, not yet. Somebody should give them a copy of Carnegie's *Gospel of Wealth*.

## CHAPTER 3

# The Spirit of Philanthrocapitalism

"I DO HAVE ONE BIG REGRET," Bill Gates confessed in the commencement speech to the 2007 Harvard graduation class. "I left Harvard with no real awareness of the awful inequities in the world and the appalling disparities of health, and wealth, and opportunity that condemn millions of people to lives of despair." He went on to describe how his eyes were opened when he read a World Bank report on investing in health in the developing world. Gates believes that a life in Africa is worth no less than a life in America, that "everybody on the planet deserves a basic level of health," and that he has an opportunity to use his vast wealth to correct a huge injustice.

This is the spirit of philanthrocapitalism: successful entrepreneurs trying to solve big social problems because they believe they can, and because they feel they should. True, it is the rare philanthropist that finds a cause in the sort of official report that Gates considers light reading. More often, they have been turned on to philanthropy by some personal experience—a family tragedy, perhaps, or an encounter with a person in desperate need. But as these philanthrocapitalists talk about what motivates them, the same themes come up time and again: they have the resources; the problem needs to be fixed; they know how to fix problems, for that is what they do all day in business.

Yet there are plenty of skeptics who question whether Gates and the new regiment of philanthrocapitalists are really driven by such straightforward, practical altruistic humanitarianism. The list of possible alternative motives is lengthy, ranging from using giving as a fig leaf to hide embarrassing or dodgy business activities, to exploiting tax loopholes, to boosting social status out of overweening vanity.

Whilst it is fiendishly difficult to know what really makes a philanthropist tick—who can see into someone else's soul?—the question is both fascinating and important. If we understand what is driving giving, it can help us to know whether today's stream of generosity will indeed become a flood. It will also tell us something about what these philanthropists really want to achieve with their money, and thus whether the fifth golden age of philanthropy is likely to reach its potential.

"I AM NOT very good at saying some things," William Gates Sr. tells a gathering of philanthropists in October 2007. The eighty-one-year-old chokes back tears that are clearly out of character and continues, "But I am very proud of my son and his wife."

The son "grew up in a home where civic engagement was in the culture," the father makes clear. Equally clear was the philosophy of wealth that was taught in the family. "Wealth is not something to be proud of— it is something that happens to you as a result of circumstances over which you have no control, a major component of which is the country in which you are born," elaborates Gates Sr.

Gates Jr. is happy to credit his family with getting him into giving. "My parents were very involved in community activities, including the national board of United Way," he recalls. "When I had started my company—we had only fifteen people—my mother said, 'Do a United Way campaign at work; expose them to the needs of the community.' I remember saying to Mom that we are really focused, busy—but I came round to it." His late mother, Mary, also wrote an encouraging letter to Melinda before her wedding to Bill, which ended, biblically, "From those to whom much is given, much is expected."

Yet although the Gates home provided Bill with a strong sense of responsibility, he insists that religious faith is not the source of his charity. "My parents went to church, as Congregationalists. But I am not religiously motivated," he says. Of course, the young Gates may have absorbed some of his wider humanitarian values from his religious upbringing. Melinda Gates is a Catholic, however, which some observers think has led the Gates Foundation to steer clear of certain projects involving reproductive health, i.e., abortion and birth control.

In contrast, Arthur C. Brooks argues in his 2006 book *Who Really Cares?* that religious faith is one of the most important reasons why people give. Indeed, he claims this explains why people on the political right give more than people on the left and why Americans give more than Europeans. Brooks is right that Americans, in general, are more generous than Europeans. Even in a ranking produced by the British Charities Aid Foundation that arguably understates American generosity, the U.S. still comes out on top (see table). It is also true that Americans are more religious than their peers across the Atlantic: in the 2000 World Values Survey, only 16 percent of Americans said they would "never" or "practically never" attend church, compared with 60 percent of the French and 55 percent of Britons.

But even if giving is correlated with faith across the population as a whole, does that hold true for superwealthy philanthrocapitalists? One of the few studies of the giving habits of the rich is Francie Ostrower's *Why the Wealthy Give*, which is based on interviews with ninety-nine donors in New York in the 1990s. "The sole factor that had a clear association with donors' willingness to characterize philanthropy as an obligation was membership in a religious congregation," she notes. "Those who belonged to a church or temple were more likely than nonmembers to see philanthropy as an obligation."

Some wealthy philanthropists are openly religious in their motivation.

---

### CHARITABLE GIVING AS A PERCENTAGE OF GDP— INTERNATIONAL COMPARISON

| | |
|---|---|
| USA | 1.67% |
| U.K. | 0.73% |
| Australia | 0.69% |
| Republic of Ireland | 0.47% |
| Netherlands | 0.45% |
| Germany | 0.22% |
| France | 0.14% |

SOURCE: Charities Aid Foundation, *International Comparisons of Charitable Giving*, November 2006.

Thomas Monaghan, who made his fortune from Domino's Pizza, is a devout Catholic whose philanthropy has included a new computer system to help the Vatican organize its finances. Much of his giving is through his Ave Maria Foundation, which makes no secret of its allegiances and whose stated purpose is to bring Catholic life and culture to the world. Much of the philanthropy of financier Sir John Templeton, a Presbyterian, goes to religious causes. There is even an organization that brings together foundations established by wealthy American evangelical Christians, called the Gathering.

As for other faiths, hedge fund boss Michael Steinhardt has given huge sums to Jewish causes. The large number of leading philanthropists who are Jewish may reflect a tendency for higher giving by wealthy members of a diaspora than their Jewishness per se (see Diaspora Giving box). Within Islam, the Aga Khan, leader of the minority Ismaili sect, has established a particular reputation for philanthropy. His programs often focus on helping countries where there are Ismaili communities, from Uganda to Tajikistan.

These are just a few examples among many. Moreover, there may be lots of philanthropists who are motivated by their faith but do not discuss their giving in these terms. Yet, compared with the population at large, remarkably few of today's biggest philanthropists claim religious faith as their primary motivation. Even Ostrower's study of New York donors does not suggest that the religious rich actually give more—they are simply more prone to feel that it is an obligation.

Philanthrocapitalists tend to be focused on results, the impact that their giving has. It can be argued that religiously motivated giving is sometimes driven more by what it does for the giver than by its impact on the recipients. A religious giver may feel he has done his duty by giving his 10 percent, regardless of whether the money has made much difference in tackling society's big problems. This point should not be overstated. Yet instrumental giving that is seen by the philanthropist as a means to an end may often be more useful than expressive giving done as an end in itself.

The Rockefellers are perhaps the greatest example of how family values can inspire great acts of philanthropy. Endowing each new generation of Rockefellers with a passion for philanthropy has become an organizing theme for the family. Each year, annual summits of the entire extended family are held, where there is formal sharing of information,

## DIASPORA GIVING

"The Jewish diaspora is the gold standard," says Noosheen Hashemi. An Iranian American who made her fortune in Silicon Valley as an early employee of Oracle, Hashemi started Parsa, a community foundation for the Persian (Iranian) diaspora in America, in 2005. Her strategy was based on a careful study of philanthropy by a wide range of diaspora.

There are four ways a diaspora can give, says Hashemi. Its members can give generally to the broader community where they now live, with no explicit connection to the diaspora. They can give to promote greater awareness in the countries where they now live of the culture of the diaspora. They can give to support other needy members of the diaspora, such as by providing community centers for their elderly and young. And they can send money back to help their home country.

So far, only the Jewish diaspora is consistently generous in all four categories, says Hashemi. The Indian diaspora has long been impressive in sending money back to India to address social needs and in promoting its culture abroad. Yet it is lagging in giving much to the broader, non-Indian community—something the Jewish diaspora is particularly good at, with its prominent support in almost every country in which it has a significant presence for everything from hospitals and universities to the arts. Studies suggest that around 70 percent of Jewish giving goes to the larger community and only 30 percent to the Jewish community. (Theresa Lloyd's 2004 study of British millionaires, *Why Rich People Give*, suggests that Jewish generosity may be motivated by a sense of gratitude. In her interviews with philanthropists, she says, Jewish donors "talked explicitly about wanting to contribute to the society that had given refuge to their families," although this was also true of millionaires from other "refugee" groups).

Sending money back home, what economists call "remittances," is now booming. Indeed, remittances from diaspora workers in rich countries sent home to developing countries now exceed government aid flows. The Filipino diaspora is particularly focused on sending money home, albeit mostly to help family members, which is not usually defined as philanthropy. The Mexican diaspora is becoming more imaginative, organizing philanthropic remittance schemes that, say, build bridges or schools in the diaspora member's hometown.

expertise, and lessons learned, and everyone is encouraged to do their part.

Brooks argues that this sort of commitment to giving is a direct result of traditional family values and that Americans give more because they are more into marriage and having children than their counterparts in Europe. For the superrich, however, there is no strong evidence of international differences in attitudes to marrying and breeding.

For the Rockefellers, the link between family and philanthropy is a symbiotic one. No doubt they have had their troubles, like any other family, but they believe that this collective focus on giving has helped them to avoid many of the problems experienced by other wealthy dynasties. The Conrad N. Hilton Foundation is one example of a family trying to imitate the Rockefeller model. The foundation is currently run by Steven Hilton, grandson of the hotelier Conrad. He is scaling up family involvement in the foundation in the hope that this will provide structure and meaning for future generations. Whether this move was directly caused by the much publicized indiscretions of his niece Paris is unclear. However, in December 2007 it was reported that Barron Hilton, a son of Conrad and grandfather of Paris, had decided to allocate 97 percent of his $2.3 billion fortune to a charitable trust that would ultimately be merged with the Hilton Foundation. This prompted numerous headlines along the lines of PARIS HILTON DISINHERITED.

Many of the newly rich worry about the negative impact that inherited wealth could have on their descendants. They do not want their money to be a curse, producing the sort of drifting, purposeless, drug-addled, trust-fund-supported "trustafarians" who, in their minds, were too often churned out by past generations of superrich families on America's East Coast and the aristocratic houses of Europe.

According to a 2001 survey of the richest 1 percent of Americans conducted by U.S. Trust, a private bank, around half of them fear that their children's initiative and independence will be undermined by having material advantages. Some 80 percent want their kids to find a satisfying career, and 65 percent want them to earn enough to support themselves entirely through their own work. Many see the family foundation as a place where their children can find a useful, fulfilling role in life, especially if all else fails.

Long before he announced he was giving away most of his fortune, Warren Buffett had said publicly that his children would not inherit the lot—instead they would get just enough to enable them to do anything, but not so much that they can do nothing, as he put it. "I don't believe in dynastic wealth," he explained when he made his gift to the Gates Foundation. He dismissed the beneficiaries of dynastic wealth as "members of the lucky sperm club," asserting his belief that America should be a meritocracy. Yet he also endowed foundations run by his children, as well as a foundation started with his late wife, Susan. Perhaps being born with a silver spoon in your mouth will become the mark of a future vocation in philanthropy.

Not everyone agrees that getting the kids involved in philanthropy is a solution to the inheritance curse. Carnegie, for one, was no fan of leaving money to the kids, even for them to give it away, because he felt that it should be used for the public good during a tycoon's lifetime and that it was bad for them: "It is not the welfare of the children, but family pride, which inspires these enormous legacies." Also, as the saying goes in the giving industry, once a person becomes a philanthropist, they have eaten their last bad meal and told their last bad joke. For billionaire money manager and author Ken Fisher, getting your heirs involved in philanthropy is as sure a way of spoiling them as handing over an unrestricted trust fund. "I don't want to create some family-name thing that is going to go on and on, and in three generations time some snotty little Fishers are going to be sucked up to for something they didn't do," he says. His gift to his descendants will be inspiration: "The main thing you want your grandchildren to realize is that if you can become rich and successful, so can they."

Their entrepreneurial spirit does seem important in the decision of many rich people to give their money away. Inheritors of wealth are more likely to keep the money, seeing themselves as stewards of the family fortune for future generations. Inherited wealth has also had time to attach itself to particular assets, in the form of family businesses or country estates, that sentiment may make it hard to sacrifice, even for a good cause. No one wants to be remembered as the family member who squandered centuries of hard-earned cash or sold the family seat. This is not true of every inheritor, of course; for example, British supermarket heir David Sainsbury has long been one of his country's leading philanthropists and has pledged to give away £1 billion during his lifetime. But generally, an original wealth creator feels less constrained than an inheritor: he made the money, and so can do with it as he pleases.

Indeed, having no family may actually be associated with higher levels of philanthropy. Many of history's greatest philanthropists, like Tudor-era donor William Lambe and Sir Thomas Guy in the eighteenth century, were childless. It is impossible to prove that this gave rise to their philanthropy, but certainly they had more cash to give away because they did not face a claim on their resources from children. Some of today's famous philanthropists are childless too. For example, it has been suggested that Oprah Winfrey's decision to fund and be heavily involved in her Leadership Academy for Girls in South Africa was driven, at least in part, by the lack of children of her own. As she told *TV Guide* in 2003, "If I were a wife and mother, I wouldn't be open to this experience. I wouldn't have had space in my life to embrace the world's children, because I'd be taking care of my own."

The 1998 study "Gay Philanthropy," by M. V. Lee Badgett and Nancy Cunningham, found that gay, lesbian, bisexual, and transgendered individuals gave more, as a proportion of their income, than the average American—presumably in part because of less pressure from putative heirs. (There is no data on whether religious members of the gay community are more generous than gay atheists, alas.) Among today's superrich, for example, Sir Elton John has certainly made his mark on philanthropy, establishing the Elton John AIDS Foundation.

VANITY IS A charge frequently leveled at philanthropists. "Giving builds up the ego of the giver," said novelist John Steinbeck, "makes him superior and higher and larger than the receiver. Nearly always, giving is a selfish pleasure." The self-made billionaire is used to being an alpha-type personality, but how best to prove his superiority? Perhaps, by giving, he can assert his dominance—not just to the recipient of his gift but also to the whole world. A century ago, economist Thorstein Veblen argued that the wealthy used conspicuous consumption to establish their social status; does philanthropy take that to the next level, as conspicuous nonconsumption?

"Wealthy donors were generally more focused on their peers, rather than those outside their class, as the audience for their philanthropy," concludes Ostrower in her study of philanthropists. Tom Wolfe, author of *The Bonfire of the Vanities*, apparently agrees and derides much of the philanthropy of the new hedge fund tycoons as ego driven. In a savage piece in *Portfolio* magazine in 2007, Wolfe reveled (among other things) in the difficulty that the hedge funders were having buying their way onto the boards of the citadels of old New York philanthropy. "Only halfway, halfway, halfway . . . *These people* have yet to actually make it into the walled city and onto the boards of the Big Four" (the Metropolitan Museum, the Museum of Modern Art, the New York Public Library, and the Frick Collection), he writes, oozing schadenfreude.

Others think the egotism of donors is more atavistic. Media mogul Ted Turner's pledge to give $1 billion to support the United Nations in 1997 led one commentator to call it "an act of pro-social dominance, a bid for status, as plain as the chest-thumping of rival silverback gorillas or the philanthropic trilling of the Arabian babbler." Comparing Turner's behavior to a gorilla may be apt, judging by the growing literature that uses evolutionary biology to explain human behavior. In *The Mating Mind*, Geoffrey Miller argues that, like hunting, generosity is an innately wasteful activity but its value rests in impressing potential mates with your fitness (in this case, by demonstrating your capacity to create surplus wealth). Hence, though giving things away may be detrimental to an individual's short-term self-interest, it may be part of an effective mating strategy. The failure to be generous can represent a failure of potency, according to Miller: for instance, Scrooge's miserliness is "self-castrating." Miller's suspicion that "few male millionaires keep their charitable donations secret from their wives and mistresses" cannot be verified empirically, but sounds plausible.

This insight can cut both ways. If philanthropists are alpha types, using their generosity to display their fitness, it may explain why so many of the rest of us own up to a nagging feeling of resentment towards them. Their giving makes us feel inferior. Our negative feelings may be our own envy. If Turner is a gorilla, he's a gorilla who tends to get the girl.

But does it matter if it is ego that is driving the rich to give money away? One risk is that such donors will be drawn to causes that are not the most needy but the most prestigious, such as the "Big Four." If so, the snobbery that Wolfe describes may have a silver lining. By locking the new giants of Wall Street out of the traditional philanthropic institutions, the old guard may deserve some credit for the new charities, schools, and sports clubs into which hedge fund philanthropists are pouring money. And these new charities may be doing a lot more good for the needy of New York than another gift to the Met would.

Also, without ego to drive them, how many rich people would give at all? As Bernard de Mandeville wrote in the eighteenth century in *The Fable of the Bees*, "Pride and vanity have built more hospitals than all the virtues together." So, raise a glass, at your $10,000-a-head black-tie gala charity dinner, to those great fundraisers, Pride and Vanity.

IN 1911, IN *The Devil's Dictionary*, the great American satirist Ambrose Bierce defined a philanthropist as a "rich (and usually bald) old gentleman who has trained himself to grin while his conscience is picking his pocket." But the pleasure of giving may be more genuine than that. "Will giving make you happier?" asks Bill Clinton at the end of his 2007 book *Giving*. Whilst he carefully makes no promises, he then lists a diverse group of givers—Bill and Melinda Gates, Carlos Slim Helú, Barbra Streisand, Rupert Murdoch, and so on—concluding that, when they were giving, they "seemed happy." After all, he continues, rhetorically, "Who's happier? The uniters or the dividers? The builders or the breakers? The givers or the takers?"

In a 1995 survey by Professor Michael Argyle of Oxford University, respondents identified charity and voluntary activity as a source of joy more important than sports and music. Only dancing, respondents said, was more joyous than giving. There is some scientific evidence that giving activates the brain's reward center—the mesolimbic pathway, to give it its proper name—responsible for doling out the dopamine-mediated euphoria often associated with sex, money, food, and drugs. This finding may pose some problem for the moral hard-liners who question the merits of any giving that is rewarded (see "Is It Possible to Be Truly Altruistic?" box).

"Asking Alberto for money was like offering an alcoholic a drink." So said a "friend" of Alberto Vilar, the philanthropist who fell to earth, according to author James B. Stewart. Vilar made a fortune by investing early in tech firms such as Yahoo! through his Amerindo investment company. By 2000, he claimed to be the "largest supporter of classical music, opera and ballet in the world," pledging over $300 million in gifts. However, he was hit hard by the bursting of the dot-com bubble and started to miss payments. Maybe it was the dopamine that prompted Vilar to keep pledging more money and insisting that he would honor his past pledges. Clearly it was something deeply, personally destructive—especially if there is any substance to the charges that it led to his arrest in 2005, accused of pilfering money from one of his investment clients, perhaps in order to meet one of his philanthropic promises. Or maybe it was pride—he was furious when New York's Metropolitan Opera "rubbed him out," removing his name from the Vilar Grand Tier after he failed to make promised payments. There is no greater public indignity

## IS IT POSSIBLE TO BE TRULY ALTRUISTIC?

"To a psychologist, I gather, if you get the warm, fuzzy feeling, you're not being altruistic, because you actually enjoyed it," says biologist and author Olivia Judson, who has grappled with the question of the evolutionary motivation for altruism. In an interview with the *Atlantic Monthly* in October 2007, she questioned whether this test for true altruism is too tough. "So to a psychologist, somebody is only being altruistic if they do something for somebody else and they don't enjoy it. I think that's a rather stringent definition, myself. I think you should be able to enjoy it."

French sociologist Marcel Mauss argues that receiving is actually the point of giving. In *The Gift*, he writes that all giving inevitably creates a social bond in the form of an obligation on the receiver to reciprocate, or lose honor. An overt example of this is the potlatch practiced in some Native American communities. Individuals gain prestige by lavishly giving away their possessions on ceremonial occasions, confident that they will get most of them back from others' potlatches. Mauss calls this "reciprocal altruism," which could also apply to striking a deal with God (in terms of rewards in heaven or on earth) when fulfilling a moral obligation to give.

British social policy pioneer Richard Titmuss criticized Mauss in his book *The Gift Relationship*, arguing that people can be motivated by a spirit of public service rather than the expectation of something in return. He uses the example of the successful system of voluntary blood donation in Britain, where the donor gets nothing except some free tea and biscuits.

Evolutionary biologist Matt Ridley concedes that some donors feel the sentiment of public service, but he still thinks that giving is reciprocal. In for a philanthropist than to have your name removed by an organization you let down.

But it would be wrong to characterize giving simply as a frenzy of dopamine and testosterone, or the ultimate ego-boosting luxury. For some philanthropists the psychological factors are more existential. The Money, Meaning, & Choices Institute was established in 1997 to explore the "psychological opportunities and emotional challenges of having and inheriting money." Stephen Goldbart and Joan DiFuria, the two California psychologists behind this project, studied some of the new, young rich who made their money in the dot-com boom at the

---

*The Origins of Virtue*, he describes generosity as "an investment in a stock called trustworthiness that later pays handsome dividends in others' generosity." So hardwired is this instinct, he argues, that we are driven to be generous by our emotions even when it does not benefit our strategic self-interest. "So when somebody votes (an irrational thing to do, given the chances of affecting the outcome), tips a waiter in a restaurant she will never revisit, gives an anonymous donation to charity or flies to Rwanda to bathe sick orphans in a refugee camp, she is not, even in the long run, being selfish or rational. She is simply prey to sentiments that are designed for another purpose: to elicit trust by demonstrating a capacity for altruism." So we may be capable of acts of generosity that are not self-interested—but they are mistakes.

Not convinced? Still want to be a pure altruist? All you need to do, argued the famously abstruse French philosopher Jacques Derrida, is to make sure that you get nothing in return and do nothing that harms your recipient (including his pride). So, as well as ensuring that you do not receive anything from the recipient of your generosity, not even thanks, you must also insulate yourself from any pleasurable feelings—even Titmuss's noble public spiritedness. Moreover, the recipient should not experience any feelings of shame, inferiority, and so on as a result of the giving process. This, Derrida concluded, means that you must never know that you have given a gift and the recipient must never know that he has received one. If you want to be truly altruistic, that is.

Oh, go on. Just enjoy it.

end of the 1990s. Many of these youthful millionaire entrepreneurs were shocked and guilt-ridden by their unexpected riches and suffered something now called "sudden wealth syndrome," a condition the two psychologists discovered. "Twenty-nine-year-olds in Silicon Valley were finding that, suddenly, they never needed to work again, and started asking, 'What is the purpose of their wealth and life?'" says DiFuria.

Chuck Feeney once said that he lived simply and had no need for most for his fortune, because "you can only wear one pair of shoes at a time." According to Feeney's biographer Conor O'Clery, the philanthropist's former business partner Robert Miller is convinced that Feeney is motivated to give by old-fashioned Catholic guilt: "He would have been a good Catholic priest because making money seemed to bother him so much."

Guilt is a negative emotion, suggesting an uneasy conscience. But some billionaires have a psychological urge that is equally powerful and more positive. Charles Handy, author of *The New Philanthropists*, attributes the growing enthusiasm for philanthropy, in part, to a need for meaning in people who have found that business success is not enough to make them happy. "There is a search for a narrative, about making a difference with your life, which is vaguely religious and gives you a buzz," he writes. Pointing to psychologist Abraham Maslow's hierarchy of needs, Handy suggests that nowadays more people are quickly getting to the stage that Maslow described as "the highest need, for a purpose beyond ourselves. They want to make a difference—it used to happen in their 60s and 70s, now it is in their 30s and 40s." (Indeed, this is increasingly true of the larger population, too: for example, witness the growing number of MBA graduates who want to work for NGOs or firms that say they have a social purpose.)

"Running a hedge fund was extremely strenuous," says George Soros, as he recalls the "kind of midlife crisis" he went through in the late 1970s. His fund had reached an unprecedented $100 million under his management. He was more than comfortably wealthy. "Was it worth it? What did I want the money for? I decided what I really cared about was open society. So I started the foundation in 1978." Philanthropy proved to be an effective tonic, says Soros, "as it gave me a new lease of life as a fund manager—my fund went to sixteen billion dollars. The two were definitely related." The only down year in his investing career was during the "midlife crisis." Soros has gone on to pour billions of dollars of his spectacular earnings into philanthropy.

SCOTTISH PHILANTHROPIST SIR Tom Hunter found the same ennui in wealth when he sold his successful sporting goods retail business. "In 1998, I was thirty-seven years old, and got a massive check. I had achieved all my goals at the time. So what is the motivation to create more wealth?" Since turning to philanthropy, Hunter has regained a sense of purpose—to grow an even bigger pile to give away.

While Sir Tom is now an enthusiastic giver, he is also remarkably frank that his first steps in philanthropy were guided not by concern for others but by tax planning. According to an interview in the *Independent* in 2006, after he sold his business for £252 million, his accountant advised him to shelter from the British taxman by moving to Monaco. When his wife, Marion, refused to leave their Scottish homeland, the accountant suggested philanthropy as the next most tax-efficient option, and so the Hunter Foundation was born. (Ironically, since then, Monaco and other "tax havens" such as Luxembourg have started to promote themselves as centers of philanthropy.) Since then, he has found more positive reasons for philanthropy and has pledged to give away most of what he expects to be at least a £1 billion fortune over his lifetime.

"Most philanthropy is tax-motivated," argues William Zabel, an American tax lawyer and writer on related matters. "The notion that charity wouldn't be hurt if you eliminated the death tax is absurd." Many wealthy people have been attracted to philanthropy by the desire to minimize their death duties. If the money is in a charitable foundation, the tax man cannot touch it—at least in America. That is why so many people who want philanthropy to flourish were opposed to the abolition under President George W. Bush of estate duties.

Even if there are tax advantages to giving, do these really negate the virtue of philanthropy? The money does have to be given away in the first place to get the tax benefit. However, the skeptics point out, there are plenty of ways that money that is claimed to be a gift really benefits the giver: philanthropy as a form of consumption, not of giving. Foundations can find family members well-paid jobs—with a car and maybe travel (for research, of course) included. In 2003, for example, the *Boston Globe* revealed that one head of his family's foundation, the assets of which had dwindled to around $4.9 million, had granted himself a 40 percent pay rise, to $1.4 million, to help cover the cost of his daughter's wedding.

In a 2005 article titled "A Failure of Philanthropy," in the *Stanford Social Innovation Review*, Stanford University political science professor Rob Reich argued that the rich can get a double benefit from giving if they use their donations to subsidize their own lifestyles through their choice of charities while also claiming a tax break. Consider, for example, a rich parent giving money to his or her children's private school and claiming a tax break. This not only reinforces the inequalities in education by further adding to the resources of successful schools in rich areas; it also rewards the rich parent for a "gift" of which their family is the main beneficiary. In other words, the tax subsidy is regressive.

In one of the biggest shake-ups in U.K. charity law, the 2006 Charities Act acknowledged that something had to be done about the potential abuse of self-serving gifts. To qualify as a charity, educational institutions must now satisfy a public benefit test to justify their tax-privileged status. This seemed to spell trouble for some of Britain's most famous schools, not least Eton College, where Princes William and Harry (among others) went to school. Eton was sufficiently concerned that it announced plans to raise £50 million to use to enroll more children from poor homes.

Philanthropy may also be self-serving because it can get what cannot be bought any other way—access to a celebrity whom the dull billionaire would never otherwise meet, say, or the best seats on opening night at the opera, or an airborne game of cards with a former president. A gift to an Ivy League university may (though the institution will deny it) guarantee your offspring a place; $1 million for an average child, or $5 million for a stupid one, is said to be the rule of thumb.

Philanthropy may also be a way for families (albeit no longer in America) to retain control of corporations, even if they don't get their hands on the profits. This was Henry Ford's original motivation for creating the Ford Foundation, when New Deal–era tax hikes raised the prospect of his heirs having to sell their controlling stake in the Ford Motor Company to pay estate taxes on his death. Even though Henry Ford II wound up this arrangement voluntarily after his grandfather's death in 1947, U.S. legislators closed this loophole with the 1969 Tax Reform Act.

Continental European law is more relaxed about this practice: witness Germany's leading Bertelsmann Foundation and Robert Bosch Foundation. In 2004, Swedish journalist Bo Pettersson upset Ingvar Kamprad, the owner of furniture behemoth IKEA, by accusing him of being the richest man in the world. Pettersson's argument is that Stichting INGKA, a Dutch charitable foundation Kamprad established with his IKEA shares in 1982, is mainly an investment vehicle for Kamprad that only gives minor donations to charity but minimizes tax and disclosure and makes IKEA immune from being taken over. In 2006, the *Economist* described Stichting INGKA as "an outfit that ingeniously exploits the quirks of different jurisdictions to create a charity, dedicated to a somewhat banal cause, that is not only the world's richest foundation, but is at the moment also one of its least generous." The magazine estimated that this foundation could be worth $36 billion, more than the Gates Foundation at that time. Its purpose? Ending hunger? Curing diseases? No: "innovation in the field of architectural and interior design."

Philanthropy that is devoted to genuinely good causes, say the critics, can still be self-interested if it is used to burnish your public reputation, perhaps to deal with negative publicity that could hurt your business. Critics attacked the motivation of John D. Rockefeller's philanthropy, seeing it as a device to help him avoid antitrust measures to break up his company. Similarly, Andrew Mellon's gift of his collection of paintings and sculpture to found America's National Gallery of Art in Washington, D.C., in 1937 has been interpreted by some as a way of protecting his fortune from President F.D. Roosevelt and the tax authorities. And of course, Bill Gates started giving on a large scale only after Microsoft was prosecuted for antitrust abuses.

One problem with this criticism is that it is impossible to refute: philanthropy tends to win public praise, so it is easy to accuse philanthropists of doing it to boost their public image. Who can say what really went on in the minds of Rockefeller, Mellon, or Gates? However, all could plausibly claim that their philanthropic plans predated the scandals that are supposed to have spurred their giving.

The only way to avoid the charge that philanthropy is a PR tool is to be ultrasecretive, like Feeney, who registered his Atlantic Philanthropies in Bermuda to avoid scrutiny (as well as tax), refused interviews, and made it a condition of any gift that his identity was kept secret. While giving in secret is encouraged by most of the world's religions, it is not necessarily practical for the superrich, since modesty can be construed as suspicious secrecy or an arrogant lack of transparency.

Even if a philanthropist wants to remain anonymous, that is becoming increasingly hard to do. In 2007 thirty-seven wealthy U.S. donors made gifts of $5 million or more (including one of $150 million) without revealing their identities, up from twenty-seven in 2006. But the University of California, Irvine, revealed the source of a $20 million gift following newspaper criticism of its secrecy. A demand for the identities of sixty-two anonymous donors to the University of Louisville Foundation to be revealed has gone all the way to the Supreme Court of Kentucky.

On balance, anonymity, for all its admirable modesty, is probably against the spirit of philanthrocapitalism. As Vartan Gregorian, long-time head of the Carnegie Corporation, put it, "I like people to be public about their generosity; it makes it more competitive if we can see who is doing what." Bill Clinton, for one, has no qualms about using competition to raise money for good causes—that is what the annual meeting of his Clinton Global Initiative is all about.

The rock star Bono says he keeps details of his philanthropic giving private for religious reasons. Yet he is full of praise for Buffett and Gates for giving publicly. "There are moments, which may come in my future, where it is a political act to put your money on the table. That is the extraordinary thing Bill and Warren have done. They have changed the rules of the game," he says. If the two richest men in the world can give away their fortunes, philanthropy is no longer a minority interest but an integral part of what it means to be a "good billionaire."

IT CAN SEEM that there are at least as many motivations for philanthropy as there are philanthropists. Each philanthropist typically gives for a range of reasons, which makes it hard to generalize. However, there appear to be two elements that dominate the new spirit of philanthrocapitalism: the belief that giving is a responsibility; and the belief that, as problem solvers, entrepreneurs can actually do something about making the world a better place. Among the superrich, there is a growing sense that philanthropy is not an option but a responsibility of wealth. As hedge fund boss and philanthropist Paul Tudor Jones has put it: "All my success was gained basically in New York City, and this was my way of repaying New York. I couldn't have done what I did anywhere else in the world."

Other philanthrocapitalists say they give back not as repayment of a specific debt but out of a general gratitude to society. True to the philosophy learned in his childhood, Gates says, "I was not lucky, in the sense that I found the [operating system] code sitting on a desk, but in terms of circumstances. That I could write the best code and hire the best people was in part due to the time and country I was born in. There is a responsibility to give something back."

An expectation that the state will take care of things is perhaps the single most important factor in the tendency of wealthy Europeans and Britons to give less than Americans. This difference was highlighted in the British investigation *Why Rich People Give*, by Theresa Lloyd, a philanthropy consultant. In her 2004 study, based on interviews with seventy-three high-net-worth individuals, Lloyd ascribes higher U.S. giving rates to the attachment of the rich in America to a more individualistic social model without universal welfare provision. But this is changing, reports Handy in *The New Philanthropists*: a European tycoon who once would have said that paying taxes was enough to fulfill his responsibilities is nowadays more likely to give back as well.

The causes that the superrich feel a responsibility to address often start with a personal experience. This was certainly true of disgraced-but-still-rich former "junk bond king" Michael Milken. The man who is often seen as the epitome of 1980s financial greed suffered from prostate cancer in the 1990s and has since given $750 million to fight the disease. The Larry King Cardiac Foundation was inspired by the veteran interviewer's quintuple heart bypass in 1987. New York mayor Michael Bloomberg managed to give up his addiction to smoking, which has inspired him to dedicate his foundation to eradicating smoking everywhere. Many people give to support the places that shaped them, especially to the community where they grew up, or their university. Tycoons such as Sandy Weill, Chuck Feeney, and Michael Bloomberg have given hundreds of millions of dollars to their alma maters. Those with less money to donate often give to the local animal shelter or donkey sanctuary after losing a family pet. Maddie the schnauzer was a source of inspiration to David Duffield as he built up software giant PeopleSoft, and later he decided to give $200 million to animal welfare organizations in her memory.

Relying on personal experience might seem to be an impediment to effective philanthropy. Surely, there is a danger that the rich will focus on their own problems and preoccupations rather than on the larger issues facing humanity. Yet in practice, for many of the superrich, personal experience leads them towards the big global problems, not away from them. In particular, compared with the population at large, today's rich often travel far more widely around the world. The typical billionaire will have a passport, or maybe two—unlike the typical American congressman. What they see on their travels, if they choose to look (luxurious ways to travel make this optional), can make them far more aware of the needs of the world than people who stay at home. Angelina Jolie, for example, says she had her eyes opened to refugee problems whilst shooting a movie in war-torn Sierra Leone.

Moreover, with the rise of the global economy and the search for new markets, business tycoons increasingly must visit parts of poorer countries where tourists never go and be more exposed to the problems people face. Swiss financier Stephan Schmidheiny was drawn deeper into philanthropy after doing business in Latin America in the 1980s. "Most countries in the region were going through economic liberalization and privatization processes that, according to official statistics, were increasing per capita incomes. And yet, in my travels through the region, I observed that macroeconomic reforms by themselves were far from sufficient in inner cities and ghettoes," he recalls.

Stephen Dawson, a British venture capitalist, also cites experience abroad as the source of his philanthropy—in his case, teaching in Madagascar after university. Hedge fund philanthropist Christopher Cooper-Hohn was affected by the sight of children scavenging on rubbish dumps when he was working as a banker in the Philippines. Maybe Gates would have started his philanthropy even sooner if he had got out more as a young man.

"THE RICH ARE not like you and me," observed F. Scott Fitzgerald. Paul Schervish of the Center on Wealth and Philanthropy agrees, not just because, as Hemingway quipped, they have more money but because their can-do attitude and their financial and other assets make them leaders and innovators in society. Schervish calls the superrich who engage in philanthropy "hyperagents: individuals who can do what it would otherwise take a social movement to do." If the social meaning of money in general is agency, he wrote in a paper "Hyperagency and High-Tech Donors," the "social meaning of wealth is hyperagency." In other words, wealth gives the rich higher expectations of their own ability to make a difference in society and greater resources with which to try to fulfill those expectations.

This reflects a sea change in attitudes over the past few decades, as wealthy entrepreneurs have risen in social status at the expense of technocrats. Go back to the 1950s, and society was run by what American sociologist C. Wright Mills called a technocratic "power elite." Highly educated, but not especially highly paid, these technocrats dominated every sector of government and business, and thus society as a whole, even in America but often more so elsewhere.

Today, it is increasingly entrepreneurs, not technocrats, who form the power elite. They are idolized on television, increasingly tracked as celebrities in the gossip pages, and expected to have solutions to big social problems. People working in government are rarely associated in the public mind with success. As Buffett explained, as he signed over most of his fortune to the Gateses, he has no doubt that they will "do a far better job in terms of maximizing the good that comes out of that money than would happen if it were dropped into the federal Treasury"—the last bastion of technocracy.

The resources of these entrepreneurial hyperagents are not limited to money. Being rich tends to bring other assets, such as access to other powerful people, that only increases their hyperagency. That is why Greg Dees of Duke University says that philanthropy today is best defined more broadly than giving away money, as "mobilizing and deploying private resources, including money, time, social capital and expertise, to improve the world in which we live."

"With wealth comes education, decision-making power, links to elites in other countries, and enormous convening power," says Peggy Dulany, the great-granddaughter of John D. Rockefeller. Through the Global Philanthropists Circle, an organization to help wealthy families learn to give more effectively, she says she is "helping philanthropists to make use of all these advantages. It is using money and connections— whether personal, family, or business—to create public benefit." If they ask, the superrich can usually get face time with both global experts and those people on the ground who know what is really going on. When wealthy donors from the Global Philanthropists Circle visited South Africa in 2002, they were shown around the jail on Robben Island by its most famous former inmate, Nelson Mandela.

In short, "richesse oblige" and a belief in hyperagency are the driving spirit of philanthrocapitalism today. The multibillion-dollar question is whether that spirit will be enough to change the world.

# CHAPTER 4

# Billanthropy

"ARE WE BIG ENOUGH TO PLAY OUR role in AIDS? Are we big enough to play our role in malaria? No, we are not big enough," says Bill Gates. "We're a tiny, tiny little organization."

This may seem an odd way to describe the world's largest charitable foundation, which by 2009 plans to employ at least a thousand people and to give away at least $3 billion a year, perhaps much more.

Yet for Gates, a better yardstick for the foundation is not other foundations but private-sector companies like his own Microsoft—with seventy-nine thousand employees and a gross profit in 2007 of $40 billion—and national governments, with their trillion-dollar budgets. Above all, it is the scale of the problems he is tackling—such as America's failing education system, in which the New York school budget alone is $20 billion a year, and even more, diseases such as HIV/AIDS, diarrhea, tuberculosis, and malaria, which take millions of lives every year, mostly in poor countries.

"How many people work on, say, brownie mix? How many people work on a soft drink? Is it possible that there should be a foundation that has a fifth as many people working on saving lives as there are working on Diet Pepsi? I don't know, maybe we are too big. Maybe we should be a tenth of what they put into improving dog food," says Gates, warming sarcastically to his theme. "Go get 0.1 percent of the scientists working on erectile dysfunction to come and work on malaria and you will be making a huge contribution.

"To me, it has to do with the scale of the problem. We've got to have the resources and employees because of the diseases," says Gates, who in his early fifties still has boundless energy and a no-holds-barred style of argument. Warren Buffett felt comfortable giving billions of dollars to the Gates Foundation, says Gates, because "Warren knew that we had taken on big enough problems that the more resources we had, the more we could get done."

To get the maximum bang from every one of the billions of bucks at his disposal, Gates has had to become the ultimate philanthrocapitalist, using every ounce of his business experience and know-how to figure out efficient ways to make a difference. "Cutting through complexity to find a solution runs through four predictable stages: determine a goal, find the highest-leverage approach, discover the ideal technology for that approach, and in the meantime, make the smartest application of the technology that you already have," he told students at Harvard University in 2007—returning to the place from which he had dropped out in 1975 to start what was to become Microsoft.

Given the foundation's scale, only by leveraging the money it has will the foundation be able to achieve its ambitious goals, says Gates. This leverage has to be achieved through the organizations to which it gives its money, which include governments, multilateral and nongovernmental organizations, social enterprises, and for-profit companies. The foundation's ability to pick the appropriate partners and manage those partnerships will determine whether it succeeds. And the need to get these things right lay behind Gates's decision to step down from his day job at Microsoft in June 2008 to dedicate himself to the foundation. "When there is three billion dollars a year to spend, the chairman probably should be full time," he says.

LIKE MANY NEWLY rich people, Gates began his philanthropy in an ad hoc manner, responding one at a time to the growing number of requests for help that arrived as word of his wealth spread. Soon, his father, William Gates Sr., started to help him figure out which of these requests were deserving. It was Gates Sr. who suggested this could be done far more efficiently through a foundation, and in 1994 the William H. Gates Foundation was born, run by Gates Sr. and endowed with an initial $94 million by his son.

During his 1997 speech in which he announced his $1 billion gift to the United Nations, Ted Turner mentioned Bill Gates by name when he attacked some of his fellow tycoons for not giving enough. Coincidentally or not, that year saw Gates start to take his giving to the next level, both by significantly increasing the amount he gave and by being more strategic in choosing what he supported. (Turner recalls saying to Gates, " 'Isn't this the best thing you've ever done in terms of fun?" And Gates replied, "Other than getting married, yes.")

This evolution began with the launch of a new foundation, the Gates Library Foundation, whose mission was to provide computers and Internet access to public libraries in poor communities in America and Canada. Sending a clear signal that he intended to be businesslike about his philanthropy, instead of relying on his father, Gates appointed a chief executive of the Gates Library Foundation: Patty Stonesifer, a former executive at Microsoft who in 1996 had been named by *Time* magazine as one of the twenty-five most influential people in America.

By the end of 1998, Gates's two foundations had combined assets of $577 million. That was an impressive rate of growth, but the following year Gates and his wife, Melinda, broke all the previous records for philanthropic donations, announcing that they would give away $16 billion. At this point—stage two of his philanthropy becoming businesslike— the foundations moved into an office building, leaving their temporary home in Gates Sr.'s basement.

In 1999, the original foundation was renamed the Bill and Melinda Gates Foundation, and the library program was merged into it the following year. The merger was intended to enable the more efficient pursuit of what were by now four missions: improving global health, raising the quality of American education, libraries, and various causes in Gates's native Pacific Northwest. Stonesifer continued as chief executive, and Bill and Melinda and Gates Sr. were the foundation's three trustees. Bill Gates Jr. continued to add steadily to the foundation's endowment.

In 2006, it restructured its activities into three main areas: global health, global development, and inequalities in the United States; Bill announced that he would work full time at the foundation from 2008; and Buffett made his gift and became the foundation's fourth trustee.

HAVING BEEN INSPIRED to become a philanthropist in part by Carnegie's writings, when Gates decided to become serious and strategic about his giving it seemed logical to try to refresh Carnegie's best-known cause: libraries. Outside each Carnegie library—often the most impressive building in town—was a lamppost or lantern that symbolized enlightenment, reflecting Carnegie's belief in giving in ways that encourage people to help themselves. Gates believed that in the Internet era, self-improvement required access to the Web—and by the late 1990s, a digital divide had opened up in which poorer communities lacked the online access taken for granted in the rest of America. "Figuring out a way to bridge that gap is important to us," he said soon after launching the libraries initiative. "We want to make sure everyone has the ability to have Internet access, regardless of where they live or how much money they have."

The new foundation took nationwide an initiative to connect libraries to the Internet that had been started locally by Microsoft's community development arm. Some cynics immediately perceived it as a marketing tool for Microsoft's personal computer software, not an act of personal benevolence. "This doesn't even qualify as philanthropy," argued one of them, Theodore Roszak, a historian at California State University, Hayward. "It's just seeding the market. You're simply lubricating future sales." By 2007, some $320 million had been given to connect libraries and train staff in all fifty American states, as well as various U.S. territories.

Gates and his staff learned a lot from the libraries about how to be businesslike in their philanthropy. Libraries offered an obvious opportunity to leverage the Gateses' dollars. There were already buildings and professional staff in the communities the foundation wanted to reach, which kept down the start-up and operating costs. Also, the cost of piloting the scheme had been borne by Microsoft, so the foundation could scale up a proven model, which is much less risky than starting from scratch. (Ideally, government would have taken on the job of scaling it up, but addressing the digital divide was not high on the priorities list of most politicians.)

Ten thousand libraries in the United States were connected to the Internet by 2003. The foundation had hoped that if it made the initial investment, communities would then reinvest to keep the connectivity going. In the end, only around 60 percent did so, upgrading to high-speed Internet access, whilst the other 40 percent have been reluctant or unable to put up their own cash, and remain connected only at slow, or inadequate speeds. Indeed, in many places, the budgetary pressure on libraries increased. "After we had put computers in public libraries, towns started to open libraries for fewer hours, which made our gift less generous than we had intended," says Stonesifer.

At this point, the foundation realized it needed to engage in advocacy work to shape public opinion. "On the positive side, we saw how we could turn the spotlight on an issue when Bill appeared on the cover of a magazine talking about libraries—which generated publicity that was equal to lots of dollars," says Stonesifer. The foundation has since focused on persuading communities of the need for public libraries and high-quality Internet access. It worked with the Institute for Museum and Library Services to research the impact of library technology—computers and the Internet—on users, and then started to grapple with the question of how to make the computers it has in place more valuable to users.

At the same time, the role played by libraries in their communities is evolving fast. More and more government forms and job applications are required to be filed online, making Internet access at libraries crucial to poorer people seeking to help themselves. And as Hurricane Katrina revealed, in many poorer areas especially, libraries were no longer nice-to-have amenities but essential community facilities, as important as first responders after the disaster.

Ten years on, how the Gates Foundation views its relationship with libraries has evolved significantly. Its focus has gone global, looking to spread connected libraries abroad, especially in the poorer parts of the world. Although the foundation's initial goal was simply to increase free public access to information and the latest technology, increasingly it sees its role as being an advocate for libraries, telling the world that the institution of the library remains relevant in the twenty-first century.

But for Gates himself, libraries were only a start. His desire to help make it easier for poorer Americans to learn led him from libraries to the challenge of improving the country's many underperforming government-funded public schools—where the obstacles to using his money to make a real difference were far greater.


IN JUNE 2000, Bill Gates's worst nightmare was a lawyer from the Bronx named Joel Klein. As Bill Clinton's assistant attorney general, Klein had convinced a judge that Gates was an abusive monopolist and that the company he had built should be broken up. Klein had always insisted that he bore no ill will towards Gates. "This has never been about punishing any individuals. This is about protecting consumers," he said when announcing his plan to break up Microsoft. And although Klein quit his job a few months later, and the judge's decision was overturned a year later on appeal, in August 2002 what Gates felt about Klein suddenly mattered a great deal.

In 2000, the Gates Foundation, George Soros's Open Society Institute, and the Carnegie Corporation had together pledged to give $10 million each to help the New York Board of Education conduct an important experiment in educational reform, by breaking some of the city's failing big schools into smaller schools. In 2002, Gates was considering much larger gifts to the city following the election of billionaire businessman Michael Bloomberg as mayor. Bloomberg had made school reform a key theme of his campaign, but in July he did something that had the potential to drive away Gates: appoint Joel Klein as the new schools chancellor to oversee his reform drive. Would Gates go ahead with his gift, given it would now be in the hands of his old enemy? "I heard that he had doubts," recalls Klein. But in the end Gates decided to put his philanthropy before personal grudges. That September, the Gates Foundation made a $1.4 million grant to start two new small high schools in the city—the prelude to further grants of $135 million between 2003 and 2007 in what became arguably the most successful example yet seen of philanthrocapitalism at work in America's schools. Gates and Klein are now staunch allies.

The need for better education is one thing on which most philanthrocapitalists agree (see "School Aid" box on pages 60–61). Indeed, education has been a favorite cause throughout the history of modern philanthropy, going back to Tudor England, where many successful merchants founded schools. In America during the Jim Crow era— which ended with *Brown v. Board of Education* in 1954, and the Civil Rights Act a decade later—thousands of schools for African Americans were built across the South, with money from the Rosenwald Foundation, created by Julius Rosenwald, president of the Sears, Roebuck and Co. department stores. Today, around one in every four philanthropic dollars goes to education, ranging from preschool to universities. By 2007, Gates had given over $2 billion to education.

Yet improving education is as tough a test of the philanthropic skills of Gates and other big givers as there can be. The sums spent by governments on schools dwarf the money available to philanthropists, who thus have to be truly creative if they are to have much of an impact.

As he has done in business, Gates takes a big picture "systems approach" to his philanthropy. "America's high schools are obsolete," he thundered in a speech to America's state governors in 2005, explaining that "by 'obsolete,' I don't just mean that they're broken, flawed, or underfunded, though a case could be made for every one of those points. By 'obsolete,' I mean our high schools—even when they're working as designed—cannot teach all our students what they need to know today." Moreover, he said, "When I compare our high schools to what I see when I'm traveling abroad, I am terrified for our workforce of tomorrow." His solution? A new three Rs to replace the traditional "reading, 'riting,' and 'rithmetic." These are *rigor* (a challenging curriculum), *relevance* (a body of knowledge that equips students to succeed in a fast changing world), and *relationship* (adults who know students, look out for them, and push them to succeed).

At first, Gates tried leverage by example, focusing narrowly on reinventing schools to create new prototypes, whose success would inspire school districts across America to adopt their methods. However, as the foundation gained greater experience—of the slow pace of change, in particular—the focus shifted from seeing schools as the main unit of change to trying to change the broader structures within which schools work, such as the entire New York school system overseen by Klein. "We needed to figure out what things we could do that would flip the system," recalls Stonesifer.

The Gates approach typically works this way: the foundation sets policy and provides funding, but others do the work on the ground. In education, it has worked with more than a hundred intermediary organizations and has cofunded programs with more than a dozen other foundations. For example, in New York a $51 million grant by Gates in September 2003 to create sixty-seven new themed small schools (each with fewer than five hundred students) was divided between seven organizations. The largest chunk of this money went to New Visions for Public Schools, an organization whose board included Klein and the local head of the teachers' union, to build thirty schools. Money also went to organizations such as Replications Inc. (eight schools), the College Board (six schools), and the Asia Society (ten schools with international themes). The Gates Foundation tries to find organizations whose methods it likes and then scales them up. New Visions, for example, run by small-school champion Robert Hughes, has started seventy-eight new schools with Gates Foundation money.

Adopting a systemic approach was not simply about the need to achieve massive change quickly. An emphasis on individual schools might also produce misleading results. When you focused on creating one good school, says Gates, it could easily be the case that "the slightly better teachers went there, slightly more money went there, slightly more motivated students went there, so it doesn't say to all the schools in the area, 'We can do that.' There have been great individual public schools for a long time, but not many great systems."

Thus, the strategy soon became to drive broad change in poor-performing school districts where there was someone at the top with a commitment to systematic reform. Bloomberg's New York proved the ideal place for a grand educational experiment. When he ran for election in 2001, Bloomberg described the school system as "in a state of emergency." The graduation rate in 2002 was alarmingly low, 51 percent of students compared with a national average of 70 percent. Most New Yorkers thought the system impossible to fix. Bloomberg campaigned for, and got, direct control of the school system, hired Klein, and started changing things—initially by taking decision making away from the patronage-heavy local school boards and then decentralizing these powers to accountable principals, and by actively breaking up big schools and piloting experimental charter schools that could be models for others.

From 2003 to 2007, New York's schools were supported by over $350 million of philanthropic gifts, of which around 40 percent was from the Gates Foundation. The money is typically start-up money, with grants lasting only for a few years, after which, assuming the new initiatives have been shown to work, other sources of funding take over, usually public money.

Klein reckons the philanthropists played a particularly important role in covering costs for things that would have been a hard sell politically if the money had to come out of public funds. For instance, he launched the New York City Leadership Academy, which trains new school principals at a cost of around $150,000 a head. As befits philanthrocapitalism, the academy—which aims to build "a team of 1,400 great principals who are true instructional leaders, who can inspire and lead teachers, students and parents in their school community," according to its Web site—was modeled in part on General Electric's John F. Welch Leadership Center. Much of its $75 million cost was provided by the Broad Foundation. "We could only have started this with private money," says Klein. "Imagine all that public money had gone to a few individuals. All the politicians would have gone crazy." Bloomberg agrees. "In New York, we spend fifteen billion to twenty billion dollars a year on education. So it is not that we are short of money. But we had to start the principal's academy with private money," he says. "Now it is in the schools budget, but that is because it is no longer a risky, untried project. It is something that works."

In 2006, in an article provocatively titled "Bill Gates Gets Schooled," *Business Week* wrote that "visits to 22 Gates-funded schools around the country show that while the Microsoft couple indisputably merit praise for calling national attention to the dropout crisis and funding the creation of some promising schools, they deserve no better than a C when it comes to improving academic performance." Gates is convinced that he deserves a higher grade. For one thing, taking risks is the essence of philanthrocapitalism, so it is no surprise that some of the experimental schools he backed fell short of expectations. But at least they were given a chance. For another, a lot had been learned about what worked and what did not. Starting new schools seems to deliver far better results than redesigning existing schools, for example, and whilst the culture tends to be much better in smaller schools, that does not necessarily translate into better performance in, say, reading or mathematics, unless the curriculum and teaching are right too.

And despite some disappointments, the overall picture was encouraging. At the small schools the Gates Foundation has funded, the graduation rate has risen to 73 percent, from between 31 to 51 percent in the schools they replaced. In New York, less than 40 percent of students in grades three to eight (ages eight to fourteen) were reading and doing math at their grade level in 2002. By 2007, 65 percent were at their grade levels in math and more than 50 percent were in reading. Graduation rates were at their highest in decades.

But even this does not satisfy those at the Gates Foundation. Despite the progress in New York, so much more is needed. "How many Mayor Bloombergs are there?" Stonesifer says, sighing. One attempt to do something about this is a campaign driven by Gates for states to agree to common rules on how to measure graduation rates and on what standards must be achieved to graduate. By 2007, forty-eight out of fifty states had committed in principle to common standards, and the foundation was focusing increasingly on getting them to translate this commitment into policy.

In 2007, the Gates Foundation, the Broad Foundation and Rockefeller Philanthropy Advisors, a consultancy, launched the campaign Ed in '08, run by former Colorado governor Roy Romer, to put nationwide education reform at the heart of the 2008 presidential election. This built on earlier advocacy work, in which the Gates Foundation has worked with Oprah Winfrey. On one *Oprah* show, Winfrey swapped pupils from

## SCHOOL AID

Whatever their political leanings, and wherever they are in the world, philanthrocapitalists tend to be working to reform the school system. In America, for example, Donald and Doris Fisher, the husband and wife cofounders of the Gap, have been big backers of education reform through their Pisces Foundation. They have been leading supporters of Teach for America, an NGO that encourages top graduates to teach in public schools for two years before starting their intended careers. Many get hooked; forty of New York's most innovative new school principals are Teach for America alumni. The Fishers have also given heavily to Knowledge Is Power Program (KIPP) schools, of which there are now fifty-seven in America. These schools engage their students from seven thirty A.M. to five P.M., and have the motto "Work Hard. Be Nice. No Shortcuts." KIPP students, 95 percent of them African American or Hispanic, consistently score above average on standardized tests.

Until his death in a plane crash in 2005, John Walton—son of Wal-Mart founder Sam Walton—promoted voucher schemes to give greater parental choice in public schools. Venture capitalist John Doerr was one of the backers of the New Schools Venture Fund, launched in 1998 to give to or invest in nonprofit and for-profit education entrepreneurs, helping them grow their organizations to scale and connect their work to broader systems change. Since the mid-1980s, Michael Milken's Milken Family Foundation has recognized thousands of outstanding teachers by giving them $25,000 Educator Awards. The achievements of the winners are widely publicized in an attempt to encourage talented a poorly performing inner-city school in Chicago and a nice suburban school. This proved a shocking experience for all concerned, not only because 77 percent of the suburban students had passed the state math exam, compared with just 0.5 percent of those from the inner city, but also because the suburban school boasted facilities such as an Olympic-size swimming pool.

"After seven or eight years, what have we done? We have done good things, but has it really changed American education? It has not. Moreover, the American public doesn't seem all that concerned," says Eli Broad, who started giving many millions to education reform at about

---

people to teach and generally raise the overall standards of the profession.

Across the pond, several philanthropists have given money to start new city academy schools in Britain—a sort of equivalent to U.S. charter schools. They include hedge fund boss Arpad Busson, who is behind the fundraising charity Absolute Return for Kids (ARK); carpet tycoon Lord Harris of Peckham; property millionaire Sir David Garrard; and Lowe advertising agency founder Sir Frank Lowe. Sir Tom Hunter has funded projects to increase the standard of leadership in the country's schools and to encourage the teaching of entrepreneurship. Vacuum cleaner tycoon James Dyson is building a school focused on reviving Britain's engineering traditions.

In India, the Azim Premji Foundation has tried to raise the quality of education in several ways, in addition to piloting educational buses that visit shanty villages occupied by migrant workers. It conducts audits of schools—looking for 100 percent enrollment, 90 percent attendance, and 80 percent achievement of basic educational standards—and gives awards to recognize and encourage high achievement. It also provides computer training to teachers; previously, the government had put a computer in every school, but many teachers ignored them, not knowing what to do with them. The foundation is investing in cutting-edge computer-based learning and rethinking how schools work, not least to foster greater community involvement and support for education. "We have influence with central government because of our brand and reputation," says Azim Premji, who certainly talks the language of philanthrocapitalism.

the same time as Gates. The goal of the Ed in '08 campaign is "to create a sense of crisis among the American public, a Sputnik moment," he says. "It is kind of a novel thing," says Gates, "trying to raise the political visibility of the problem and really challenging the candidates to have an agenda and speak out about it."


"EVERYBODY ON THE PLANET deserves a basic level of health. Six million children die needlessly each year; there are four and a half million adult deaths due to the best technology not being available." says Gates. His belief that every life is of equal value is why global health—shorthand for "health in poor countries"—and development are his foundation's top priorities, even ahead of education in America. He can think of no more striking example of lives being valued unequally than the differences in access to basic health care between rich and poor countries. Most needless deaths occur in poorer countries, where resources are not available to provide adequate health care. At the start of the twenty-first century, barely 10 percent of the $75 billion or so being spent globally each year on medical research addressed the health problems of the poorest 90 percent of the population. "The need is mind-blowing in its scale," Gates says.

As an example of how a disease can cause a massive number of deaths primarily due to economic inequalities, consider malaria—the mosquito-borne killer that Gates has pledged to wipe out. As Melinda Gates reminded a Malaria Summit hosted by the foundation in October 2007, thanks to technical and policy breakthroughs, by the late 1960s the battle against malaria seemed well on the way to being won; the annual death rate had been cut from 3.5 million in the 1930s to about half a million. Yet now, more than 1 million people die each year from the disease. What went wrong? "Malaria changed from a disease that afflicted a broad range of countries to a disease that affected only poor countries. It changed from a celebrated cause of our scientists and politicians to a source of suffering that the rich world was willing to accept and the poor world was helpless to prevent," she explained.

Malaria is but one of several diseases whose impact is felt overwhelmingly in poor countries. Each year, tuberculosis claims 2 million lives, HIV/AIDS another 2 million. Over 1.9 million children die each year from respiratory infections, and 1.6 million from diarrhea. The

Gateses aim to fight all these diseases with a strategy, in the true spirit of philanthrocapitalism, built on an understanding of the forces of supply and demand—in particular, the lack of effective demand for basic health care from poor countries because of their poverty.

"Most things in world health are improving because technology is improving. But there is a huge market failure on the research side," Bill Gates says. "The market failure is that there are no economic signals that cause people and money to be put to work on, say, developing a malaria vaccine, which in terms of the human condition, should be one of the top medical activities, well above, say, curing baldness or erectile dysfunction." Gates is trying to leverage the foundation's money by changing those economic signals—for instance, by funding research into drugs for the neglected diseases of poorer countries and strengthening demand by persuading governments and others to put up money to buy the drugs that result from this research.

These diseases have certainly been neglected by governments, the pharmaceutical industry, and philanthropists. When the Gateses made an early gift of $15 million to fund research into malaria, he says, "we more than doubled the amount of private money going into it." Indeed, one of the main yardsticks by which he judges his success is that the total amount of money going to improve global health is growing. Anything less would mean that others were simply free-riding on Gates, taking advantage of his generosity—some $8 billion given to global health causes by 2007—to reduce their own contributions. "We would be a failure if we weren't increasing the overall money going into global health," he says. "And we are increasing it, very, very substantially."

In 1993, Gates read the World Bank's annual *World Development Report*, a dense 348-page document subtitled *Investing in Health*. He could not put it down. He saw that there were deadly diseases that were "simple to eliminate," such as trachoma, which causes itching eyes and can result in blindness. Soon he was making donations, such as $100 million to fund vaccinations, and turning his attention to the most deadly diseases. He became so enthusiastic about what could be done that, before long, he says, "People would see me at cocktail parties and wonder 'is he going to come up and talk to me about TB?' I was the Tuberculosis Guy."

TB Guy soon became Global Health Guy, as he embarked on an ambitious strategy against many diseases. As with most of his other philanthropy, Gates provided the money, in a host of creative ways, that others put to work. The foundation adopted a pragmatic approach, directly funding what it could and using its convening power and voice to catalyze others to act, thereby leveraging its money. In choosing partners—and often several are involved in any one project—Gates and his team have a clear sense of the relative strengths and weaknesses of different sorts of institutions. In this division of labor, the private sector generally provides good partners in research and development (R&D) and production. Governments and public-sector multilateral organizations are good for financing the purchase of health care products and distributing them to the needy—but not for R&D.

One headline-grabbing initiative was the Grand Challenges in Global Health project that the foundation launched in January 2003. Partnering with the U.S. government's Foundation for the National Institutes of Health, Gates issued an open invitation to researchers around the world to propose ideas for making "important advances against the diseases of the developing world." In October that year, fourteen grand challenges—ranging from developing vaccines that do not need refrigeration to preventing insects from transmitting disease—were selected from over a thousand ideas, which were then developed into proposals that competed for grants of $200 million. In 2005, the foundation put up a further $250 million.

Where possible, the aim is to create successful models that can be replicated and scaled up. One example is a partnership with pharmaceutical giant GlaxoSmithKline (GSK), which Gates hopes will become the template for how Big Pharma will contribute to solving global health problems in future—its past contributions, typically driven by short-term commercial priorities, being for the most part underwhelming. Since 2000, the Gates Foundation has worked in partnership with GSK on microbicides to prevent the spread of HIV/AIDS and on eradicating malaria. "Our foundation pays the cost of the clinical trials; GSK bears the opportunity cost. They're pulling top scientists off of work that could lead to more lucrative discoveries," says Gates. "Since they're not in the business of doing break-even R&D, it's the most you can ask a big company to do and still have any expectation that the CEO will keep his job." Already, this partnership has produced a promising malaria drug for infants.

The foundation has also worked closely with nonprofit organizations on health issues. These include long-established NGOs such as Seattle-based PATH, which, among other things, runs the Malaria Vaccine Initiative for Gates and is reckoned to have received more cash from the foundation than any other organization. Then there are newcomers such as the Institute for OneWorld Health, a nonprofit drug company formed in 2000 by social entrepreneur Victoria Hale. When OneWorld Health discovered an old drug that it thought could cure kala-azar, a parasitic disease of the internal organs that kills two hundred thousand people a year mostly in India and Bangladesh, Gates funded drug trials. When these worked, the foundation used its clout to help navigate the notoriously bureaucratic Indian regulatory system whilst working on a partnership to get the drug to the needy with the David and Lucile Packard Foundation, which had an existing distribution capability in the affected areas.

The Gates Foundation has also been the driving force behind numerous public-private partnerships with governments and multilateral organizations. In 2000, it announced the launch of an HIV/AIDS prevention and treatment program with the government of Botswana, Harvard University, and a big drug company, Merck. In 2003, an estimated 37 percent of the population of Botswana between the ages of fifteen and forty were infected, the highest rate in the world. When Bill and Melinda Gates first visited Botswana that year, there were 5,000 people on the program, receiving antiretroviral drugs. By 2006, there were 79,490. By then, the program was being used as a model to be spread across Africa, thanks in part to funding from the U.S. government under the President's Emergency Plan for AIDS Relief (PEPFAR). George W. Bush launched the ambitious $15 billion scheme in 2003, not least as a result of lobbying financed by Gates.

Another public-private partnership that Gates says has been "super-successful" is the Global Alliance for Vaccines and Immunisation (GAVI). Launched in 2000 at the World Economic Forum in Davos, Switzerland, GAVI brings together governments of rich and poor countries, the World Health Organization, UNICEF, the World Bank, research institutes, NGOs, and other foundations with the goal of saving children's lives by expanding mass vaccination programs. By 2007, an estimated 2.9 million lives had been saved.

"GAVI was our first toe in the water—when we said, OK, it's not just us spending our money wisely and bringing in smart people that do things; it's us as one of the conveners of U.N. agencies which will help developing governments to create an initiative," recalls Gates. Then followed the Global Fund to Fight AIDS, Tuberculosis and Malaria in 2002, which mobilizes funds to fight those diseases—though first the foundation learned a valuable lesson about leverage. In 2000, Gates had given a five-year grant of $750 million to start GAVI, assuming that this would encourage others, notably rich country governments, to add their money to the pot. Some eventually did so, but at a snail's pace. When Gates repeated the gift in 2005, he was still calling for others to do more. He did not make the same mistake with the Global Fund: before making his initial $100 million gift (later increased to $650 million), Gates waited for other donors, in particular the governments of several rich countries, to pledge large sums of money. By the end of 2006, the Global Fund had committed $7 billion in 136 countries.

The Gates Foundation applied this lesson again in 2007 when it joined with five governments to pilot an innovative new funding mechanism to incentivize drug development. The Advance Market Commitment (AMC), administered by GAVI, guaranteed that $1.5 billion would be available to buy a vaccine to protect children against pneumococcal disease, which kills more than a million people every year. This AMC greatly reduces the risks to drug companies of investing in the development of such a vaccine and thus makes such development more likely to happen. If the pilot succeeds, more AMCs backed by more governments are likely to follow.

THE GATES FOUNDATION is now among the biggest sources of funding for global health. Even before Buffett's gift, it had a larger annual global health budget than the World Health Organization, a U.N. agency. As the foundation's influence has grown, so too has the volume of criticism—albeit most of it in private, as nobody wants to be caught biting the hand that might one day feed them.

For some who have worked on global health for far longer than Gates, excitement at how his giving has reenergized their field is outweighed by resentment at the new billionaire on their block. "What does a computer software guy know about health in poor countries?" they mutter. He is funding projects that were tried and found wanting years ago. He pours money into countries without thinking about how it will distort how people behave, sucking people (doctors!) out of more important work into his better-paid jobs. And he is so American—staffing his foundation with people who used to work for the U.S. Centers for Disease Control and Prevention, the U.S. Agency for International Development, the National Institutes for Health, and the Clinton administration. And so, miserably, on.

In August 2005, some of the more substantial of these criticisms found concrete expression in a leading medical journal the *Lancet*. Anne-Emanuelle Birn, a professor at the University of Toronto at Scarborough, penned a blistering attack on the Grand Challenges initiative, arguing that Gates "has turned to a narrowly conceived understanding of health as the product of technical interventions divorced from economic, social and political contexts." History suggests, Birn wrote, that "problems of international health demand a combination of social, political and healthcare models," particularly to reduce poverty—the best way to improve public health. By focusing narrowly on finding better drugs for particular diseases, she noted, the role of the Grand Challenges initiative would be "probably a limited one."

The brickbats were out again in January 2007, from Pulitzer Prize winner Laurie Garrett of the Council on Foreign Relations in the influential journal *Foreign Affairs*. In an article titled "The Challenge of Health," she argued that unless the "recent extraordinary rise in public and private giving" is directed at "tackling public health in general instead of narrow, disease-specific problems" poor countries could be "pushed even further into trouble, in yet another tale of well-intentioned foreign meddling gone awry." Again, her theme was that focusing on particular diseases—so-called stovepiping—was less effective than a broader approach based on building up the overall health care systems of poorer countries. Stovepiping "tends to reflect the interests and concerns of the donors, not the recipients," she argued. For instance, foundations may direct money and attention towards easier-to-deal-with infectious diseases at the expense of financing more important and complex work to improve maternal health.

Moreover, as well as the brain drain of health workers from poor countries to better-paid jobs abroad, workers were being tempted out of more useful jobs into the narrow areas targeted by donors. In Malawi, from 2003 to 2007, the government had lost 53 percent of its health administrators, 64 percent of its nurses, and 85 percent of its physicians—mostly to foreign NGOs, largely funded by the U.S. or British government or the Gates Foundation, which "can easily outbid the ministry for the services of local talent." Garrett's article was not explicitly targeted at Gates, though as his foundation is the best-known proponent of eradicating specific diseases, she clearly intended to influence him.


GATES HAS NO doubt about the importance of technological solutions, though he rejects the notion that he is focused on technology at the expense of broader systemic challenges. Medical innovation is at an exciting point, he believes, noting many similarities to the early years of the personal computer revolution. "This is a fairly unique time in global health," he says. "If you look on the margin at where can medicine do something dramatic in the next fifteen years, global health and infectious diseases are where the most dramatic things can—and with any luck, will—happen."

True, there is not much to show for this so far in terms of new drugs, though that is probably just because drug discovery and development is a lengthy process that can easily take a decade or more. Gates thinks a trickle of promising products may soon become a flood and says "very good progress" is being made on at least ten of the twenty deadliest diseases; solutions should be expected within ten years, perhaps sooner. "Sometimes when we look at the drug discovery pipeline, we think if things go well, we will have a lot of problems with success," he says, thinking about the challenge of getting all those new drugs to the people who need them.

"Delivery is the elephant in the room," says one top Gates Foundation executive, privately conceding that critics may have a point when they say that drug discovery could be the easy part of improving global health. Gates says he has given plenty of thought to distribution. "My favorite book is *Disease Control Priorities in Developing Countries*, because it really goes through the system—what should be done at primary care and what should be done at secondary," he says, a claim about a World Bank publication that would be implausible coming from anyone else. There are real choices to be made between improving the drug and improving the delivery system—say by spending time getting better refrigerators out in the villages to preserve the drugs. "The last thing you want to do is make a vaccine and not have the refrigerators." Already, the foundation has invested heavily in improving vaccination systems.

Gates says that he has studied enough of the history of public health to know it is not just about technology. Broader elements of economic development are needed. "Just pure sanitation is a huge thing. If you look at the dramatic improvement in infant mortality in the United States, it's not when antibiotics come along; it's when toilets and tennis shoes come along," he says, insisting that his foundation "was always destined to be about more than just financing drug discovery."

Even so, the extent to which it has had to be about more than that has surprised some of his closest colleagues, such as Stonesifer. "We expected to concentrate on developing drugs and so on. We were a bunch of product-development people! We assumed others would focus on getting the products out there. We believed science would allow these problems to be solved. But governments meant a 'last mile' problem in the villages," she recalls. "Maybe it was good we didn't know about this—as we wouldn't have started."

The many difficulties of investing in health care systems help to explain why the foundation is focusing more narrowly than its critics would like. One of the key elements of philanthrocapitalism is an obsession with ensuring that money is put to good use. It is hard for philanthrocapitalists to have much confidence about how money given to the governments of many poorer countries will be used. "We don't just write checks and say to the health ministry, 'Here's a bunch of money. Do what you want,'" says Gates.

The foundation has come to play a leading role in shaping international policy on global health, having initially avoided doing so. Gates says the initial reluctance was deliberate, and always intended to be temporary. "In the first few years, we were just learning the area, and we decided that we weren't going to go out and say, 'OK, USAID, DFID [the British Department for International Development], superrich world-development agencies, you should do this, change your aid programs in this or that way.'"

This learning process has entailed much hard work. Gates describes the problems of global health as "hypercomplex," involving all sorts of "complicated path dependency." Never mind the difficulty of drug development; understanding how money flows through the international global health system is mind-boggling. "I don't even know every U.N. organization yet, though I think maybe in a few years I will," he says optimistically.

Even so, he notes, "We've gained in confidence. We've seen the vacuum that's there. We've seen the opportunity, that when you come forward in leadership, things can happen." Gates's decision to work full-time at the foundation was in large part so he could devote more energy to that global leadership role. Here, his experience at Microsoft was instructive. "There was a certain purity at Microsoft, when I used to just write code and avoided managing and hiring and all that stuff. Then I realized that if I want to have a lot of impact, I would have to learn how to hire people, give speeches, talk to customers," he says. "There's a ton of things to do, but that's how you have the largest impact."

AS A FULL-TIME philanthrocapitalist, Gates will have the chance to take the effectiveness of his giving to a new level. In many respects, everything so far has just been preparation for big things that lie ahead. The bulk of his own fortune remains to be put to good use, and there is all that money from Buffett, which will be in full flow by 2009. He faces many challenges.

One is organizational growth. Getting bigger will have clear practical advantages, not least when negotiating partnerships with governments, NGOs, or private companies. "Say that five years ago, Big Pharma's global health activity was X, today it is about 5X, and I'm looking for it to be about 50X. When it comes to me sitting down with a Pharma company and saying, 'Hey, here is the thing that would be great to do,' do you think that our size hurts us? Do you think a bunch of tiny foundations could do that?"

Scale should also allow the foundation to address problems in deeper ways. Indeed, Buffett has made it clear that this is what he wants. "His general philosophy is to take some big problems and go deep on those, as opposed to go broad," says Gates, who shares this attitude, unlike many in the giving business. "The world of philanthropy would be better off if foundations took half the things they are doing and focused their energy and attention on them," he says. "In the economy you get that type of specialization—you just have to because the competitive feedback says, 'OK, you just have to live this stuff and be the best.' But most philanthropies try to do too many things."

Even so, finding sensible places to use the money was hard enough when there was only $1.3 billion a year to give away. At $3 billion, it will be far tougher—and the amount could quickly become far bigger than that if there is any truth to rumors that Buffett's will requires all of his gift to be used within ten years of his death. "Gates has got a big problem," says his friend and ally Michael Bloomberg, "because the money he has to give away is so large. It is hard to monitor it. He will have to split the money among lots of organizations. How many people is he going to need to do it?"

The Gates Foundation is quadrupling its staff, which brings obvious risks of a loss of focus and an increase in bureaucracy. Gates managed a larger and faster-growing workforce at Microsoft, but maintaining discipline and focus is far harder in a foundation than in a business, where the need to make a profit tends to concentrate minds on the task at hand. Recruiting staff with the right skills is also trickier than in business because of the Gates Foundation's unique position straddling the public and private sectors. (Indeed, questions were raised about the foundation's due diligence process after successive heads of its Global Health program later came under scrutiny in Congress over allegations of misconduct in their previous jobs.) Gates will need to take care that the foundation's move into swanky new headquarters in downtown Seattle does not become the wrong sort of symbol, just as in the corporate world, building a new luxury home is often a sign of becoming too comfortable and complacent. Other big foundations have already made that mistake. And Gates will have to manage this transition without the help of Patty Stonesifer, who in 2008 decided to step down as chief executive of the foundation.

Although Gates says the foundation will remain focused on the core activities it was engaged in when Buffett gave that money, one of those was very new: global development. This is about helping to eradicate poverty, a goal that should please those critics of the foundation who think its focus on diseases is too narrow. The foundation could go in many different directions to promote development, ranging from technical solutions that might, say, increase the productivity of small farmers to asking tough questions about corruption and the distribution of power. The foundation has already started work on promoting the growth of microfinance—financial services for poor people—and in 2006 it launched, in partnership with the Rockefeller Foundation, a new Alliance for a Green Revolution in Africa, opening offices in Kenya and hiring a staff including, some of the time, former U.N. secretary general Kofi Annan.

Such scale brings other challenges, not least in how Gates relates to other foundations and organizations. In February 2008 the *New York Times* published an internal memo from the World Health Organization's malaria czar, Arata Kochi, which complained that Gates's money was creating a "cartel" in health research. Even with the best intentions, Kochi argued, "a lot of money leads to a monopoly, and discourages smaller rivals and intellectual competition." If the power of the Gates Foundation is enough to worry a U.N. agency, its effect on other philanthropists may be even greater. Many observers of the philanthropic world think that when Gates shows an interest in addressing a problem, others who have been addressing that problem, or are considering doing so, back off. This may be because of the ego of the other philanthropists, who perhaps justifiably think their giving will not get much attention when it is (almost inevitably) far smaller than the sums dispensed by Gates. Or it may be that they simply believe that, with Gates on the job, the problem is being dealt with so their money can be better used elsewhere. As Bloomberg cautions, "One of the beauties of private philanthropy is you get a diversity of agenda. If everyone colludes and agrees what is good, you lose the advantage private philanthropy has over government spending."

In business, Gates may appreciate the virtues of crowding out the competition—though he has always resisted the antitrust charges brought against Microsoft—but in global health, for example, he says his approach is the more, the merrier. "You should start a foundation and go after a malaria vaccine. I would applaud you. Go for it! It's not like a market, where you say, 'Someone else is doing this stuff, you know,'" he says.

Even so, he acknowledges that problems can be created by his foundation's scale and that he faces an important challenge in managing the expectations of other foundations—and, for that matter, governments and businesses that have money to give. "We have to be careful because in, say, global health, we do so much that if we go into a new area, it can confuse others as they try to figure out how to align around us. We need to be clear about what we want to take the lead on and where we are happy to be supportive."

He welcomes others taking a lead on some issues, as Bloomberg is doing on eradicating smoking worldwide. "Of the diseases we are working on there are a bunch that if somebody emerged who was really serious about that disease and was really bringing a whole new level of resources to it, then it would make sense for us to go and get behind some of the things that they are doing," says Gates. He talked with Bloomberg, for instance, "about how do we benefit from his leadership and make sure that what we are doing in this area is helpful to him."

Figuring out exactly what role to play in the global governance system will also pose significant challenges, particularly if the foundation increasingly plays a formal role in it, based on a model pioneered at the Global Fund, where the Gates Foundation sits on the board alongside sovereign governments. The governance of the fund was designed to address some of the deficiencies of the traditional United Nations approach, which is often bureaucratic and slow. The representative of the Gates Foundation and a representative of business were included on the fund's twenty-person board, provoking a lively debate about how to ensure proper accountability to the public that will only grow if this model spreads.

Advocacy will play an ever bigger role as the foundation tries to change things through politics, both by lobbying governments and shaping public opinion, in rich and poor countries alike. There will be a lot more partnering with campaigning NGOs and celebrities such as Bono and Oprah, as well as Gates using his own celebrity to draw attention to necessary changes, says Stonesifer. But it will also draw attention to the foundation's growing influence, which may make it subject to greater criticism and demands for accountability—all the more so as the public comes to see Gates as the leader of a growing movement of philanthrocapitalists.

Gates will help himself, and other philanthrocapitalists, by ensuring that his foundation is as transparent as possible and subjecting its activities to rigorous public performance analysis. He has promised to be open about the foundation's failures, of which he expects plenty—given that taking risks is one of the philanthropist's comparative advantages over a government, business, or mass charity. Among other performance and transparency initiatives, in 2007 he gave $105 million to the University of Washington to research the performance of global health work, including that of his foundation. It remains to be seen how willing the university will be to tell a major funding source that he is doing something badly (perish the thought).

Unlike some philanthrocapitalists, Gates is steeped in the history of philanthropy. He has often sought advice from veteran philanthropists such as David Rockefeller, whose grandfather is an inspiration to Gates. Gates admires J. D. Rockefeller's willingness to take on big, tough issues and pursue them, often against the conventional wisdom of his day, doggedly for the rest of his life. Like old man Rockefeller, he says, "We're going to stick with it. We're not just like, oh, this is our disease this year until we make a bit of progress. This is it for the rest of my life. We are going to go after these things. And if we have the luck of success, then maybe we'll get to pick something else. But this deserves our total focus."

## CHAPTER 5

# Investors for Good

"IF YOU ARE LOOKING FOR A SPOUSE," says Warren Buffett, the trick "is not looking around for somebody who is amenable to change and that needs change the most. The trick is to find someone that is going to be fine just as they are." The richest man in the world since 2008, when he overtook Bill Gates, was giving relationship advice by way of illustrating his approach to investing—and at least since June 2006, to philanthropy. This boils down to choosing the right people, and organizations, at the right time, and letting them get on with doing what they do best.

When Buffett, a sprightly, bespectacled septuagenarian, buys a company—he has purchased forty or fifty, by his count—he doesn't expect the people running it to do things any differently, he says. That would be "like getting married and expecting your spouse to change. It's not a good idea." This folksy style of speaking and his fine record have won the boss of Berkshire Hathaway many fans among professional and amateur investors alike.

"Warren will be remembered not only as the world's greatest investor, but the world's greatest investor for good," predicted Gates, after Buffett pledged most of his fortune to the Gates Foundation. Gates chose his words carefully. Buffett regards his gift as an investment in changing the world for the better, not just as an expression of concern. The view that philanthropy is an investment in solutions to society's biggest problems lies at the heart of philanthrocapitalism. And just as there are different ways of being a successful investor, there are different ways of bringing an investment mind-set to philanthropy.

FINANCE HAS BEEN one of the leading sources of wealth creation in the past few decades, making fortunes for Buffett and many other, lesser billionaires, a growing number of whom are now significant philanthropists. Indeed, it is hard to think of an industry that has produced more of the new army of philanthrocapitalists—perhaps not even the Internet technology industry that made Gates the world's richest man for a time.

'Twas ever thus, since Renaissance financiers such as the Fuggers in Germany used their spectacular profits from financing the crowned heads of Europe to build the world's first social housing project, the Fuggerei, which still stands in the city of Augsburg. Or the eighteenth-century British financier Thomas Guy, one of the people who profited most from the newly invented joint-stock capitalism. A bookseller by trade, Guy would probably have remained in comfortable mercantile obscurity were it not for some large and extremely well-timed investments in the subprime mortgages of his day, seamen's pay tickets, which he converted into shares in the South Sea Company and then sold before this, the original stock bubble, burst in 1720. He then spent his fortune on a range of philanthropic projects, most notably a bequest in his will to found the new London hospital that still bears his name today.

Every corner of today's financial world has produced significant philanthropists. From banking, there is Sandy Weill, who built Citigroup into what was for a time the world's most valuable financial services company and who has given $250 million to Cornell University. From private equity, among others, there is Sir Ronald Cohen, the Egyptian-born Jewish cofounder of the giant British firm Apax Partners. As well as endowing the Portland Trust, which aims to promote peace between Palestinians and Israelis through economic development, Cohen has helped shape Britain's more encouraging policy towards philanthropy, not least as chairman of the government's Social Investment Taskforce. Following the IPO in 2007 of the Blackstone Group, the private-equity firm they cofounded, Pete Peterson endowed a foundation with $1 billion and Steve Schwarzman gave $100 million to the New York Public Library.

The most public sign of the link between philanthrocapitalism and the finance industry in recent years has been the annual transatlantic fundraising battle of the hedge fund tycoons, between the Robin Hood Foundation in New York and Absolute Return for Kids (ARK) in London.

Robin Hood hosts its annual fundraiser each spring in New York's huge Javits Center, where some four thousand hedge fund managers pay up to $25,000 for a ticket and donate millions of dollars: in 2007, twenty-three hedge funders each gave $1 million to support a new teacher-training institute in New York. They also bid for various exclusive lots. The 2007 auction included the chance to sing with rock band Aerosmith (which went for $400,000), three dinner parties prepared by celebrity chefs ($1.3 million), and an inside-track luxury trip to the Beijing Olympics as guests of the NBC television network (thanks to cajoling by comedian Jon Stewart—"For two million dollars you get to stand in front of tanks" and "Let's show these Communists what we're made of"—this eventually went for $2.2 million).

In London, much the same thing happens at the dinner hosted by ARK, which in 2007 featured a speech by Bill Clinton, music by Madonna and Prince, and an auction that included dinner with Mikhail Gorbachev and a day on the set of the next James Bond movie. In 2007, Robin Hood again "robbed" the rich to help the poor far more effectively, raising $72 million to ARK's $53 million. Since it was founded in 1988 by hedge fund billionaire Paul Tudor Jones, Robin Hood has distributed over $500 million to various organizations fighting poverty in New York City. ARK was founded in 2002, by Arpad Busson, the Swiss boss of $12 billion hedge fund EIM. Busson was inspired by Tudor Jones, whom he worked for in the 1980s. ARK has so far raised over $100 million for projects including finding better homes for children in Romanian orphanages, providing antiretrovirals for South African children with HIV/AIDS, and founding charter schools in Britain.

As true philanthrocapitalists, many of these financial titans apply to their giving some of the business practices that made them rich. That thought may horrify those who see finance as a business that is parasitical and paper shuffling, rather than fundamentally value creating. Perhaps sometimes it is, especially when periods of irrational exuberance result in bubbles. Yet in the past few decades there has been a revolution in finance that has allowed a much deeper understanding of risk and generated more efficient ways of managing it. This has resulted, overall, in a massive increase in the productivity of capital, the lifeblood of capitalism, and has benefited most of us, by driving faster economic growth, as well as handsomely rewarding its most capable practitioners.

One powerful insight that financiers can bring to philanthropy is a sophisticated understanding of leverage, which is essential if philanthrocapitalism is to live up to its promise. Today's new philanthropists, from Gates down, know that however large their personal fortunes, they are dwarfed by the financial resources at the disposal of governments and for-profit companies. To make a real difference, they need to leverage their resources by concentrating them where they can generate maximum bang for the buck.

In finance, leverage refers to increasing the potential upside on an investment by borrowing. In philanthropy, leverage means increasing the returns on an investment by targeting money where it has a disproportionate impact. This requires rigorous analysis of the conditions and systems underlying social problems in order to find tipping points or bottlenecks where more money generates a significant multiplier effect, often as a result of philanthropists partnering with other organizations, from nonprofits to the state.

Finance also brings valuable insight into how to turn an idea into a successful organization: venture capital has inspired perhaps the best-known term in the lexicon of philanthrocapitalism, *venture philanthropy*. It can also shed light on how to pick winners, as Buffett has done so successfully for so long.

WHEN BILL GATES asked his new (sort of) boss to "fill us in on your management style," Buffett joked that "to start with, it's not very stylish." In philanthropy, as in investing, Buffett believes in a division of labor, to allow people to specialize. After pledging to give away his fortune, Buffett recalled how in 1956, on returning home to Omaha after serving his apprenticeship in investment in New York, he had "sat down with seven people who gave me $105,000 to manage. Those people made the judgment that I could do a better job of amassing wealth for them than they could do themselves." That was a good bet, to say the least. Then, fifty years later, Buffett "sat down and thought about who could do a better job of dispersing wealth than myself."

This approach was "really quite logical," he says. But it was also revolutionary, because "people don't often have that second sit-down." When it comes to wealth management, Buffett says, they "eagerly turn their money over to people who have a certain expertise, experience. But they don't seem to think about doing that very often in the philanthropic world." Instead, he says, too often people hand over responsibility for dispersing their wealth to their "old business cronies or some local pals at the country club or whomever, or even a professional staff that may take over the agenda."

Buffett's business philosophy is a form of "value investing," in which he focuses on firms that are not merely good value but also of the highest quality, with enduring competitive advantages—typically dominant players in an industry, such as Walt Disney and Coca-Cola. Here, the parallels with his philanthropic "investment" in the Gates Foundation could hardly be clearer. "I do the same thing in business as I am doing in philanthropy—associating with people who are more talented than me at what they are doing."

As his marriage metaphor suggests, as an investor, Buffett looks for managers who are already talented and trustworthy. And because they tend to become very rich when Buffett buys their firm, he also wants managers who are motivated by more than money—who, like him, are going to get out of bed and "tap dance" to work. "I look for people who are in love with what they are doing, are turned on by what they are doing, and let them get on with it." In philanthropy, he believes, the search for talent "should be more important than in other areas such as investment management, where the game really is not as tough."

In outsourcing his philanthropy to Gates, he is backing a talented executive whom he knows extremely well. Since their first meeting, in 1991, the two men have sat on boards, played golf and (obsessively) bridge together, and chewed the fat about many aspects of life, not least philanthropy. Buffett regards Bill and Melinda as two people "who are ungodly bright, whose ideas have been proven, who already have shown an ability to scale it up and do it right."

Perhaps he is just being modest, but Buffett insists that he would be "terrible" at the nuts and bolts of philanthropy, which is why he is outsourcing it to the Gateses. The Gateses are more willing to make mistakes than he—which he regards as one of their strengths. The best philanthropy often involves taking risks, and more risk means more failures, as well as (hopefully) more successes.

The Gateses are also more inclined than he is to be patient. "Feedback on philanthropy is too slow," Buffett complains. "I like immediate feed-back. I'm the kind of guy, if I walk in the ice-cream store, I want a triple-dipper right there." In philanthropy, "you have to have a longer view than that. You have to take delayed results in many cases. Now, [the Gateses are] going to be impatient to get the best results they can, but it is a different game in that respect. And they're very well suited for it." The Gateses are also likely to be around far longer than Buffett; as he puts it, "their judgment aboveground is going to be a lot better than mine six feet under."

Equally important to Buffett may be the fact that he says he is "having so much fun doing what I'm doing." (His gift is structured to be transfered to the foundation in relatively small annual parcels during his lifetime, so he can remain at Berkshire Hathaway to concentrate on maximizing the value of his gift, which is in the form of shares in the firm.) Certainly, he suspects he wouldn't enjoy the daily grind of giving money away half as much as he enjoys making it. Plow through a company annual report? Yes, please. Read a "one-hundred-and-ninety-two-page book on disease"? Leave that to the Gateses. Nor does Buffett have any desire to "listen to as many people with as many different opinions as Bill and Melinda enjoy listening to," he admits. "There are a lot of people whose opinions I really don't want to listen to, you know. So you have to be a little more diplomatic perhaps than I am."

Buffett is convinced that this investment approach is the way for him to get the most good for his money. No matter that he would never bet so much of his money on just one firm when investing—nor that if he had instead spread more of it around one or two other well-run foundations they might have provided the Gates Foundation with some useful competition.

Many investors see Buffett as a role model. Will the same be true of philanthropists? Buffett's decision to give his money away to someone else's foundation is revolutionary but is it also replicable? Perhaps his gift will mark the birth of a philanthropic marketplace in which wealthy people who want to give effectively without having to be overly involved will invest in successful foundations established by other philanthropists. When the Gates Foundation agreed to accept his money, it did not expect others to follow Buffett's lead. Indeed, it was caught by surprise soon after when a young boy sent his pocket money. Resolutely egalitarian, the foundation decided to accept the money. A few other foundations have said they would be happy to help other billionaires like Buffett who do not feel the need to start a new foundation with their name on it. Buffett says he knows twenty or so billionaires for whom his investment approach to philanthropy might make sense. That would do for starters.

NOBODY LIKES TO be called a locust. Yet that was the fate of Christopher Cooper-Hohn in 2005 after his hedge fund joined an attack on the management and strategy of Germany's stock exchange operator, Deutsche Borse. This attack was so successful that it cost Deutsche Borse boss Werner Seifert his job and led to the abandonment of a planned acquisition of the London Stock Exchange, the economic foolishness of which had prompted the attack by Cooper-Hohn and his fellow "locusts"—as one of Germany's leading politicians controversially branded them. Such criticism has not deterred Cooper-Hohn from launching further assaults on other venerable institutions. In 2007, it was his criticism of ABN AMRO that triggered a lively takeover battle for the Dutch bank, from which Cooper-Hohn's hedge fund profited handsomely, as it had done from the Deutsche Borse affair.

Perhaps the most striking thing about this particular "locust" is his hedge fund's name. When not celebrating their founder, or his favorite place, hedge fund names are typically something suitably aggressive, intimidating, red-in-tooth-and-claw capitalistic: Tiger, say, or Pirate, or Cerberus. By contrast, Cooper-Hohn's sounds positively cuddly: the Children's Investment Fund (TCI). And with good reason: when Cooper-Hohn decided to start his own hedge fund, after enjoying spectacular success working for a leading American fund, from the start he structured it to be philanthropic, automatically giving away a large part of the money it makes to help children.

The hefty fees charged by hedge funds—typically, 1 or 2 percent annually of the total funds under management, plus a 20 percent slice of any profits generated by the fund during the year—have been widely criticized, not least by Buffett, who called them "grotesque." But Buffett should be more approving of Cooper-Hohn's arrangements. One third of TCI's annual management fee of 1.5 percent of the assets in the fund, plus half of every percentage point of profit the fund earns each year above a minimum return (net of fees) of 11 percent, automatically goes to the Children's Investment Fund Foundation (CIFF).

Cooper-Hohn launched CIFF at the same time as the hedge fund, in December 2003. (However, his philanthropy began a year earlier, through a family foundation.) Starting with $700 million, the hedge fund had about $14 billion under management by April 2007, and $1.4 billion had already been allocated to CIFF. This was far more than Cooper-Hohn had imagined possible and made it one of Britain's biggest charities. In 2006 alone, over $400 million was donated to the foundation, making Cooper-Hohn arguably Britain's most generous philanthropist.

Given the growing political hostility towards hedge funds, especially activist ones such as Cooper-Hohn's that pick fights with established firms and respected bosses, this built-in philanthropy may provide him with useful protection. As a July 2007 *Economist* article notes, in today's increasingly difficult circumstances, "the decision to funnel TCI's profits to the poor looks less like an act of insane generosity than a remarkable piece of far-sightedness." Yet few doubt the sincerity of Cooper-Hohn's philanthropy. The son of a Jamaican car mechanic and a secretary, he studied accounting and economics at Southampton University in England and then took a banking job in the Philippines. While working there, he saw children scavenging on rubbish dumps for food, and the image stayed with him.

The hybrid fund-and-foundation structure was devised over dinner at a London restaurant with his American wife, Jamie Cooper-Hohn—who studied public administration at Harvard and then worked for various charitable organizations. She oversees the day-to-day management of the foundation, though her husband is on the board and, she says, "our pillow talk largely revolves around the children, his investments, and our foundation grants and pipeline." Prospective investors interviewed her as thoroughly as her husband, as the philanthropic mission was a key part of the hedge fund's sales pitch.

Cooper-Hohn is determined to pursue his philanthropy with his trademark businesslike intellectual rigor, as his wife puts it, "making long-term, well-researched investments and bringing a private-sector approach into development."

CIFF's mission is to "demonstrably improve the lives of children living in poverty in developing countries through strategies that will have lasting impact on their lives and their community." Note the words "demonstrably," "strategies," and above all, "lasting impact." After CIFF exits a project, says Jamie Cooper-Hohn, the children it has worked with should be healthy and have the ability to protect themselves and their families from disease. They should be equipped to provide for themselves and their families' nutrition, education, and health.

Initially, CIFF supported a "portfolio" of projects focused on four main issues and five countries, each selected for "its ability to have an impact." The issues CIFF chose were children affected by HIV/AIDS, emergency humanitarian assistance, education, sanitation, hygiene, and water in the countries of Ethopia, Kenya, Malawi, Uganda, and India. In 2007, this approach was replaced with a more flexible one, focused on regions and the overall impact on the child, rather than specific issues.

CIFF has three main objectives: demonstrable impact on children, large-scale and sustainable change, and influence beyond CIFF's direct investment—in other words, our old friend, leverage. To this end, the foundation focuses on identifying and overcoming obstacles and bottlenecks where a relatively small amount of money can make a big difference. And it works with a wide range of partners, from traditional charities such as Save the Children and Médecins Sans Frontières (Doctors Without Borders) to newer charities such as the Elton John AIDS Foundation and the Clinton Foundation, along with private-sector drug companies and governments. Its 2007 restructuring was designed to increase its ability to achieve transformative change. Having been disappointed that providing good projects with "mezzanine finance" did not result in dramatic growth, CIFF is now focused on agreeing with governments in advance that if a project it funds achieves the hoped-for results, it will be scaled up dramatically using public funds.

To measure its performance, CIFF initially used a series of standard indicators. On health, it looked at mortality rates, vaccinations, and the frequency of cases of malaria, diarrhea, and respiratory infections. On nutrition, measures included a child's weight and the amount of fruit, vegetables, and protein in diets. On education, it tracked attendance and the grade level completed. However, in 2007 the couple and the CIFF board realized that many of these metrics were unsuited to the projects the foundation was backing. Many of the metrics were relevant only to children aged five and under, whereas much of CIFF's money went to older children. New measures are now in place.

Initially, the couple, still in their early forties, expected to run the foundation with no overhead, so that all the money would go straight to good causes. They certainly did not want an "army of professional staff."

Yet, says Jamie Cooper-Hohn, they soon realized that you get what you pay for.

While not an operating foundation, CIFF now has a growing team of professionals, including several based in the countries where it is funding projects. A lot of energy goes into helping the organizations it funds to "think ambitiously and draw up a credible business plan."

Like many philanthrocapitalists, the couple experienced a culture shock as they moved from the world of money making to that of giving. "With virtually all the larger, established international NGOs with which CIFF has come into contact, we have found a similar set of challenges in attitude and approach," says Jamie Cooper-Hohn. (Equally, many NGOs that have come into contact with the couple privately admit to culture shock of their own. One senior NGO executive says he has found Mrs. Cooper-Hohn, in particular, overly aggressive and sometimes too simplistic in her approach to complex problems, though he concedes that overall her impact has been positive.)

For example, NGOs typically fight CIFF's requests for transparency, especially over how they implement and monitor progress of a project. This has included not telling CIFF about key staff changes, important funding information, and alterations to program plans, as well as generally resisting giving CIFF access to programs and related data. One organization, recalls Jamie Cooper-Hohn, "refused my request to be present when an external evaluator presented the data on the program we were funding."

Nor is much effort made by NGOs to achieve market efficiencies (say, by ordering supplies in bulk, possibly in coordination with other NGOs, to reduce costs), she says. She has found there is "no or minimal effort" to share the lessons learned from an initiative with other organizations, or even within the same organization; nor is there much effort to use these lessons to change public policy or raise additional funds.

CIFF has taken several steps to address these culture clashes. Before the start of a grant-proposal process, it now devotes far more energy to explaining to NGO executives its approach to making grants and what it expects from its grantees. In particular, CIFF makes it clear that the grant process will probably take significant time and require several drafts to get the project right. (Some critics say this results in paralysis by analysis, and accuse the couple of taking too long to put their money to work. They reply that it takes time and much thought to ensure that the money is spent effectively.)

In exchange for this increased effort by the NGO, says Jamie Cooper-Hohn, CIFF offers several things in addition to cash, including an "indefinite commitment to work with the organization." It also offers a means to take risks and to scale up quickly and aggressively when a program strategy is working; additional support to solve the NGO's capacity issues (for instance, by hiring consultants or investing in infrastructure); and introductions to other potential sources of funds.

CIFF has been criticized for not giving enough money away, though this is surely due to the amount of money it has growing unexpectedly fast, and to a desire to think things through and to learn before scaling up. Already, CIFF has suffered disappointments. For instance, projects designed to help children by raising the income of parents succeeded in raising incomes, but this had no demonstrable impact on the well-being of the children.

As of 2007, CIFF's greatest success was a partnership with Bill Clinton to enable children with AIDS to be properly treated with antiretroviral (ARV) drugs. As many as half a million children die of AIDS annually, and children represent 10 percent of those who need access to ARVs. In 2005, thanks to an earlier initiative led by the Clinton Foundation, the numbers of adults on ARVs was rapidly accelerating. Data from developed countries showed that children receiving the same treatment could live very long and healthy lives. Yet there were virtually no children on ARVs in the developing world, and the few that were being treated were generally getting broken pieces of adult tablets (not a very effective way to manage dosage).

Through its research, CIFF identified three bottlenecks to children receiving proper pediatric ARVs: the high cost of medicines, a lack of medical staff willing to treat children, and a failure of political will. After unsuccessfully approaching several other organizations, CIFF succeeded in persuading and funding the Clinton Foundation to extend to children its existing project, which provided ARVs cheaply to adults by negotiating low prices for bulk purchases with generic drug makers.

Clinton began negotiating with generic drug firms, starting with Cipla, to identify a volume of demand at which the company would produce the medication for children at a reasonable margin of return. The company would not go ahead without an official statement of protocol from the World Health Organization and UNICEF—something that had not been resolved in three years of discussion. Happily, perhaps encouraged by Clinton's involvement, this was swiftly forthcoming. Cipla agreed that it could put ten thousand children on medication at an annual price of $180 per child (comparable with the price of adult medication). CIFF led a consortium of fourteen foundations and individuals that contributed $4.4 million to underwrite the program of drugs and training. The program was launched in countries where, after CIFF guaranteed the initial market demand, other sources such as the Global Fund to Fight AIDS, Tuberculosis and Malaria, would pick up the rest of the cost. Within nine months, twelve thousand children in sixteen countries had begun treatment.

"The strategy was to create a market," says Jamie Cooper-Hohn. That had sufficient impact to convince the Clinton Foundation to start looking for ways to expand further, which led to what she calls a "stunning stroke of leverage." The French government was persuaded to use an air travel tax, which was combined with contributions from multiple European countries through a program called UNITAID, to pay for drugs for an additional one hundred thousand children to initiate treatment in 2007, two hundred thousand children in 2008, and universal coverage thereafter. Further negotiations plus economies of scale later drove down the annual price to under $60 per child.

Although the bulk of the money now comes from other sources, and the role played by the Clinton Foundation was immense, none of this would have happened—or at least, nowhere near as quickly—without the catalytic impact of CIFF's identification of the bottlenecks and its seed money. Next CIFF hopes to have a similar impact through its deliberate approach to grant making by virtually eliminating the transmission of AIDS from mother to child. Beyond that, the couple has high hopes for raising the quality of education for hundreds of thousands of needy children. Not bad going for a "locust" and his wife.

CIFF HAS MUCH in common with the hedge fund philanthropy of the Robin Hood Foundation and ARK—the latter two's gala fundraising auctions being one of the few points of difference. To pursue its goal of reducing poverty in New York City, Robin Hood tackles issues including education, homelessness, and mental health. It describes its approach as follows: attack the source, by identifying and going after poverty at its roots; add value, protecting and leveraging investments by helping programs become more effective; and get results, by evaluating programs, measuring results, and refusing to "settle for less than the best."

In 2005, Robin Hood paid over half a million dollars to Philliber Research Associates to collect data on its programs. To oversee its own analysis, it awarded its in-house economist a salary of $300,000 a year—large by foundation standards. (Robin Hood's founders, like their counterparts at ARK, cover all the organization's overhead costs so all monies raised at its events go directly to its projects, which encourages donors to give generously.)

Robin Hood's metrics are widely admired, not least by business titans such as Jeffrey Immelt, the boss of General Electric. A poorly performing program may attract additional resources if Robin Hood thinks it can be turned around, especially in the form of managerial support, consultants, and other advice. Or the program could be cut off; each year roughly 10 percent of the programs supported by Robin Hood lose their funding.

"Whatever we are doing, there is measurability, accountability, a strong business approach," says ARK founder Arpad Busson, a Swiss national who first achieved fame outside the hedge fund industry by fathering two children with supermodel Elle MacPherson and later dating movie star Uma Thurman. Like other philanthrocapitalists, Busson says, "At ARK, we like to leverage. This is because we come from the hedge fund world. We try to form a partnership with a government or supranational entity to leverage what we can do with our little money, to get scale."

Sometimes Busson thinks ARK can achieve the most leverage by giving money to other organizations, and other times by running a project itself—so unlike CIFF, it is an operating foundation in at least some of what it does. One of ARK's top projects is "deinstitutionalization—closing orphanages in Romania." By 2006, it had closed seven and "ran the largest fostering program in Romania." Romania was "sent a strong message by the European Union to sort out its orphanages," says Busson, who saw that as an opportunity for ARK to achieve leverage by partnering with the Romanian government.

ARK is also involved in education in the U.K., where it is committed to building several schools, modeled on the top twenty charter schools in America. Here, the potential leverage lies in establishing a model for successful state education in inner-city areas that the government will then scale up across the U.K. However, the government's decision to experiment with academies in partnership with the likes of ARK has generated a great deal of controversy and opposition from supporters of the status quo. As is sometimes the case, one person's leverage is another person's unwanted intervention.

"VENTURE PHILANTHROPY" MAY be the best-known phrase in philanthrocapitalism, but it is hardly new. Its first recorded use was in 1969, when it was mentioned during a congressional hearing by a representative of old philanthropy, John D. Rockefeller III, grandson of the Rockefeller Foundation founder.

What he meant by venture philanthropy was an adventurous, risk-taking approach to funding unpopular social causes. In the mid-1990s, however, a more narrowly defined, focused form of venture philanthropy emerged, mirroring the techniques of Silicon Valley's venture capitalists, who by then were starting to be widely admired for their ability to quickly turn a bright idea into a large, successful business.

Before the development of the modern venture capital business, which now extends far beyond Silicon Valley, it was largely a matter of luck whether someone with a bright idea could find the necessary investment capital and tap the necessary business expertise to build a successful company out of it. By bringing the three elements of idea, capital, and business expertise together in one place, venture capitalists have been able to incubate many a new business and to grow them much faster than would be the case otherwise. The venture firm Kleiner Perkins Caulfield & Byers, for instance, nurtured now-huge companies such as Sun Microsystems and Amazon.com. John Doerr and Vinod Khosla, two of the people behind the success of Kleiner Perkins, are now notable philanthropists, particularly engaged in the battle against climate change.

In America, the leading exponent of venture philanthropy is generally reckoned to be Mario Morino, an early software millionaire, who in 2000 launched Venture Philanthropy Partners (VPP). Another is Paul Brainerd, the cofounder of Aldus, a pioneer of desktop publishing, who started Social Venture Partners in 1997. Outside America, the leader is probably Stephen Dawson, one of Britain's first Silicon Valley–style venture capitalists, and cofounder, in 2002, of venture philanthropy fund Impetus Trust.

Morino's fortune has its origins in a software business, Morino Associates, that he started, in the classic way, in his basement. He later merged the firm into Legent, which in 1995 was acquired by Computer Associates in what was then the largest ever IT takeover. An early investor in the firm was General Atlantic Partners, the private-equity arm of Irish American billionaire Chuck Feeney's foundation, Atlantic Philanthropies. After Legent, Morino worked for a while as a venture capitalist with General Atlantic.

In 1992, having achieved, as he says, "a comfortable net worth, by anyone's standards," Morino turned his attention to philanthropy. He had watched the working-class immigrant neighborhood where he grew up "fall apart" as manufacturing jobs disappeared, and realized he needed to do something. Given his background, he decided to focus on learning and community. To figure out the best way to help, he spent eighteen months in 1993–94 meeting about seven hundred people, including the legendary management thinker Peter Drucker. By that time, Drucker's work was increasingly focused on improving the effectiveness and managerial excellence of the nonprofit sector (see "The High Priest of Philanthrocapitalism" box on pages 94–95). At one small private meeting, recalls Morino, Drucker argued that "there is little true innovation; we just think what we're doing is new, but chances are that it has been done numerous times before and we just don't know about it." From this, Morino inferred that "true success may lie more in solid execution than pure innovation." He was also struck by Drucker's conviction that there was a growing social entrepreneur movement and that the "challenge and benefit to society would be to convert this movement into a true force for change."

In 1994, Morino created the Morino Institute, which focused on figuring out how the Internet and Internet-driven economy could bring about positive social change. Then he launched VPP, to "help great leaders build strong, high-performing nonprofit organizations" that improve the lives and increase opportunities for children and young people in low-income families around Washington, D.C.

By 2007, VPP had invested most of its first fund, of $30 million, and was raising a second fund of $50 million—although central to Morino's philosophy is the belief that money is only part of the solution, and perhaps only a small part. His approach is to concentrate a potent mix of money, expertise, and personal contacts on the organizations VPP supports. Morino's connections are certainly impressive. His VPP cofounders are Internet entrepreneur Raul Fernandez and Mark Warner, a venture capitalist who went on to become governor of Virginia and then, briefly, a likely contender for the Democratic presidential nomination. Among the investors in the first $30 million fund were twenty-six technology and business leaders, including AOL founder Steve Case.

Although Morino operates much like the best venture capitalists, the straight talking Italian American says he regards most VCs as "highly mercenary. The good ones are those who think long-term, but most VCs shoot the people they invest in after eighteen months if things aren't going to plan." Morino is all about long-term commitment, not least of his time—since 1993, he says, his nonprofit work has taken sixty to ninety hours a week, which, he admits, is "not a casual investment." (Though he remains actively involved, VPP now has new leadership "with an ever-decreasing dependence on me"—evidence that the organization has become established as a "self-standing entity," something Morino claims as his greatest success.)

VPP's goal is to help organizations in the dangerous middle ground between small and efficient and large and efficient. Lots of remarkably efficient organizations have $2 million to $3 million budgets and ten or fewer staff, says Morino. And at the top of the pyramid, there are "giant nonprofits, which are every bit a corporate model and don't need any help." The real challenge is the "organizations in between, the breakthrough organizations. These often have a model that works to some degree but lack the capital and talent to grow and expand. There is an acute shortage of talent."

VPP invested its first $30 million of capital in twelve nonprofits involved in activities ranging from running a charter school to addressing multicultural problems. Morino says proudly that VPP has helped them recruit "over twenty executives and over twenty board members and to raise more money. Of the seven organizations we have taken from a business plan to a multiyear plan, five now have a chief operating officer—which in the nonprofit sector is really rare."

One of the key challenges for any venture capitalist, and by extension, venture philanthropist, is to back the right people. Staying the course is arguably even tougher in the nonprofit world than in business, so one of the things Morino looks for in a person he backs is evidence that they have an "enduring motivation" for their work, such as religion or a life-changing personal experience (often a family tragedy or a close call). "Is there a value set that is enduring? Is it faith based, or trauma based—the two most common drivers of successful nonprofit leaders? If we can't find one of those linkages, we push them hard to think about what is driving them, because without that, they won't endure," he says.

Like a good VC, a good venture philanthropist spends a lot of time mentoring those running the organizations he or she invests in. "I test, probe, listen, observe, adapt, and try again, and this goes on as a continuous-loop process," Morino says. It is also important to be candid about, and learn from, your mistakes as a venture philanthropist—and to "check in your ego at the door."

Keeping an ego in check does not come easily to many of the new breed of philanthropists, says Morino. They can "bring a remarkable en-trepreneurial spirit, the ability to see problems and opportunities that nobody else can see—to find a novel way to solve a problem. They bring money, leverage, networks, risk-orientation, focus on impact, a desire to find inflection points." Yet, says Morino, at the same time, the new rich have "often got their money very fast, and they get intoxicated with their own brilliance. They expect to quickly achieve similar results in another sector. They forget that they have been very fortunate, and that other sectors may be more complex."

This ego factor is one reason why venture philanthropy has so far grown quite slowly, says Morino. He reckons that, as of 2007, there were fewer than ten genuine venture philanthropists in America and "only two or three with real money." Modestly, Morino says that the "leader is the Edna McConnell Clark Foundation, which does twenty-five million dollars a year in venture grants," including to thriving organizations such as the Harlem Children's Zone project, which works to improve the lot of youngsters in some of New York's most deprived neighborhoods. Yet, ironically, the Edna McConnell Clark Foundation refuses to describe itself as a venture philanthropy organization, not least because, it says, the phrase "carries substantial 'freight' from its origins in the commercial sector."

Morino agrees that being businesslike as a philanthropist, which he favors, is not the same thing as treating nonprofits as if they are businesses. Here, his thinking has evolved a lot over the years. The social sector, he says he has learned, is "far more dependent on relationships than systems. It is about social complexity not business complexity." And many of the skills that make you successful in the business world can work against you in the social world: "Business values quickness, brashness, confidence. In the social sector, if you take out a BlackBerry in a meeting, that is a sign of disrespect." At first, admits Morino, "I spoke too brashly about our work and unnecessarily created ill will within the foundation and nonprofit worlds, making our work more difficult. I believe what I was saying was right and needed to be said, but I could have done much more to learn from those who had come before me and could have been more respectful in expressing my views."

Political sensitivity, and an ability to work with bureaucrats and community leaders, is also crucial, given the importance of public funds and perhaps legislation in scaling up organizations nurtured by venture philanthropists to a size at which they can have serious impact. In other words, these "soft" skills are necessary to achieve leverage. "You can't overstate the importance of government funding," says Morino. "The need to get public money flowing in your direction is a big challenge."

Acceptable management practices are also different in the social sector, where the notion that "our people are our most valuable asset" is perhaps taken more seriously than in the business world. "In business you can take out a whole team. You can't do that in this world," Morino says. Another danger is that, whereas in business, the best venture capitalists are highly attentive both to what customers want and to the mission of those running the firms in which they invest, in philanthropy they can be tempted to become social engineers and to think they know best. "You should not try to change someone's mission," says Morino. "The hardest thing to get across is that we genuinely want to partner with them. There has been too much one way: here's the money, here's the rules. You need to invest in respect, have true respect for who you are working with."

VPP was an inspiration for Stephen Dawson, the pioneer of venture philanthropy in the U.K. After graduating from university and working as a development volunteer, Dawson turned his attention to making money with the venture capital firm ECI, which was founded in 1976 and has invested successfully in small and medium businesses in industries ranging from specialty alcoholic drinks to mobile telephones. "In 1997 I read an article in the *Harvard Business Review* about what business could do for charity," recalls Dawson. "I had always thought of getting back into development, and I was starting to scale back my involvement in ECI, so I finally had time to think about philanthropy."

In 2002, Dawson cofounded Impetus Trust with Nat Sloane of the consulting firm Accenture. They invested their own money and raised more from other venture and private-equity firms, consciously trading on their reputations in their pitch to donors—as Dawson puts it, saying, "You can trust us because we come from the same background as you."

Mindful of the potential culture clash between the business and nonprofit worlds, they deliberately hired their chief executive from the charity sector. Impetus plans to build a portfolio by investing in about four organizations a year for about four to five years each, with the aim of taking these organizations through a step change, whether rapid expansion, turnaround, or merger (that rarest of things in the nonprofit sector).

By 2007, Impetus had a portfolio of ten investments, with a cash value of about £4.5 million, addressing issues such as reintegrating ex-offenders, supporting people with eating disorders, preventing gang violence, and promoting sexual health in black and minority communities. "We had worried at the outset whether contributing expertise would be useful and appreciated by grantees," says Dawson, "but it has been a great success." By 2007, Impetus's partner charities had already increased their income by 20 percent and the number of beneficiaries by 50 percent.

As well as pushing venture philanthropy in the U.K., Dawson also cofounded the European Venture Philanthropy Association (EVPA) in 2004. By 2007, the EVPA had sixteen full members in nine countries, including the splendidly named Fondazione Oliver Twist, an Italian venture philanthropy firm focused on preventing social exclusion, learning disorders, truancy, and delinquency. "The venture philanthropy scene in Europe is fragmented and experimental," says Dawson, who is optimistic despite conceding that so far "only about half a dozen organizations are really doing it." He is keen to pass on what he has learned because, as he says, "there are zero barriers to entry in philanthropy, and it is easy to make mistakes."

Another innovative approach to venture philanthropy is being embraced by groups of philanthropists, who jointly decide what to support and monitor how their money is used. A notable example of this sort of group venture philanthropy is the Silicon Valley Social Venture Fund, known as SV2. Launched in 1998, as an innovative arm of the venerable Silicon Valley Community Foundation, it aimed to show newly wealthy tech entrepreneurs and others how they could be effective philanthropists.

SV2 was founded by Laura Arrillaga-Andreessen, then a business student and herself a second-generation philanthropist—her father is one of the largest donors to Stanford University, having earned a fortune from owning much of the land in Silicon Valley. Arrillaga-Andreessen was concerned that, whilst vast fortunes were being accumulated by Silicon Valley entrepreneurs at a far younger age than ever before, their giving was very low. This was due not to "cyber-

## THE HIGH PRIEST OF PHILANTHROCAPITALISM

Peter Drucker, who died in 2005 at the age of ninety-five, is generally acknowledged to be one of the greatest ever writers and thinkers about management; indeed, he is often credited with inventing the very discipline of management. He also deserves to be remembered as the original guru of philanthrocapitalism.

Drucker wrote thirty-nine books, among them *The Concept of the Corporation, The Practice of Management, The Future of Industrial Man,* and *Post-Capitalist Society.* An advocate of "scientific management" and "management by objective," he made famous the term "knowledge worker," reflecting his fascination with the growing importance in the modern "knowledge economy" of people who work with their minds, rather than their hands.

In his later years, the Austrian-born Drucker became increasingly focused on the nonprofit sector, which he saw as having a crucial role in building community and gluing society together, yet needing better management. As well as being one of the first writers to spot the rise of social entrepreneurship, he worried about the lack of ethical leadership provided by many top business executives and other wealthy people. He was a particularly fierce critic of the soaring pay packages awarded to mediocre corporate executives, often as a reward for firing rank and file workers, warning that "this is morally and socially unforgivable, and we will pay a heavy price for it." In advocating better management of nonprofits, he stressed that stinginess," she believed, but to their lacking any idea of how to give. SV2 sought to give them a philanthropic model by developing a network through which they could learn with and from their professional peers.

SV2 partners, who now number about two hundred, ranging from twenty-somethings to sixty-somethings, must commit to give a minimum of $3,000 a year. They work as a group to identify nonprofit organizations that they can strengthen and help to grow. They use a venture capital approach, giving cash to a nonprofit start-up, sitting on its board of directors, and monitoring its performance, which they describe as the return on the investment.

Each year, SV2 awards one "STRENGTH" (Socially-minded Team Responsible for Enabling Non-profits to Grow and Thrive) grant and

this was not to make them more like businesses but rather to enable them to be more true to themselves and their mission.

In much of this work, Drucker was supported by philanthropist Bob Buford, who in 1990 founded the Peter F. Drucker Foundation for Nonprofit Management (now the Leader to Leader Institute). Buford, who made his fortune from cable TV companies, has funded several organizations intended to "transform the latent energy of American Christianity into active energy." For over twenty years, Drucker mentored Rick Warren, helping the pastor of the Christian evangelical Saddleback Church in California apply management principles to create an organization designed to cater effectively to the spiritual needs of today's society.

Drucker believed that the best leaders are "purpose driven." Warren, whose book, *The Purpose Driven Life,* has sold over twenty-five million copies, has become a regular participant in the World Economic Forum in Davos and the Clinton Global Initiative, where he rubs shoulders with other philanthrocapitalists and urges them to bring down the "five global goliaths": spiritual emptiness, egocentric leadership, extreme poverty, pandemic diseases and illiteracy, and lack of education. His church has become a partner with the Gates Foundation, among others, in the Malaria No More campaign to eradicate the mosquito-borne killer. This mixture of philanthropy, capitalism, and religion that Drucker helped to produce is certainly novel, yet it is also a sign of the times.

commits to working with the organizations it supports by providing time and intellectual capital—arguably far more valuable than the cash grants, which by philanthropic standards are not large. In 2007, after debate at a series of meetings running from January to September, the SV2 partners decided to focus that year on education, with a grant of up to $150,000.

In 2007 it was also announced that SV2 would be spun off from the community foundation and placed under a new parent, the Individual Philanthropy Institute. Although SV2 claims that its grants of over $2 million so far have made a big difference to the organizations it has supported, its greatest impact may be the training it has provided to some of its wealthier partners, who have gone on to be significant philanthropists in their own right. They include Jeff Skoll, the former boss of eBay; Jerry Yang, the founder of Yahoo!; and Marc Andreessen, the founder of Netscape (and now Arrillaga-Andreessen's husband). Perhaps that is the ultimate venture philanthropy: investing in creating effective philanthropists.

"THE BOTTOM-LINE QUESTION," says Mario Morino, "is does this activity result in effective, meaningful change?" It is the same question that every true philanthrocapitalist asks, constantly, and that some can answer with more confidence than others. In some ways, the parallel with venture capital is discouraging. Where are the philanthropic counterparts of the giant firms created by venture capital, such as Google? Does the lack of such counterparts mean the comparison to venture capitalism is ultimately inappropriate, or perhaps that its practitioners do not take it seriously enough? Is the ambition to build a philanthropic giant really there?

Morino's conclusion from VPP is an unequivocal yes: venture philanthropy can deliver meaningful change. One small but significant example: In the summer of 2002, an investment rationale and recommendation (IRR) for supporting the See Forever Foundation & Maya Angelou Public Charter School was presented to the VPP executive committee (which works much like the investment committee of a venture capital firm, reviewing and approving proposed investments and monitoring progress). The IRR perfectly conveys the essence of philanthrocapitalism: success is not measured simply in terms of the "growth plans" and "extraordinary leadership" that will allow the foundation to open three new schools, quadrupling the number of people it serves, but also through the leverage of "replication," which has the "potential to change a sector" and "influence public policy and funding decisions."

"Five years later, at the end of our investment in See Forever, we can clearly see that the organization is achieving its aspirations on all fronts, and there is a high likelihood they will exceed the expectations we all had," says Morino in 2007. Moreover, this success had the potential to achieve far greater leverage. The work of the See Forever Foundation and of the Friendship Public Charter School (also a VPP investment partner), by showing that an urban school could succeed, is "resetting the bar for performance of what is possible in the field," he says. "Their sheer achievement has the potential to send a ripple effect across scores to hundreds of other nonprofits, and hence, benefit thousands to tens of thousands of children and youth."

Whether it is the high engagement of the venture philanthropists, the data obsession of the hedge funders, or the homespun wisdom and knack for backing long-tem winners of Warren Buffett, approaches that have already driven a productivity revolution in capitalism now promise to do the same in the world of philanthropy. Yet not all fortunes are made using such disciplined, measured methods of investment. Billions have also been earned by a group of usually flamboyant, occasionally eccentric, and always individual entrepreneurs, whose original, sometimes seemingly cavalier ways of making money are now being applied to their giving.

## CHAPTER 6

# The Vision Thing

"I THINK THE U.N. IS STRONGER TODAY than it was then. I just feel it is stronger," says Ted Turner in 2007, ten years after the media mogul made headlines around the world by pledging $1 billion to support the United Nations. "Sometimes you just need one friend to stand up. Kofi [Annan] said it was a real psychological boost to employees. There was a lot of talk a decade ago about the U.S. pulling out of the U.N.; you don't hear that a lot now."

Turner is one of a group of philanthrocapitalists whose skill in business is taking big bets based on big ideas, an approach that also characterizes their giving. The contrast with the data-obsessed hedge fund philanthropists could hardly be greater. Whilst some of them won't give away a penny without months of due diligence and clear, readily monitorable goals, Turner picked a cause that is certainly of huge importance to humanity but whose progress he will never be able to prove with hard evidence. Pushed on whether he is really sure his gift was worth making, he laughs and says, "I don't know. You want to think you made a positive difference," in a way that makes it clear he thinks the question itself is silly. It is hard enough to demonstrate success of any sort in the big-picture things that the U.N. is involved in, much less the impact of a particular financial contribution to the organization's work.

Turner's philanthropy is all about vision, just like his approach to business. "What's the greatest achievement in science?" he asks. His answer: "Putting a man on the moon. What's the greatest achievement in medical science? Getting rid of smallpox. What is the greatest scoop in journalism, so far? CNN and the first Iraq war."

Back in 1980, many regarded Turner as crazy when he launched CNN, a global twenty-four-hour news channel. All that changed on January 17, 1991, when CNN's unique footage of America's opening attacks on Baghdad turned it into a gold mine. "I was watching it with Jane Fonda, who was my wife at the time," recalls Turner. "It was at prime time. I looked at the other channels—there was Dan Rather, just talking; Peter Jennings, just talking; Tom Brokaw, just talking. Then I turned back to CNN, and *bang, pow*, all the lights in the Baghdad sky. The next day I made three billion dollars—well, at least, CNN was worth a lot more."

"I'm not a technical person," says Turner. "But I'm about as good as they come on seeing the big picture." Yet make no mistake: despite the intangibility of his cause, Turner, the so-called Mouth of the South, is a philanthrocapitalist. "Don't say philanthropy is giving it away," he says. "I consider it an investment—an investment in the future of humanity. I'm not giving it away." The inescapable difference between being a visionary businessperson and a visionary philanthropist, however, is that the businessperson's vision is ultimately rewarded with profits, if it is any good. There is no such unequivocal affirmation for the visionary philanthrocapitalist.

It only took Turner a few minutes to decide to make his U.N. gift, and its size. By some accounts, he did it because he was in need of something headline-grabbing to say during a speech he was to give after receiving a Global Leadership Award from the United Nations Association, an organization that backs the U.N. But that quick, impulsive decision, too, is typical of his approach to business. Executives who used to work for Turner say that he has always suffered from a sort of attention deficit disorder: you might get only five minutes to pitch an idea to him, after which he would often make his decision—even if it was a multimillion-dollar proposal. In our interview it was hard to keep him focused on philanthropy. "Bill Gates told me once, 'Thank you for drawing my attention to philanthropy,'" he says in one monologue; then, "Men should be banned from public office for a hundred years"; then, "You'd look ten years younger if you wore a hairpiece."

In his business career, this limited attention span might be blamed for some truly bad decisions, such as his enthusiasm for the 2000 merger of

Time Warner (by then the owner of CNN) and AOL, which cost Time Warner billions of dollars. But, equally, it did not stop him from making some hugely successful bets, such as creating CNN, and later, becoming the largest private landowner and bison farmer in America. As his executives say, with a mixture of resignation and respect, "That's just the way Ted is."

Turner became interested in philanthropy when he heard somebody at a "do-gooder meeting in Washington" talk about how philanthropy had helped to bring his family together. In 1990, Turner created a family foundation, involving his children, that focused on the environment, education, and poverty, reflecting the famously liberal Turner's belief that "you can't have a world for very long where ten percent of the people have ninety percent of everything; it's not stable, and it's not right either." He says he has also given away around $250 million to oppose the proliferation of nuclear weapons—another cause whose progress is fiendishly hard to measure. "The only way to prevent nuclear proliferation is for every country that now has nuclear weapons to give them up," he argues.

Why did he decide to "invest in humanity" by supporting the U.N.? Embarrassment at U.S. foreign policy seems to have played a large part in his decision, just as it did when, after America decided to boycott the 1980 Moscow Olympics in protest at the Soviet invasion of Afghanistan, Turner launched the Goodwill Games to bring together athletes from every nation and thereby make the case for peace through sport. At the time, bashing the U.N. was all the rage in a Republican-run Congress, and as a result, America was not paying its agreed-upon contributions to the U.N.'s coffers and was in arrears to the tune of $1.5 billion.

"People say to me, 'Why the U.N.? It's a great big bureaucracy.' Well, of course it is. But what are we going to do about these problems without it?" says Turner, who believes that "if the U.N. wasn't here today, we'd have to invent another one. Without the U.N., there would have been a world war." One of the clearest indicators, for Turner, that his gift has been successful is that the American public has recognized this: opposition to the U.N., he says, seems to have declined in recent years, and some progress has been made in Congress to make good on America's unpaid dues.

Turner was reviving a tradition of American philanthropists trying to build the institutions of world government. "At last there is no excuse for war," proclaimed Andrew Carnegie in 1905. "A tribunal is now at hand to judge wisely and deliver righteous judgment between nations." Sadly, the Permanent Court of Arbitration of The Hague Conventions that he was trumpeting has never lived up to Carnegie's great hopes, but the Peace Palace in The Hague that he funded to house the Permanent Court is now also home to the International Court of Justice of the United Nations. The Rockefeller family went one better, giving eighteen acres of land in Manhattan to be the site of the new U.N. headquarters in New York, which opened in 1950.

Nonetheless, Turner's gift was a surprise to the U.N. as much as anyone else. For a while, it wasn't clear whether the U.N. could actually accept the money, coming from a private citizen rather than a state (and not devoted to a purchase of land or bricks and mortar). Governments were responsible for paying their U.N. dues, not businesspeople. "You have to be creative when you give to an international institution," says Turner. The solution was to create an independent foundation that could channel money to the U.N., and to reassure Turner, ensure the funds were not eaten up by bureaucracy. Turner had been careful in his choice of words when he made his pledge; he was giving to "U.N. causes," not directly to the U.N.

This arrangement broke new ground for the organization. "It was good of the U.N. to let me call it the U.N. Foundation, to let me use the U.N. name and logo," recalls Turner. "I asked Kofi, 'What if I turn out to be a nut?' A week later it was approved." Turner is often accused of making this gift for egocentric reasons, but the name of the foundation, at least, seems suitably, if uncharacteristically, modest. "I didn't get to change the name of the U.N.: Ted Turner's U.N.—I wouldn't mind," he says, a tad wistfully.

Another of Turner's gifts as a businessman has been to appoint talented executives who could compensate for his own lack of focus on the details. As soon as he announced his gift, he called Tim Wirth, a former Democrat senator, and asked him to lead the U.N. Foundation. "At first, the U.N. thought partnership meant 'you give us the money, we spend it'—the traditional institutional response," says Wirth. "Partnerships are very hard to manage. It took a while for the U.N. and related institutions to figure out what we wanted to do, and for us to figure out what we wanted."

One of Wirth's first challenges was to organize a campaign to improve the U.N.'s image within America and thereby create pressure on Congress to pay its U.N. dues. "There was a need for an NGO to come to the defense of the U.N. in the U.S. It is probably one of the most important things we do. The U.N. can't defend itself. It would look silly if it had to hire lobbyists to go to D.C.," says Turner.

As well as promoting the U.N., the foundation initially decided to focus on women's reproductive health, children's health, climate change, and the environment. After a couple of years, the foundation's board started to address the question of how to achieve scale, and, says Wirth, "realized that our biggest leverage is our network, the U.N.'s convening power." The foundation helped immunize four hundred million children against measles, in conjunction with UNICEF and the Red Cross; supported the campaign to eradicate polio led by Rotary International; and raised millions of dollars for the Nothing But Nets bed-nets campaign to fight malaria. It has played a leading role in putting together the program for action on climate change championed by U.N. secretary general Ban Ki-moon and got involved with UNESCO in a project to further engage the private sector in the conservation of World Heritage Sites. With the World Health Organization, it has formed a partnership with Vodafone, Palm Pilot, Salesforce.com, and Google to track public health data, which is input into handheld devices, wirelessly transmitted to a database, and mapped online; after testing this in three countries starting in 2006, the plan is to roll it out in thirty countries.

In all these initiatives, a key challenge for the foundation has been "to find the right people within the U.N. who can get things done," says Wirth. "But there are entrepreneurs within the U.N. system."

Having been surprised once by good fortune, the U.N. soon realized that philanthropy was a potential golden egg for an organization that constantly feels strapped for cash and enthusiasm. In March 1998, it established the U.N. Fund for International Partnerships (UNFIP), which, under director Amir Dossal, oversaw the relationship with the U.N. Foundation. It also set out to forge alliances between the U.N. and other philanthropists, NGOs, and businesses, which have included logistics company TNT, Coca-Cola, and Vodafone. UNFIP is not just a channel for money; it is also a route for donors to meet and potentially influence the secretary general and other decision makers. The creation of the U.N. Foundation and UNFIP may be the start of a trend to give significant philanthrocapitalists a recognized role in the global governance system, like the Gates Foundation's seat on the board of the Global Fund to Fight AIDS, Tuberculosis and Malaria.

UNFIP's first success in moving beyond Turner to other philanthropists occurred in September 2006, when the first annual Global Creative Leadership Summit was held in New York, the result of a partnership between UNFIP and the Louise T. Blouin Foundation. A Canadian who built up a trade magazine and classified advertising publishing empire with her husband, Louise Blouin MacBain has involved herself in the arts and philanthropy since their divorce in 2001. Timed to coincide with the annual U.N. General Assembly, the Global Creative Leadership Summit is a stark contrast to the diplomatic negotiations taking place across town. Described as "a unique platform for the best minds of our generation," the futuristic gathering throws together leading artists, scientists, politicians, business leaders, and other interesting thinkers in blue-sky discussions of topics ranging from "Inside the Brain of the Terrorist" to "The Body, Health, and Globalization."

Pledging $1 billion is one thing, handing over the money quite another. The disastrous performance of the combined AOL Time Warner, and the general troubles of the stock market following the bursting of the dot-com bubble, did serious damage to Turner's fortune. For a while, it seemed that he would be unable to honor his pledges. "I'd lost eighty percent of my wealth; it didn't look like I'd be able to afford it," Turner says. Happily, the U.N. was able—and willing—to reschedule the payments, allowing him to hand over the remaining money at a slower pace. Turner had also helped to raise significant sums for the U.N. from others, so the need for his money was less pressing. In October 2006, the U.N. Foundation announced it had received the promised $1 billion—$600 million from Turner and the rest from others he helped recruit. "Now, so much money is coming into the U.N. from other sources. It is stronger when others give, because it is not just me," he says.

How much life will there be for the U.N. Foundation after Turner, who says he will have no more money to give once he finally hands over the remaining $400 million he had promised? The original plan had been to shut the foundation when Turner's money ran out, but now there is growing interest in keeping it going for much longer, says Wirth: "Is there someone out there who is a big U.N. fan who would like to take it on?" (So far, Wirth concedes, there have been no other big individual donors to the foundation, since "they all view this as Ted's deal.") As ever, Turner is optimistic that the foundation will continue to thrive, despite the lack of hard data to back him up. "It's so clear to so many people that the U.N. Foundation is a good idea," he says.

SIR JOHN TEMPLETON has broken new ground in the spheres of both God and Mammon. It took a peculiar optimism to invest in European stocks in 1939 at the outbreak of the Second World War, particularly when nearly a third of the shares were in firms that were already bankrupt. Yet this sort of high-risk investing at "points of maximum pessimism" characterized Templeton's career, and made him a billionaire. He went on to become one of the pioneers of global finance. After the successful foray into postwar Europe, he established Templeton Growth Ltd., a mutual fund that enjoyed enormous success by diversifying globally when most investors stuck to U.S. stocks.

Templeton's philanthropy bears all the hallmarks of his approach to making money, including a willingness to trust his instincts and to invest in things that others would not touch. Not for him the detailed impact analysis and obsession with metrics that drive so many of the philanthrocapitalists from the financial sector. Templeton chose to bet big on the greatest intangible of all: God.

Templeton rejected from the start the idea that religion and science are in conflict. "We are trying to persuade people that no human has yet grasped one percent of what can be known about spiritual realities," he once explained in an interview with *Financial Intelligence Report*. "So we are encouraging people to start using the same methods of science that have been so productive in other areas, in order to discover spiritual realities."

He is best known for awarding the annual Templeton Prize for Progress Toward Research or Discoveries About Spiritual Realities, which seeks to reward those who have revealed "holy truths." The first winner of the Templeton Prize was Mother Teresa in 1973. Subsequent winners include American evangelist Billy Graham, Soviet dissident Aleksander Solzhenitsyn, and theoretical physicist Paul Davies. Whether out of principle or for PR reasons, the value of the prize is pegged to stay just ahead of that of the Nobel Prize: the Templeton Prize was worth $1.6 million in 2008.

His main philanthropic vehicle, the Templeton Foundation, was established in 1987 to be a "catalyst for scientific discovery on what scientists and philosophers call the 'Big Questions.'" Like the Templeton Prize, the foundation primarily bets on individuals, disbursing around $60 million per year on scientific projects that explore spiritual issues.

Templeton's goal of reconciling religion and science has made him some serious enemies among militant atheist scientists. In his bestseller *The God Delusion*, Richard Dawkins takes several shots at the Templeton Prize, describing it as "a very large sum of money given . . . usually to a scientist who is prepared to say something nice about religion." Others have accused the Templeton Foundation of propagating "intelligent design," a theory popular among some Christian fundamentalists that purports to disprove scientifically the Darwinian idea that humanity is the result of Godless evolution. The foundation says it has funded both sides of that debate and has since come to the conclusion that the science behind intelligent design is unsound and has ceased to fund it.

In a 2007 article in the left-wing magazine the *Nation*, Barbara Ehrenreich veers between alarm and ridicule as she attacks Templeton's "most famous baby," the "young field of Positive Psychology, launched by University of Pennsylvania's Martin Seligman after his five-year-old daughter accused him of being a 'grouch' and he resolved to improve his outlook." Ehrenreich then dismisses what she calls the Templeton Foundation's "stickiest project of all—an $8 million grant to create the Institute for Research on Unlimited Love, that last being defined by Templeton Sr. as 'total constant love for every person with no exception.'"

Note the reference to Templeton Sr.—for it is John Templeton Jr. who gives the critics far more cause for alarm than his father. "Put all this happiness and optimism together with John Templeton Jr.'s political agenda," writes Ehrenreich, "and you could come up with some pretty paranoid scenarios: for example, that the Templeton Foundation is a plot to numb Americans into smiley-faced acquiescence to the status quo. And could it be a coincidence that Templeton helped finance the re-election of the most optimistic President we've had since Ronald Reagan?"

Templeton Sr.'s critics, from Richard Dawkins down, like to brand him as a hard-line right-winger supporting traditional conservative causes such as religion and free markets. But this may be a more apt description of his son. Templeton Jr. has been in charge of the day-to-day management of the foundation since 1995, with his influence over it growing as his aging father declined. A determinedly evangelical Christian and political conservative, Templeton Jr. gave $1 million of his own money to found the right-wing think tank Let Freedom Ring in 2004. He also campaigned enthusiastically for the election of George W. Bush as president and for the American-led invasion of Iraq.

Critics of Templeton Sr. should note that he has set stringent rules on how the foundation should be managed after his death. These include clear instructions that his son may be ejected from the foundation's presidency if he is found by an independent evaluation to have failed to pursue his father's vision in nine out of ten areas. More fundamentally, wacky though some of the causes Templeton has supported may prove, one of the great advantages that philanthropists have is their ability to back unfashionable or unconventional ideas, to think outside the box. Philanthrocapitalists can afford to take risks that others cannot. Searching for spiritual truths is certainly not an activity that government is qualified to do. Perhaps Templeton's money will prove to be wasted. But if he is on to something, and somehow funds the discovery of the meaning of life, perhaps history will judge him to be the greatest visionary philanthrocapitalist of all.

NO CHALLENGE SEEMS too daunting for Sudanese telecommunications tycoon Mo Ibrahim. He made a huge bet on bringing the mobile phone to Africa and won big. Now he is plowing a chunk of his fortune back into an even bigger challenge: transforming Africa's notoriously dysfunctional politics.

One reason Ibrahim is willing to take risks on a continent where no one else would is that he is an African himself. Another reason is that he knows an opportunity when he sees one. After starting out as a telecommunications engineer in Sudan, he went to Britain to study and joined British Telecom in the early days of the mobile phone, then branched out into consultancy. He sold his consulting business to Marconi for more than $900 million in 2000 and combined his areas of expertise to create Celtel, which soon became one of Africa's biggest mobile phone operators.

Celtel has arguably done more for the lives of ordinary Africans than much of the aid that has flowed over the decades from the rich governments of the West. Mobile phones have challenged the monopoly of the inefficient, state-controlled fixed-line telecoms dinosaurs, which had kept the telephone as an expensive luxury in much of Africa. The continent now boasts more than a hundred million mobile phone subscribers, a number that is growing not just in the wealthier nations like South Africa. In countries recovering from civil war, mobile telephony is proving the fastest way of bridging the digital divide with the rest of the world: consider the Democratic Republic of Congo, for example, where there are only ten thousand fixed-line subscribers but more than one million mobile phones.

Mobile phones boost entrepreneurship and economic activity by reducing the cost of connecting with suppliers and customers. (Ibrahim is excited about the potential for mobile phones and mass entrepreneurship to deliver even more dramatic growth and poverty reduction in the future, in Africa as well as elsewhere, and in 2007 he established a $150 million fund to invest in African business.) Mobile phones are also being used in innovative ways to provide health care advice to remote communities, to help people to receive money from relatives abroad, and so on.

And they are profitable too. In 2005, a Kuwaiti telecoms operator bought Celtel for a cool $3.4 billion, making Ibrahim an even richer man. More remarkably, given the commonplace corruption in Africa, Ibrahim also claims that this business triumph was achieved ethically, without paying bribes. This is no idle boast: it is the key to his philosophy of using philanthropy to transform African politics. Ibrahim has applied his business methods to his giving—not by distributing a one-dollar mobile phone but by launching a crusade against corruption. Having learned that what mattered more than anything else in Africa was politics—bad governments are bad for business and even worse for citizens—he launched the "largest prize in the world." Winners of the Mo Ibrahim Prize for Leadership receive $5 million up front, plus a $200,000-a-year pension for life. Only former presidents and prime ministers from Africa need apply.

Given the widely held view of African leaders as expert milkers of the public finances, this idea struck many people as crazy. But that may be the point. Ibrahim believes there are good leaders in Africa, but they don't get the credit they deserve. His prize will draw attention to the good leaders whose deeds are often obscured by the (usually more fascinating) bad ones. It is also tougher to be an uncorrupt leader in Africa than elsewhere, Ibrahim argues: once you're out of power there are no multimillion-dollar deals for your memoirs, no $100,000-a-speech lecture tours, and no one offering you nonexecutive directorships.

Of course, even the largest prize in the world is not really going to do much to incentivize leaders who face the more immediate daily pressures of political survival. Five million dollars would be pocket change for the leader of an oil- or diamond-rich country who could potentially channel billions of dollars into a secure offshore bank account. Yet the prize has a more subversive purpose: to build a public debate within Africa about leadership and how to improve it.

The first winner of the Mo Ibrahim Prize for Leadership, awarded in October 2007, was Joaquim Chissano, former president of Mozambique. The judges, chaired by the Ghanaian former U.N. secretary general Kofi Annan, did not simply announce the result; they explained in detail how they had reached their conclusion. This included drawing on the work of a team of experts from the John F. Kennedy School of Government at Harvard University, hired by the Mo Ibrahim Foundation to measure the performance of every African government on issues such as human rights, rule of law, and sustainable economic development and publish the results as the Ibrahim Index of African Governance. The Ibrahim Foundation says it will repeat this exercise each year, to provide every African with an impartial view of how his or her government is getting on. Oh, and if the panel of judges is unable to find a worthy winner, it is happy not to award the prize. That would send a particularly clear message.

Not everyone in Africa appreciates Ibrahim shining a light on leadership in their continent. "It's a wonderful initiative, but it may continue to stigmatize us," says Sam Jonah, a Ghanaian mining tycoon. "You see Mo go on al-Jazeera or the BBC saying, 'How do African leaders sleep at night?' But Enron and WorldCom were not African companies. Given the current state of the world, everywhere needs an overdose of leadership. Mo should make his prize global." Well, maybe. Ibrahim responds that he is an African, though he would welcome philanthropists in other parts of the world creating similar prizes for their own continents. He has also been careful to ensure that there is an African majority on his panel of judges (of which he is not one), lest anyone suggest that this is the former imperialists standing in judgment over Africa again.

It is in the nature of this initiative that Ibrahim, like Turner, Templeton, and other big-picture philanthrocapitalists, will never be able to prove that his giving made a difference. Even if the quality of African leadership improves, it will be impossible to say if the prize and performance measurement played a part. Yet Ibrahim thinks it is worth a bet, and all he has to lose is some money—of which he has plenty.

WE WILL NEVER know how close British billionaire Sir Richard Branson came to preventing the bloody war in Iraq, but the instantly recognizable bearded boss of Virgin certainly tried. In early 2002, he recalls, "I was thinking, 'How can we find a graceful way out for Saddam Hussein?' I happen to know Nelson Mandela well. He had spoken out against the war. We talked about him going to Iraq, speaking to Saddam, confronting him with the truth. Maybe he could go into exile in Libya, the same way [1970s Ugandan dictator Idi] Amin went to Saudi, and we could avoid war." If anyone could talk sense to Saddam, surely it was Mandela, the saintlike statesman who, as South Africa's first black president, had overseen the country's miraculously peaceful postapartheid transition to majority rule after his release from jail.

But before he could fly Mandela to Baghdad, presumably (given Branson's famous addiction to publicity) in a Virgin jet, the invasion had begun. Mandela had wanted his mission to be blessed by South Africa's president, Thabo Mbeki, and by Kofi Annan, the then U.N. secretary general, who in an earlier version of the plan (which Annan rejected) was to accompany Mandela on the trip. "By the time he got their blessing, the bombing had started," says Branson, who admits that they did not let the U.S. or British governments in on their plan because "the Americans seemed so gung-ho about war that they might have advanced the timetable."

That near miss got Branson's entrepreneurial juices going. His business career has been all about seeing big, high-profile opportunities and taking risks to achieve them, from signing the Sex Pistols to Virgin Records to launching his transatlantic airline. "Gates is using his business skills to create vaccines. We are using our business skills to create solutions to issues we care about," he explains. To Branson, his ability to generate publicity and his unique global brand are a valuable source of leverage for his philanthropy. "I have financial resources and a public profile. I can pick up the phone to anyone in the world and get through."

One day, Branson recalls, his friend Peter Gabriel, a musician and human rights activist, gave him the germ of an idea when he said that "problems in African villages are resolved by the elders; the global village needs global elders." To transform the idea into action, Branson quickly arranged a couple of strategy meetings on his Caribbean retreat, Necker Island, where he persuaded a group of wealthy philanthropists to fund a new group, the Elders. Some of these tycoons lost interest when they realized they had been invited for their money, not because they were going to be appointed Elders.

The idea of creating elders for the global village is certainly imaginative and addresses a clear need—especially given the deficit of credibility in the existing institutions of global governance, not least because of the failings of the U.N. (for all Turner's efforts). But Branson understood that launching a self-appointed group presented a huge branding challenge—along the lines of "who do these people think they are?" Wisely, he did not include himself as an Elder, nor the other philanthropists who agreed to back the group. Instead, he asked Nelson Mandela and his wife, Graça Machel, to appoint the first Elders. Branson describes the Elders group as an attempt to extend the brand of Mandela beyond his current frailties and limited remaining lifespan: "Mandela is not going to live forever. How do we replace, continue him?"

This strategy certainly worked in the recruiting phase. "I was skeptical to start with. But there is something compelling about an invitation from Madiba [Mandela's pet name to close friends] and Graça, asking us to carry forward their vision of the world," says Mary Robinson, a former president of Ireland and now an Elder. Yet she wanted more reassurance than just the involvement of Mandela. Before agreeing to join, she says, her biggest need was "to be sure we would be independent." The philanthropist founders have provided $18 million for the first three years, which the Elders can spend as they wish. Independence is crucial to the Elders brand. "We are all independent, beyond looking for votes, which means we can speak honestly to people in difficult situations, such as conflicts," says Robinson, who, at age sixty-four, says she is "far too young to be an Elder."

The Elders group was launched in July 2007 on Mandela's eighty-

ninth birthday. As well as Robinson and Annan, the twelve Elders included former U.S. president Jimmy Carter; South African archbishop
Desmond Tutu; and Muhammad Yunus, the Bangladeshi Nobel Peace
Prize–winning founder of the Grameen Bank, which provides small
microcredit loans to millions of poor people. A place is reserved for
Burmese democratic leader Aung San Suu Kyi, whose house arrest pre-
vents her participation.

"I don't think any of this could work without the root, which is
Madiba and Graça," says Robinson. "Richard and Peter Gabriel managed to persuade the right person on the earth to put this together.
Madiba gives this tremendous initial credibility, though soon we will be
judged by what we do with that." Hopefully, she says, "our credibility
will reinforce each other's work." Brands need constant investment, in
philanthropy as in business. The challenge now is to figure out how to
use that brand to greatest effect. Nobody has yet figured out what the Elders will have to do to be judged a success, or a failure. Only time will
tell if they can prevent future wars like that in Iraq, but they seem determined to try: on their first mission they visited Sudan, to advise on how
to end the genocide in the Darfur region.

Where Branson the man stops and Branson the business starts is impossible to say. Virgin's cool consumer brand is in large part a reflection
of Branson's personality and his adventurous, risk-taking lifestyle,
which has led him to set balloon flight records, bungee jump off buildings, and dress as a woman to promote his businesses. And though bits
of the Virgin empire have at times been sold to the public or other
investors—often later to be bought back—much of it is owned by Branson, so philanthropy conducted by Virgin holdings can be credited to
him. On the other hand, critics note that Branson is very efficient at figuring out how to use his web of companies to keep his tax bill as low as
possible. And they suspect that his embrace of social causes may be
driven more by generating positive publicity that increases the value of
his companies than by achieving real impact.

Branson started young. At age seventeen, he set up an advice service
for students, which he says is "still going strong after thirty-five years."
In the early 1980s, as fears grew about the spread of AIDS, he launched
and controversially marketed Mates, a brand of condoms, because he
considered the existing condom producers too lackluster and the government's AIDS-awareness campaigns woefully inadequate.

## ALL SHALL HAVE PRIZES

The nineteenth-century Swedish munitions baron Alfred Nobel is the most famous prize giver—an act of atonement for the invention of dynamite, so the story goes—rewarding annually since 1901 achievements in physics, chemistry, medicine, literature, and peace (the economics prize is not actually a Nobel Prize).

Prizes to incentivize innovation also have a long history. The race to win a £20,000 prize offered by the British Parliament in the eighteenth century for a solution to how to measure longitude, and the struggle of clockmaker John Harrison to convince the government-appointed panel that he had won, is described in Dava Sobel's 1995 bestseller, *Longitude*. Charles Lindbergh flew the Atlantic in 1927 to win a $25,000 prize offered by Raymond Orteig, a hotelier.

Now they are back in fashion. The breakthrough moment came when SpaceShipOne won the $10 million X Prize, created by Peter Diamandis, for the first privately funded space flight. In October 2006, the X Prize Foundation launched its second prize, for genomics: $10 million to the first inventor able to sequence a hundred human genomes in ten days. In March 2007 it launched another $10 million prize, for designing "super-efficient cars that people want to buy." By 2012, the foundation plans to launch a further ten prizes, worth a combined $200 million in areas ranging from space and medicine to education, energy, and entrepreneurship.

Philanthrocapitalists believe that incentive prizes can potentially leverage their money many times over. According to Diamandis, offering a prize means that "ten to forty times the amount of money gets spent" trying to solve the problem than is spent on cost of the prize. Transatlantic flyers spent a combined $400,000 to win the $25,000 Orteig prize; the twenty-six teams competing for the $10 million spaceflight prize spent $100 million. Larry Page, one of the Google founders, is a big fan, and has given money to the X Prize Foundation. "Larry says that if he were to give to a university, he'd get about fifty cents on the dollar of value, maybe two dollars if there are matching funds," says Diamandis. "But he says he gets ten-times leverage by launching a prize, and one-hundred-times leverage by supporting a prize-giving organization."

Prizes may also attract the efforts of those whom old-style grant-making processes fail to reach, such as people outside mainstream research institutions and corporate life. Better still, because it only pays out when a problem is solved, a prize has the additional advantage of transferring the cost of failure to others.

Setting the right terms on which a prize is awarded can be tricky. In general, incentive prize criteria need to be clear and sensible—easier in science than in woollier areas such as social policy. The efficiency of a car engine can be defined in terms of a miles-per-gallon equivalent. But, as the X Prize Foundation may soon discover, coming up with a clear, testable, and useful challenge in, say, education is difficult. Developing guidelines for such hard-to-measure prizes is one reason why the foundation says it needs $50 million for its operating costs, which will support a staff of forty "prize experts" who will identify suitable prizes, write the rules, and try to generate public excitement.

In one notorious case, a nanotechnology prize was devised by legendary physicist Richard Feynman for designing a micro-engine. The prize was won but the successful solution was not replicable, and was thus of no use. The X Prize Foundation plans to prescreen all applicants, to reduce the risk of them coming up with prize-winning solutions that won't generate the intended social impact. That risks deterring the sort of out-of-the-box thinkers that prizes may be the best means to attract, however, though the X Prize Foundation says that it "wants to attract mavericks" and by May 2007 had already received over three hundred expressions of interest in its new automotive prize.

The X Prize Foundation insists it will be able to design suitable competition rules. "Anything worth achieving can be stated as a goal and measured," says Tom Vander Ark, who became president of the X Prize Foundation after leaving the Gates Foundation. A good prize, he says, must be important, offer significant benefit to humanity, and be measurable and fundable (the reward needs to reflect how much it would cost to develop the solution).

Yet even clear rules and a big prize may not deliver the desired result. From 1994 to 1999 the Rockefeller Foundation offered a $1 million prize for a cheap, reliable test for sexually transmitted diseases. The offer expired without being claimed.

Branson has also declared war on climate change—which, given how much carbon he pumps into the atmosphere from his Virgin aircraft, has provoked some cynicism from his critics. At the 2006 Clinton Global Initiative, it was widely reported that he had promised to give $3 billion to develop noncarbon fuels. Actually, critics pointed out, he had promised to invest, not give, the future profits for the next ten years (an unspecified sum) from his Virgin transport businesses to develop alternative fuel technologies.

Even Branson admits there is more than a little self-interest in this decision, though he argues that in this case what is in his self-interest coincides with that of humanity as a whole, for "if it succeeds, we needn't feel guilty about driving cars or going on holiday." Moreover, he says that if money was driving this decision, he might have invested differently: "If I had three billion dollars to invest, just to make money, I would not risk it all on a hopeful attempt at a breakthrough in clean fuel. Maybe investing in oil would be less risky."

In February 2007, Branson followed Templeton and Ibrahim by offering a prize, the Virgin Earth Challenge. It builds on a long tradition of "incentive prizes" that was revived recently by the X Prize Foundation (see "All Shall Have Prizes" box). On climate change, "we are close to the tipping point of irreversibility," Branson says. "There is only one solution: get carbon out of the atmosphere. Yet there are no scientists researching how to do it, as they have no incentive." To remedy this, he announced that the $25 million prize would be awarded—bear with us—to the inventor of a "commercially viable design which will result in the net removal of anthropogenic, atmospheric greenhouse gases each year for at least ten years without countervailing harmful effects. This removal must have long term effects (measured over, say, 1,000 years) and, most importantly, must contribute materially to the stability of the earth's climate."

This is a long shot, to say the least, and one that conveniently generates lots of positive publicity whilst not costing Branson much money at all unless the prize is awarded—which even he admits is "less likely than likely." But surely pursuing high-risk, high-return strategies is what entrepreneurial capitalism is all about. Attempts such as these to apply that approach to philanthropy deserve to be encouraged. Turner, Templeton, Ibrahim, and Branson may turn out in the end to have poured billions of dollars down the drain, but what if they triumph against all reasonable expectations? As Branson puts it, if someone can come up with a commercially viable way of removing greenhouse gases, and so win the prize, that will be "the best check I've ever written."

# CHAPTER 7

# Philanthropreneurship the eBay Way

AN ARGUMENT BROKE OUT AT A gathering of Silicon Valley philanthropists in November 2004. On one side was Pierre Omidyar, billionaire founder of auction Web site eBay; on the other, Muhammad Yunus, whose pioneering work to extend loans to poor people through microfinance is credited with lifting millions out of poverty. Two years later, in an article in the *New Yorker* a few days after he received the Nobel peace prize, Yunus recalled the dispute. "He says people should make money. I said, 'Let them make money—but why do you want to make money off the poor people? You make money somewhere else. Here, you come to help them. When they have enough flesh and blood in their bodies, go and suck them, no problem. But, until then, don't do that.' "

At issue was Omidyar's belief that microfinance could lift millions more people out of poverty, far quicker, by running it for profit rather than as a nonprofit like the Grameen Bank founded by Yunus in Bangladesh in 1974. The two men had clashed at the home of legendary venture capitalist and philanthropist John Doerr, who was hosting the meeting as a fundraiser for microfinance. Omidyar had declined to add his own money to the $31 million that the other philanthropists had pledged to Doerr's scheme to underwrite a loan guarantee that would be used to encourage banks in poor countries to lend more, and at lower interest rates, to local microfinance institutions. Instead, Omidyar left the meeting convinced that, if it was pursued as a for-profit business, microfinance could reach a massive scale. He calculated that meeting the needs of all the potential poor borrowers would require about $60 billion—way beyond the capacity of the traditional charitable and government donors. "There is not enough nonprofit and aid capital in the world to get microfinance to the scale it could achieve. Relying on nonprofit capital, not self-sustaining business models, is a big mistake," he says.

Omidyar's interest in profit is not a mark of a lack of generosity—he has pledged to give away most of his fortune. Instead, it reflects his view that the entrepreneurship of the business world needs to be applied to social problems and that often, but not always, this should involve harnessing the profit motive. This belief is shared by the other man behind the success of eBay, fellow billionaire Jeff Skoll, who is now probably the leading philanthropist promoter of the social entrepreneurship movement.

The fact that Yunus is admired by many as the world's leading social entrepreneur shows how controversial it is to apply entrepreneurial approaches from business to the social sectors. Figuring out the appropriate roles of for-profit and nonprofit activities in social entrepreneurship will be crucial to the success of philanthrocapitalism. Mastering this philanthropreneurship is a challenge that is attracting not only Omidyar and Skoll, but also many other entrepreneurial philanthropists.

OMIDYAR AND SKOLL became philanthropists early in 1998, when they strolled into the offices of the Silicon Valley Community Foundation offering a remarkable gift: a $1 million block of shares in their company, which was soon to go public. Their only condition? That the foundation keep the shares for a year, so that selling them did not disrupt the initial public offering by creating downward pressure on the price. This was an unusual offer, one that had been rejected by several other foundations, but this time it was accepted. A year later, when the foundation sold the shares in eBay, it banked $40 million. This remarkable act of generosity by two men then in their early thirties, and yet to bank any significant amount of money for themselves, was a sign of things to come.

"As a kid, I wanted to make a difference," recalls Skoll, a dual citizen of America and his birthplace, Canada. Having created the ("fairly generic") eBay Foundation, which focuses on the local community around the firm's offices across North America, Skoll, eBay's first employee, started to get excited about philanthropy when he "began meeting people who were doing something small and successful, but had a vision to extend what they were doing to have a big impact on society: social entrepreneurs. It hit me that there was something different about this form of philanthropy—they were nonprofit in nature but entrepreneurial in spirit, very different from old-style nonprofits. So I started the Skoll Foundation to support them."

With its annual Skoll Awards for Social Entrepreneurship, the foundation provides social entrepreneurs that it thinks are on the cusp of significant growth with "mezzanine finance" of $1 million spread over three years. In 2003, having realized that there was a lack of rigorous knowledge about the subject, he endowed the Skoll Centre for Social Entrepreneurship at Oxford University's Saïd Business School. His goal was to create the world's leading academic institution focused on social entrepreneurs. The following year, the Saïd Business School hosted the first of what has quickly become the main annual gathering of leading social entrepreneurs, the Skoll World Forum on Social Entrepreneurship—a mixture of learning, networking, and celebration that Skoll calls "Woodstock for social entrepreneurs."

Muhammad Yunus may be the best-known social entrepreneur, but there are many others who are starting to achieve significant impact. One who has received money from Skoll is John Wood who quit Gates's Microsoft in 1999 to start Room to Read, which is following in the footsteps of Andrew Carnegie by building libraries (and schools) across the developing world. Appealing to the businesslike approach of philanthrocapitalism, Wood uses what he calls the "Starbucks test" to pitch for funds, pointing out that in 2007, its eighth year, Room to Read opened 1,600 libraries and 155 schools, more "outlets" than the global coffee giant managed at a similar stage in its development.

The two key aspects to being a social entrepreneur are having a social purpose and being entrepreneurial. The classic definition of an entrepreneur was written by the eighteenth-century French economist Jean-Baptiste Say: an entrepreneur is a person who "shifts economic resources out of an area of lower and into an area of higher productivity and greater yield." By that yardstick, a social entrepreneur is someone who shifts resources into areas in which they have a greater benefit to society.

The leading academic authority on the subject, Duke University's Greg Dees, offers a longer definition. A social entrepreneur, he says, "plays the role of change agent in the social sector" by adopting a mission to create social value (not just private value); relentlessly pursuing new opportunities to serve that mission; engaging in a continuous process of innovation, adaptation, and learning; acting boldly, without being limited by the resources at hand; and showing heightened accountability to the constituencies served and for the outcomes created.


SOCIAL ENTREPRENEURSHIP IS a slippery concept, despite the best efforts of scholars such as Dees to define it. The role of profit is particularly controversial, with some hardliners saying that social entrepreneurship cannot be for profit. Certainly, in the early years of social entrepreneurship, the focus was on how to be as effective as a for-profit entrepreneur whilst remaining fully within the nonprofit sector.

Yet, according to Omidyar, the success of eBay itself is a challenge to old black-and-white ways of thinking about the relationship between the profitable, the entrepreneurial, and the social. After all, eBay is a hugely profitable firm built on promoting trust amongst a market-based "community" of users, many of whom have had their lives changed by becoming entrepreneurs selling to a vast global marketplace. Reflecting on this has changed how both Omidyar and Skoll go about their philanthropy. Both now mix nonprofit and for-profit investing as part of their philanthropreneurial mission to do good.

Omidyar recalls thinking about the "impact that eBay had on individuals, through self-empowerment, and asking, why limit our efforts to plain charity?" Earlier he had started a traditional foundation that could only give money away, and in 2004 the French-born entrepreneur merged this foundation with his private investment office, naming the new organization Omidyar Network. This new entity was free to do everything from making grants to political lobbying (not allowed at traditional tax-exempt charitable foundations) and investing for profit—as long as in doing so it was trying to create social good. "We didn't want to be limited to one tool, traditional philanthropic grant making; we wanted an expanded tool kit," he says.

Omidyar structured the organization to avoid different "silos" forming between grant making and profit making. It has a single investment team, with members from the nonprofit and for-profit sectors. Profits from the for-profit arm will be plowed back into future investments or giving. Omidyar descibes himself as "pro-market, anti-big-government, skeptical of traditional philanthropy." The focus of Omidyar Network, he says, is "individual self-empowerment—economic, social, political. Our approach to making the world a better place is to encourage individuals to be involved, empowered. It is a large-scale, market-based approach to making the world a better place."

Omidyar Network has focused much of its effort on supporting the growth of microfinance, especially since Omidyar got inspired at that meeting at Doerr's in November 2004. It has also invested in several other for-profit social-impact businesses. One is Meetup.com, a platform for bringing together communities based on shared interests, such as stay-at-home moms, owners of Pekinese dogs in New York, or separated parents in Ohio wanting equal access to their children. Another investment is in Prosper.com, a peer-to-peer lending marketplace where people can loan their own money directly to others. Another is InnoCentive, an "open innovation" company that takes research and development problems, frames them as challenges, and invites people to solve them. It gives cash awards for the best solutions that meet the challenge criteria. This, says Omidyar, has a "triple-win model: the company whose problem gets solved gets a win; the inventor gets a cash prize; InnoCentive gets a fee."

To further foster entrepreneurship, in 2008 Omidyar Network also started to focus on public policy. "Effective government is crucial to social impact. So we will invest in strengthening governments and institutions," says Omidyar. He is particularly keen on the agenda of strengthening the property rights of poor people, as described by the Peruvian economist Hernando de Soto in his book *The Mystery of Capital*.

Skoll shares Omidyar's view that philanthropists can pursue social good through for-profit activities as well as giving, although he chooses not to combine these approaches within a single organization. He believes there is a huge opportunity for leverage by supporting movies with a social message; that, he hopes, will shape public opinion and so shift resources. In 2004, he created Participant Media to make for-profit movies with a social message; the firm's slogan is "changing the world, one story at a time." Participant Media achieved instant success with movies such as *Syriana*, about the oil industry; *Good Night and Good Luck*, about McCarthyism; *Fast Food Nation*, about obesity; and above all, Al Gore's Oscar-winning documentary about the threat of global warming, *An Inconvenient Truth*. Later successes include two movies about Afghanistan, *The Kite Runner* and *Charlie Wilson's War*.

## SILICON CHIPPING IN

Pierre Omidyar and Jeff Skoll are following in the footsteps of many of Silicon Valley's earlier winners. The grandfathers of tech-industry philanthropy were Bill Hewlett and Dave Packard, founders of the eponymous computer maker. According to *Bill and Dave*, Mike Malone's 2007 biography, although they "didn't really begin the philanthropic work for which they became famous until after they had retired from HP, both had been making donations of time and money . . . almost from the day they left the garage" where they started their firm (establishing a model for many later tech entrepreneurs).

During their lifetimes, Dave Packard and his wife donated $1 billion to their foundation, which will rise to $4.7 billion thanks to bequests after their deaths. The David and Lucile Packard Foundation continues to distribute many millions of dollars a year to causes such as population control, environmental protection, preschool education, and universal health insurance for children. The similarly sized William and Flora Hewlett Foundation is involved in supporting global development and the performing arts, as well as environmental and educational issues.

"By making philanthropy of some kind an almost mandatory next career step for high-tech tycoons," Malone argues, Hewlett and Packard have inspired others to give "ten times" more than the sums they have personally donated. These others included two of the men behind the next big tech firm to emerge in Silicon Valley, chip maker Intel. In 2001, the firm's cofounder Gordon Moore established the Gordon and Betty Moore Foundation, which has grown to a similar scale as the Hewlett and Packard foundations and focuses on environmental conservation and science, as well as projects in the San Francisco Bay Area, such as nursing and land preservation. Andy Grove, Intel's fourth employee and for many years its chief executive, endowed a foundation in 1986, focused on education, women's health, and medical training and technology.

Skoll is more interested than Omidyar in finding a third way between nonprofit and for-profit. He judges the success of Participant Media not just according to how much money it makes. "The aim is for it to be a sustainable business. Everyone else in Hollywood has a single bottom line. For us, it is social return plus financial return," he says. Participant

Media is focused on the same issues as the charitable Skoll Foundation, including the environment, health, human rights, institutional responsibility, peace and tolerance, and social and economic inequality. "I hope it is compelling enough entertainment to get people hooked and into the issues, and to make enough money to be sustainable."

The Skoll Foundation has also been involved in the nonprofit support of movies, paying to translate the film *Gandhi* into Arabic and to screen it across Palestine in the hope that it would inspire more-peaceful, constructive protest and bring closer a political settlement in the Middle East. Well, it was worth a try.

OMIDYAR AND SKOLL have been guided in their thinking about social entrepreneurship by Bill Drayton, who in 1978 founded Ashoka, an organization devoted to finding and fostering social entrepreneurs worldwide that has become a favorite investment vehicle of some of the leading philanthrocapitalists, including the eBay billionaires. "Like many of the world's greatest givers, Bill Drayton is not well known outside the global NGO community. But to those who believe in the power of private citizens to improve society, Drayton is a hero," writes Bill Clinton in *Giving*.

Like the social entrepreneurship movement as a whole Ashoka began by trying to apply entrepreneurship in the nonprofit sector, only embracing the profit motive more recently. Ashoka started with an annual budget of $50,000 and named one Indian social entrepreneur as a "fellow." Now it has built a network of eighteen hundred fellows in sixty countries, with a budget of $30 million a year.

Drayton, who still thinks like the McKinsey management consultant he once was, reckons there are four stages in the life cycle of a social entrepreneur; apprenticeship; launch; takeoff—"an extended period in which entrepreneurs consolidate their organizations and continue to refine and spread their ideas until they become widely adopted"; and maturity, when "entrepreneurs have had demonstrable impact on their fields." According to *How to Change the World*, David Bornstein's book about the rise of Ashoka, early on Drayton chose to focus Ashoka's effort and money on what he considered "the moment of 'greatest magic and maximum vulnerability,'" namely the takeoff point at which "a small investment of resources and collegial support could produce maximum gains."

Drayton admits that social entrepreneurship is not especially new. His organization is named after King Ashoka, a benevolent Indian ruler from the third century B.C. who unified much of South Asia and pioneered innovations in both economic development and social welfare. Another of Drayton's heroes is St. Francis of Assisi, whose followers, the Franciscan monks, inspired wealthy families in fifteenth century Renaissance Italy, such as the Medici banking dynasty, to create the world's first microfinance institutions, *monte de pietà*. These civic pawnbrokers lent small sums of money to the poor, secured against such items as a cap, knife, or book. (The motivation was not entirely wholesome, however: they hoped that these organizations would starve Jewish moneylenders of business and drive them away.)

According to Drayton, what was an inspiring exception in the past has become almost a mass movement today. In recent years, the number of social entrepreneurs has grown to such an extent that he believes they are driving a "productivity miracle" in what he calls the "citizen half of the world." This is due, in Drayton's view, first, to a shift in the global economy away from government provision towards more-efficient private provision (by both for-profit and nonprofit organizations); and second, to a parallel surge in the efficiency of the nonprofit sector—which now has global revenues of well over $1 trillion a year—because of the rise of social entrepreneurship. Today, the "social half of the world is becoming as entrepreneurial as business," says Drayton.

This controversial claim (how on earth do you measure the productivity of the social sector to know if it has increased?) is music to the ears of philanthrocapitalists such as Omidyar and Skoll, who recalls that, when he first became aware of it in the 1990s, social entrepreneurship "was like the business world in the 1890s, before the infrastructure to support it was developed." Today, Skoll thinks that the transformation of social entrepreneurship into something as efficient and effective as contemporary business is well under way.

Skoll and Omidyar are not alone in providing support to social entrepreneurs. For very-early-stage social entrepreneurs, a leading backer is Echoing Green, established in 1987 by partners of General Atlantic, a private-equity firm started by Chuck Feeney to provide seed capital for social entrepreneurs. Since then, the New York–based organization has invested around $25 million in nearly four hundred and fifty social enterprises in thirty countries, including Teach for America, City Year, College Summit, and Mental Disability Rights International.

Even more selective is the Schwab Foundation for Social Entrepreneurs, endowed by Klaus Schwab, the founder of the World Economic Forum, and his wife, Hilde, in 1998. Once a year, the foundation has brought together one hundred or so of the leading social entrepreneurs from around the world to share insights, train them, and honor their achievements. A handful of the best have been chosen to join with the world's wealthy elite at the World Economic Forum in Davos, where they can showcase their work and, they hope, secure the financial backing and connections they need to grow.

Today, courses in social enterprise are taught at many of the world's leading business schools, whose students increasingly want to work in jobs with a purpose beyond merely making money. In his bestselling book, *The World Is Flat*, Thomas Friedman wrote an enthusiastic chapter about the ability of social entrepreneurs to find innovative solutions to society's problems, concluding, "if it's not happening, it's because you're not doing it."

IF BEING AN entrepreneur is about taking risks, then philanthropreneurship means being willing to take risks in the people and ideas you back with your giving. A common criticism of traditional philanthropy by social entrepreneurs is that it has tended to be too risk averse. Drayton certainly thinks so. In the early days of Ashoka, he approached many of the leading American foundations for seed money. "I went to lots of traditional foundations, and they all said no. We cut across all their stovepipes," he recalls. "Not one of them would risk any money on this idea. How could they miss it?" Moreover, he adds, for social entrepreneurs to receive such a negative response is "absolutely typical. Only fifteen percent of the social entrepreneurs in the Ashoka network have had any support from foundations in their first five years. Whenever a foundation says it is like a venture capitalist, you have to stifle a laugh."

In Ashoka's first five years, Drayton says, he "could not get one public foundation in the U.S. to support us with one cent." Instead, he relied on friends and other contacts for finance. Yet eventually traditional philanthropy gave him a huge break in 1984, when the John D. and Catherine T. MacArthur Foundation awarded him a MacArthur Fellowship, worth $200,000 over five years. This so-called genius grant, which came with no strings attached, proved crucial in allowing him to focus full-time on Ashoka.

A personal connection helped secure backing from the influential Rockefeller Brothers fund. This was followed by a big breakthrough: significant grants from the Rockefeller Foundation to launch Ashoka in Africa. Nonetheless, it is living, entrepreneurial philanthropists whom Drayton is happiest to count as supporters. "Business entrepreneurs really get what we are about. Two thirds of our funds are from business entrepreneurs. We would be completely sunk without their support. They are also fun to deal with," he says.

One of Drayton's most generous backers was Swiss billionaire Stephan Schmidheiny, one of Europe's most influential philanthropists. A financier, with an estimated fortune of $3.1 billion, his philanthropy began in the mid-1980s when, in partnership with the Archbishop of Panama, he set up FUNDES, an organization to promote small and medium enterprises to create jobs for the underprivileged. He played a big part in positively involving some business leaders in the fight against climate change in Kyoto. In 1994, he founded Avina, which supports Latin American social and business leaders in their efforts to implement sustainable development projects. But, on a transatlantic flight, he read an article about Ashoka and realized that "I had not invented anything new, after all. My idea already existed." He then formed a partnership with Ashoka to help it expand throughout Latin America.


"THE PHILANTHROPIST WHO has had the biggest impact on Ashoka is Pierre Omidyar," says Drayton. Not only has Omidyar given millions of dollars to Ashoka, enabling it to grow faster, he has also helped by applying his business insights to the organization. "He keeps asking us questions, always very good questions," explains Drayton.

Much of the appeal to philanthrocapitalists of social entrepreneurs over other people in the social sector is that they speak, more or less, the same language, says Omidyar. To businesspeople, discovering the nonprofit sector, in particular, for the first time can come as a nasty surprise. "Every businessperson who first engages in the nonprofit sector goes through a lot of growing pains, disappointments. It is a very different kind of sector, a different cultural environment."

As well as evoking innovation and change, the term social entrepreneur resonates with two core beliefs of many philanthrocapitalists: first, that the social sector badly needs a dose of business rigor; second, that traditional funders of the social sector, whether government or philanthropists, have failed to challenge the sector's often-lackluster performance by getting nonprofits to hire top talent and insisting on management best practice. Omidyar, Skoll, and others rightly want to make improvements on both these fronts, although, as they are also starting to discover, it is crucial that they do not emphasize being entrepreneurial at the expense of being effective.

For the philanthropist, finding the few good new ideas among the many bad or limited ones that many of today's army of self-described social entrepreneurs propose is not easy. And even if an idea becomes a successful start-up, the philanthropist could have to deal with the problem that the entrepreneurial skills of the founder may be ill suited to the demands of managing effectively at scale. Another danger is that by focusing on start-ups, philanthrocapitalists may overlook big opportunities in already-established social sector organizations, such as helping these organizations improve their performance.

In recent years, several articles have appeared in the *Harvard Business Review* that analyze nonprofits through the same lens that is used to assess the efficiency of for-profit businesses. For instance, in a 2003 article, Bill Bradley, a former Democratic presidential hopeful, and two McKinsey consultants claimed that in America alone, there was a "$100 billion opportunity" for the nonprofit sector to improve its efficiency through better management.

This inefficiency is reflected not least in a failure to grow. Since 1970, more than 200,000 nonprofits have opened in the United States, but only 144 of them have achieved annual revenues of at least $50 million, write William Foster and Gail Fine in the spring 2007 issue of the *Stanford Social Innovation Review*. By contrast, the average founding year of the ten largest American nonprofits is 1903. In the for-profit world, companies such as eBay, Amazon, and Google have grown into global giants in under a decade.

One crucial way in which the high-growth nonprofits differed from the rest was that they built a professional organization. Among other things, this required a focus on bringing in top talent, which can be more difficult in the nonprofit culture than in a for-profit business. Too often, nonprofits are reluctant to pay well because foundations and other funders regard that as excessive overhead, rather than an investment in essential human capital.

Some striking data on this is provided in *Forces for Good: The Six Practices of High-Impact Nonprofits,* by Leslie Crutchfield and Heather McLeod Grant. Rather than focus on monetary measures of success, such as annual revenues, they conducted a survey of thousands of nonprofit executives to find the twelve nonprofits that were judged by their peers to have had the greatest impact. Successful nonprofits are willing to compensate generously to attract and retain top talent, the authors found. Ten of the twelve paid at the higher end of the nonprofit pay scale: in 2005, the chief executive of the Heritage Foundation (a conservative public policy think tank) earned $600,000 and the chief executives of America's Second Harvest (which works on hunger relief) and the Environmental Defense Fund (a green advocacy group) each earned over $300,000.

Jim Collins, a management guru who wrote the bestselling business books *Built to Last* and *Good to Great,* says getting the right people is arguably even more important in the nonprofit world than it is in business because it is often harder for nonprofits to get rid of employees once they are "on the bus." Business leaders can fire people more easily and can spend money on buying talent.

One social entrepreneur who has found a way to secure top talent is Wendy Kopp. In 1989 she founded Teach for America, a nonprofit organization that gets graduates from top universities to spend the first two years of their careers teaching at schools in poorer districts. Kopp made it clear from the start that only the best candidates would do. By 2005, over ninety-seven thousand people had applied to work for her organization, but only fourteen thousand had been accepted. Kopp's ability to pick and choose boosted her credibility with philanthropic backers and enabled her to raise more money. Teach for America is one of the top twelve high-impact nonprofits identified in *Forces for Good,* which highlighted that it had achieved the most rapid growth of all of them, reaching an annual budget of $40 million less than fifteen years after it was formed.

One of the areas in which Omidyar Network expects to be increasingly active is helping socially oriented organizations better manage their talent. "Financial capital is only one lever. Scaling is not just about money; it is having the right people," says Omidyar. "We would like to offer organizations help in thinking seriously about deploying human capital."

Collins has long argued that there are great organizations in the nonprofit sector, just as there are in the for-profit world—although in both sectors, the vast majority of organizations fail, by some margin, to achieve greatness. But even Collins says that how nonprofits are financed leaves much to be desired. In this respect, philanthropic foundations are often to blame because of the way in which they fund the organizations they support, which can reflect an obsession with cost control and compliance with the funder's particular goals.

On the other hand, social entrepreneurs themselves, whether nonprofit or for-profit, may often be ill-suited to growing an organization to scale. The inspirational talents that are invaluable for a start-up can become fatal flaws in bigger organizations that require a more managerial approach. Persuading an inspirational founder to move on to allow a professional manager to lead the organization to the next level tends to be even harder in a nonprofit than a for-profit, where at least leaving can be generously remunerated.

In this respect, today's social entrepreneurs may be no different from one of their great eighteenth-century predecessors, Thomas Coram. A sea captain by trade, he spent his early years in New England building ships and on his return to England was so horrified by the sight of abandoned children dead and dying in the streets of London that he established the city's Foundling Hospital to care for them. Without money to fund the institution himself, Coram set about raising donations from the wealthy, applying the principles of the "joint-stock philanthropy" of the day. Many of his supporters were women (his original petition to the king included seven duchesses, eight countesses, and five baronesses), apparently a tribute to the old sea captain's rugged charm. Yet, as with many of today's social entrepreneurs, Coram's talents as an entrepreneur and fundraiser did not extend into the more boring responsibilities of management. His readiness to criticize others, plus his fruity language, drove the trustees to fire him from the board in 1742, three years before the hospital opened its doors. But by then, his most important socially entrepreneurial contribution had already been made.

Omidyar and Skoll both agree that even before raising the profit question there is a huge opportunity to improve the process of allocating philanthropic capital to social entrepreneurs, thereby enabling them to build substantial organizations. That is what Skoll is doing with his mezzanine finance, and Omidyar through his support of Ashoka. Traditional foundations are particularly poor at this sort of capacity building. "In the business sector, people are very comfortable with the idea of investing in an organization and the need to build up its infrastructure. In the social sector, the tendency is to invest only in a program; there is very little investment in building organizations," says Collins, who has extended his bestselling analysis to the nonprofit world with the essay "Good to Great and the Social Sectors."

In the for-profit world, there are powerful market pressures that drive organizations to be more efficient. What constitutes good performance is clear: profit. Despite many attempts, the nonprofit world has yet to find a comparable universal yardstick. The for-profit world also has mergers and acquisitions that (mostly) allow faster growth and remove poor performers. There is no merger-and-acquisition market in the nonprofit world. Philanthropists could help by encouraging consolidation, says financier and philanthropist John Studzinski. "In homelessness work, I'm a great advocate of consolidation. There are about forty homelessness projects in London; only eight are any good," he says.

Some of the more venerable nonprofits think that they offer better value for money than new start-up social enterprises and they are starting to attract funds from the new generation of philanthropists. Charles MacCormack, since 1993 the head of Save the Children, fears that the new philanthropists will focus too much on social entrepreneurs, and so miss out on the expertise and scale of established charities and NGOs. "I end up talking to many of these new people along the way, the megadonors who are trying to create their own organizations from scratch," he says. "But they could get better impact and leverage by partnering with Save the Children, or Care, or UNICEF, as we already have the sunk costs of staff, offices software, and so on." He hopes that a "certain number of these donors will come to realize that it makes more sense to work with an existing entity than start a new one." Indeed, some already are. In the past five years he has seen "a dramatic increase in giving to

Save the Children from superrich philanthropists, led by the Gates Foundation, but also Soros, Hewlett, the U.N. Foundation, the Elmer Foundation, and CIFF." In that time, the charity has gone from getting two thirds of its funding from government to one third.


THE RISE OF social entrepreneurship has coincided with a growing recognition by the nonprofit sector of the virtues of the for-profit model, says Omidyar. "Sustainability is key. Nonprofits have recognized that their cost of raising capital is horrendous compared to the for-profit world. The nonprofit world has said, 'Here is what business can teach us: scale, sustainability, impact,'" he argues. Microfinance is the testing ground for his belief that for many nonprofits, and social problems, the best strategy is to harness the profit motive.

There are already examples of for-profit microfinance institutions that have been extremely successful, notably Banco Compartamos of Mexico, which in 2007 went public with a market capitalization of $1.5 billion (see "Microfinance the Mexican Way" box on pages 132–33). To encourage others to follow the for-profit route, Omidyar gave $100 million in 2005 to Tufts University, his alma mater, which he stipulated should be invested in for-profit microfinance within three years. This gift, he says, was about "creating a marketplace around microfinance, to match investors and people who need capital." At first, it was not clear if this unprecedented gift could actually be invested as Omidyar wanted but "we are finding more and more investment opportunities," he says.

Omidyar peppers his conversation with references to Adam Smith. He even has a bust of the eighteenth-century Scottish author of *The Wealth of Nations* in his office. A crucial point in the evolution of his thinking about philanthropy came, he says, when "I rediscovered Adam Smith, who said that in the right environment, the right kind of business model will inevitably lead to social benefit by pursuing traditional financial goals." As Omidyar explains, "It can be very difficult to measure a nonprofit's social impact. On the other hand, it is very easy to measure a for-profit's financial performance. Financial performance doesn't necessarily equate to social impact, but if there is a correlation, it can be a very useful indicator."

This leads to his key conclusion: "We need to change the way people think about business—to see that it is not inherently evil but inherently good." Not that this means there is no role for the nonprofit sector, or for government, which has the important duty to "create the right environment, through public goods, regulation," according to Omidyar, who is confident that this message is starting to be heard. "My sense is that the social sector has acknowledged that, in the end, having a social impact is not the exclusive preserve of nonprofits. Whether you are a nonprofit or for-profit, you need to be scalable, need to be sustainable, need to focus on customers and outcomes. No one in the nonprofit sector disagrees."

Ashoka is picking up Omidyar's message by helping for-profit companies work with nonprofit organizations to create win-win situations. Drayton calls these partnerships "hybrid value chains," which sounds daunting but is taking off in practice. One example involves Cemex, a Mexican cement giant, and groups representing slum dwellers, which are working together to provide more efficient ways of buying cement to build extra rooms on houses. "Hybrid value chains are going to change the world because they are so profitable," says Drayton.

Ashoka has also hired some bankers to explore how to engage capital markets in social change. Its program of "social financial services" has two goals; to engage with the mainstream banks and to provide more-efficient funding for social entrepreneurs. One product of this is the Eye Fund, created by social entrepreneur David Green and Deutsche Bank.

"Traditionally, social enterprises have been too small to be interesting to the capital markets," says Green, who has worked since 1983 to find low-cost solutions to eye problems in poor countries. The Eye Fund aims to overcome these problems by aggregating the revenues of many small social enterprises that generate cash by providing affordable eye care to people in poor countries. The goal is to borrow an initial $20 million from commercial lenders and thereby fund a "sea change in the growth to scale of eye care, instead of incremental growth," says Green.

It is still early days for philanthropreneurship. The debate about when to give money away and when to invest it for profit is likely to continue for many years. Certainly, nonprofit activities will remain a big part of social entrepreneurship and philanthropy. Most social entrepreneurs need grant support at the outset to get an idea off the ground—much as any business would need start-up finance. The dilemma for the philanthrocapitalist is when to let go and move to a for-profit model.

A big opportunity for philanthropists may be to back ideas that, if they succeed, would profitably solve social problems, but which have a

---

## MICROFINANCE THE MEXICAN WAY

"Microfinance is one of the first areas where we will see the philanthropist play an unexpected role, as a creator of industries," argues Carlos Danel, the joint chief executive (with Carlos Labarthe) of Banco Compartamos. "Ours is a story in which this modern type of philanthropist has played a key role."

Compartamos started out in 1990 as a nonprofit, lending to people in the poor Mexican states of Oaxaca and Chiapas. But it had a hard time growing because of the scarcity of funding. In 2000, it had only sixty thousand clients. But that year it became a for-profit—and has not looked back. By 2007 it had over eight hundred thousand clients. In April that year Compartamos sold 30 percent of its shares in an initial public offering. By then, "our goal was to show mainstream capital that a social venture can be a successful business and create social value too," Danel says.

The decision to turn for-profit was not an easy one, and 2000 was a time of temptation to pursue a different path. Vicente Fox, the newly elected president of Mexico, knew Muhammad Yunus and was a keen advocate of microfinance. "He set up a big fund, and said that twenty-five percent of it would be given to us—free money!" recalls Danel. "We refused, as we wanted to build a track record with the market. This was a critical point in testing our model. The easiest thing to do would have been to take the state's money, especially as banks weren't lending to us at that time."

Compartamos does not serve the very poorest clients, unlike Yunus's Grameen, which even makes interest-free loans to beggars. Danel acknowledges that there may be limits to the scope of for-profit microfinance. "We focus on market segments C and D—not the poorest segment, E, as microfinance is not an effective tool there," says Danel. "It is really only for the working poor. The entire industry in Mexico only has fifteen percent coverage of the C and D market, so there is still plenty of opportunity to grow." Some critics complain that the interest rates charged by Compartamos are too high, but Danel says that if the rates were lower, it would not be able to so quickly grow the number of clients it serves.

The philanthropist who played a crucial role in the history of Comparta-

higher risk of failure than commercial providers of capital, including
venture capitalists, are willing to bear. Bearing the risk of ascertaining

mos is Alfredo Harp Helú. A cousin of billionaire Carlos Slim Helú, he was
an owner of Banamex, a retail bank, which was sold in 2001 for $12.5 billion
to Citigroup. He met Danel in 1994, a turbulent year in Mexico, in which
Harp Helú was the subject of a high-profile kidnapping. Afterwards he decided to take the activities of his foundation to a new scale, and was soon
Latin America's leading philanthropist, giving away millions of dollars a
year. He became the biggest individual investor in Compartamos and was
"instrumental in making us more of a financial institution than an NGO,"
says Danel. In many ways, Harp Helú became a mentor to the joint CEOs,
like the best sort of venture capitalist.

Which raises a question: Given it is now a for-profit business, surely
Compartamos should have been funded by a real venture capitalist, not a
philanthropist imitating aspects of venture capital? In an ideal world, perhaps, concedes Danel, but that was not an option in the real world. "Forget
social entrepreneurs—all entrepreneurs in developing countries struggle to
raise venture capital, even for simple for-profit businesses. Venture capital is
extremely hard to come by in developing markets, especially seed capital."

Danel believes that Omidyar, Gates, and other philanthropists can now
have a big impact on other nonprofits by "bringing to bear their business
expertise, by treating the people they work with as business partners who
they are helping to work their way out of reliance on the donor community.
It is easier for these philanthropists to do that than public donor institutions with more bureaucratic structures [such as the World Bank], and with
no obvious alternative use for the capital. But they need to be smart. If they
don't see themselves as enablers of microfinance institutions moving to
the private sector, they could crowd out private investors by sending a signal that there will be perpetual reliance on philanthropy."

Danel reckons that "there are similar opportunities in health care, education, and housing for the very poor—if it can be demonstrated that there
is a profitable business model." Cell phones, which have grown fast in developing countries and are run for profit, are a good example of how profit
can help achieve scale and drive social change.

whether the idea can be pursued profitably is well suited to philanthropy. If the idea is a dud the money can be counted as a donation to
the cause of increasing human knowledge; if it only works as a nonprofit, philanthropists can choose to keep funding it; whilst if it succeeds, the philanthropists can let for-profit investors take it to scale
while they, having played a crucial catalytic role, can put their philanthropic risk capital to work elsewhere.

That said, there remains much learning to be done, as both Skoll and
Omidyar would be the first to admit. In 2007, Omidyar restructured
Omidyar Network yet again, hiring Matt Bannick to be its managing partner. Bannick was previously president of eBay's international division and
was brought in to provide more drive and entrepreneurial spirit.

In the philanthropic world, there has been much discussion of whether
Omidyar's actions live up to his rhetoric. Some critics accuse him of

## INVESTING IN SUCCESS

It is hard to think of a clearer example of how the worlds of social entrepreneurship and business are coming together in new, somewhat para-
doxical ways than Endeavor. Founded in 1997 by Linda Rottenberg, who
had led Ashoka's Latin American expansion from Buenos Aires, and Peter
Kellner, an investor mentored by Bill Drayton, Endeavor is a nonprofit
whose sole purpose is to help for-profit entrepreneurs become more successful.

At first, Rottenberg's requests for initial funding for Endeavor were
turned down time and time again by traditional foundations, which "kept
saying that building the middle class is not something they want to support." Happily, Stephan Schmidheiny's Avina foundation seeded Endeavor
with $500,000, and later Endeavor won backing from various wealthy busi-
nesspeople, not least at a glitzy annual gala in New York at which it hands
out Entrepreneur of the Year awards.

Endeavor organizes groups of wealthy businesspeople in developing
countries, who mentor potential "high-impact entrepreneurs" chosen by
Endeavor as they seek to grow their businesses. Having started in Latin
America, Endeavor had operations in eight countries after ten years and a
network of 266 entrepreneurs (out of over 15,000 candidates that the organization screened). The firms started by Endeavor's entrepreneurs had

indecision and too frequent changes in strategy, which has fueled a high rate of staff turnover. Asked to list the top five challenges facing the organization, one former executive at Omidyar Network, who quit out of frustration, says that the first was the "arrogance and naivety" of the leadership: a "lethal combination." Omidyar himself had not even visited a working microfinance institution until 2007. Second, the former executive says, the leadership was "very condescending to nonprofits, and was always wanting to be different for its own sake." Third, it had no stick-to-it-ness—the organization had a "different flavor every week, both substance and peoplewise." Fourth, there was "too much talk with no action and no proven results." Lastly: "clueless, kiss-up leadership."

Such comments are not atypical. However, Omidyar thinks the criticisms are greatly overdone. "We are still relatively new to this business of delivering social value," he says. "We like to work with people who like

---

combined revenues of $1.9 billion, had raised equity capital of $908 million, and had created over thirty-eight thousand jobs.

Endeavor initially focused on countries where a few families or firms dominated the economy, making it hard for entrepreneurs without preexisting wealth to gain a foothold. The aim was to create role models for aspiring entrepreneurs in those countries to inspire them to follow their dreams. "Entrepreneurship should be America's best export," says Rottenberg, who thinks her model can readily spread to many more countries as a sort of "McDonald's of entrepreneurship."

But why has Endeavor opted to be a nonprofit reliant on philanthropy to cover its costs, rather than a for-profit able to raise commercial funds to back its entrepreneurs with cash as well as mentoring? Rottenberg says that being a nonprofit helped win the trust of entrepreneurs who may have been reluctant to enter a relationship with a foreign for-profit organization and that several attempts by others to create for-profit equivalents of Endeavor have failed.

In 2007, Endeavor's strategy unexpectedly started to generate a financial return of sorts: several of the entrepreneurs it mentored gave, or pledged to give, Endeavor some equity in their firms as they were taken public or sold. This was a thank-you, designed to give the organization a sustainable business model—and proof, perhaps, that you reap what you sow.

learning new things, and a lot of learning requires change"—which explains some of the high staff turnover. "Any organization that is learning is going to have turnover. Given the goal of long-term social impact, it would be wrong to take short-term decisions designed to reduce turnover and so compromise the long-term objective."

Meanwhile, Skoll had spent much of 2007 thinking: "I got to a point where I felt I'd been running things—eBay, my foundation, my investment group, Participant—and I hadn't taken time out since school to just step back and figure out what is next, how I can be more effective." He decided to "travel a lot, to see what the big problems are." He visited social entrepreneurs in the field, attended the Clinton Global Initiative, and planned to spend some time with the Elders group, which he decided to help fund. "I want to sit with people who have experience, ask their advice," he says.

"I'm determined to point social entrepreneurs and, candidly, any type of entrepreneurs, at finding solutions to climate change," he said shortly after visiting India in August 2007. His tour was conducted by Rajendra Pachauri, the head of the Intergovernmental Panel on Climate Change—which soon afterwards was jointly awarded the Nobel Peace Prize with former U.S. vice president Al Gore. What Skoll saw convinced him that "climate change is a much bigger problem than I had thought." Moreover, he says, "the two billion people at the bottom of the pyramid will one day want to burn fossil fuels; if we lose those people to fossil fuels, we lose the battle against global warming."

One example of a potential solution that Skoll saw firsthand in India was a profit-driven way to beat climate change called the "solar franchise." In principle, in every village, someone would buy or be granted the solar franchise, put a solar panel on his or her roof, and sell other villagers use of the electricity generated by it, for recharging their electronic devices and so forth. "The idea is to let the profit motive take it to scale," he says.

And it is not just Omidyar and Skoll who are learning. Muhammad Yunus used his 2007 book *Creating a World Without Poverty* to promote the idea of "social business." "A social entrepreneur may have some cost recovery; a social business entrepreneur recovers 100 percent or more, and so can move from the philanthropy world to the business world," he says. "Philanthropy money is limited by resources. Business is less vulnerable."

Yunus still disagrees with Omidyar over how far the for-profit model can go in solving the world's problems but, as a champion of entrepreneurship, he is happy to let the market decide. "Let's have more competition between self-centered business and those trying to do good," he says. May the best business model win.

## CHAPTER 8

# Picassos, Genomes, and Ivory Towers

"I CAN'T REALLY EXPLAIN WHAT THEY do; I've no background in medicine or science," admits Eli Broad of the research institute that bears his name. This seems a strange confession for a philanthrocapitalist who has invested $200 million in arguably the world's leading center for research into the human genome, the Broad Institute. But Broad plans to give more: "I will probably end up endowing it," he says. Broad is also a big supporter of the arts. He has amassed a two-thousand-piece collection of modern art, including work by Jean-Michel Basquiat, Joseph Beuys, Cindy Sherman, and Jeff Koons. He once made headlines when he paid $2.5 million for a Roy Lichtenstein painting with his American Express card, earning 2.5 million air miles. In 2008, he decided to make his Broad Art Foundation the permanent owner of his collection, with a mission to lend its works to museums around the world. (The name of the institute and the arts foundation, like that of its benefactor, rhymes with road, not lord.)

Is this just a septuagenarian's vanity, a rehashing of old-style giving, or further evidence of how today's business-minded donors are reshaping philanthropy? Some critics question whether giving to the arts, or even to scientific research, can be justified at a time when billions of people are too busy struggling to stay alive to think about such abstract things.

For much of his life, Broad's philanthropy was small and low-key— "just writing checks," he says, including to his alma mater, Michigan State University. That changed in 1999, as his full-time business career neared its end. Now, his foundation has a staff of around sixty people. He says his approach is to "see all we do as an investment, not a gift. We are looking for returns. But like in the venture capital business, not everything you back is a winner."

Broad and some of his fellow tycoons regard giving to the arts and higher education as entirely in keeping with their modern, businesslike, impact-driven approach. That said, there is an increasingly lively debate among leading philanthrocapitalists about how best to make a difference through giving to these high-minded and often thoroughly intangible causes.

Broad is trying to apply to his giving the risk-taking methods that twice made him a billionaire—first, by turning KB Home into one of the world's leading house builders and then by turning SunAmerica, once a lackluster insurer, into a leading force in retirement savings products. In both cases, key ingredients to his success were his deep understanding of the structure of an industry, his ability to spot emerging trends that would reshape that industry, and the nerve to back his own judgment with serious amounts of money. In home building, for instance, he saw the opportunity to get rid of basements, as the end of coal heating made them unnecessary, and the need to add parking spaces, anticipating the boom in car ownership.

Broad acknowledges that science and the arts are not the most pressing issues for philanthropy. For him, school reform is the "number-one priority" because it's "the biggest challenge America has; our economic security and standard of living are at stake." But that doesn't stop scientific research being his "priority 1b".

Whereas Broad's approach to school reform has been deliberate and top-down—including focusing on training school principals and board members, and more recently joining with Bill Gates in the Ed in '08 campaign to promote change through national politics—he admits that his approach to medical science has been "opportunistic." The Broad Institute is led by Eric Lander, a charismatic scientist who is now overseeing the world's most ambitious attempt to figure out how to use the masses of bioinformation generated by genomic researchers to dramatically improve the effectiveness of medicine.

From its impressive, modern seven-story offices, complete with interactive museum, in the heart of Cambridge, Massachusetts, the Broad Institute has become a model of philanthrocapitalism for the way it has brought all the different organizations in Boston and Cambridge that work on the genome together to collaborate. Getting Harvard and MIT to be part of a combined institute was remarkable enough. But the institute has also brought on board seventeen local teaching hospitals as well as the private sector, creating an open, collaborative, cross-disciplinary effort that is unprecedented in the range of experts it can call on and its ability to carry out projects at any scale. One indication of the potential of this collaboration: the city of Boston has "the highest fraction of concentrated talent in the life sciences that exists anywhere on the planet earth," observes former Harvard University president and former U.S. treasury secretary Larry Summers. This includes the top five institutions in the world measured by their ability to attract peer-reviewed science funding.

Philanthropy has played a crucial role in the emergence of the science of genomics. The field is a case study of today's increasingly complex interaction between government, for-profit businesses, and philanthropy. Long before Broad got involved, the human genome work on the Charles River had received much needed funds from the White-head Institute for Biomedical Research at MIT, which was endowed in 1982 by Edwin Whitehead, a scientific and clinical equipment tycoon. His plan was that his free-standing, privately funded institute, operating independently at the heart of a university, would become the model for similar ventures. ("It's easier to make $100 million than to give it away," Whitehead complained after initial attempts to start the institute had been opposed by critics who argued it would undermine academic independence.) The Whitehead Institute is now part of the Broad Institute, which has also received a $100 million donation from the Stanley Foundation to research psychiatric aspects of genomics. The London-based Wellcome Trust has also given heavily to genomics, as has the Gordon and Betty Moore Foundation.

At the same time, huge amounts of taxpayer dollars have also flowed into genomics, notably through America's government-backed National Institutes of Health. In the 1990s, the flow of government and philanthropic money surged, not least due to an apparent competitive threat from Craig Venter, a scientist who set up a for-profit research firm and was widely believed to be plotting to map the genome in order to exploit it for financial gain. Venter has always insisted that he intended to make the genomic information publicly available through a foundation, whilst his for-profit company would merely seek money-making uses of the information. Nevertheless, public and philanthropic money was devoted, successfully, to beating Venter in the race to crack the genome code, in order to ensure that this hugely valuable breakthrough would be readily available to the public. Some experts think Venter's participation, and the response from government and philanthropy, caused the genome to be mapped at least five years earlier than it would otherwise have been.

As well as the human genome, Broad's other scientific interests have had personal and political motivations. He has given generously to research on inflammatory bowel disease since his son fell ill with Crohn's disease. And it was his infuriation at the policies of George W. Bush that prompted him to become, he says, "maybe the largest private funder of stem cell research, certainly in California, perhaps North America." Here he was trying to fix what he saw as a problem with government policy. "Because of the federal government ban on funding stem cell research, any center that received federal government funding of any kind, for anything, could not accept the $3 billion funding approved in a California ballot initiative. So I decided to invest in new buildings in which California-funded research can be done," he says.

Broad is not alone among today's tycoons in giving huge amounts of money to research and to universities. In 2001, Intel cofounder Gordon Moore donated $600 million to the California Institute of Technology. Bill Gates has given over a hundred million dollars to the University of Washington to monitor progress in improving global health. Michael Bloomberg has donated hundreds of millions to the medical arm of Johns Hopkins University. In 1996, Oxford University opened a new business school endowed by, and named after, Syrian businessman Wafic Saïd, and in 2005 it opened the James Martin 21st Century School with a $100 million gift from Martin, a British technologist and futurist. Indian mining and metals tycoon Anil Agarwal has pledged to give $1 billion to create the Vedanta University in Orissa state, India, which he says will be the equal of the world's best. And so on.

Likewise, many of Broad's fellow philanthrocapitalists share his enthusiasm for supporting the arts. One notable recipient is New York's recently expanded Museum of Modern Art, which raised $725 million from donors. Commemorated in galleries named after some of them, they include many of the financiers who have made their fortunes during the recent golden age of capitalism: private-equity legend Henry Kravis, billionaire Lehman Brothers boss Richard Fuld, hedge fund tycoon Leon Black, and billionaire investor Sid Bass, among others.

Giving money to support the arts and academic research is as old as philanthropy itself. In Renaissance Europe, wealthy trading families such as the Medici were benefactors of Michelangelo and other great artists. Many of the world's leading museums and art galleries were built on philanthropic gifts, often of the founder's collection of paintings or artifacts. And although most of the world's ancient universities started as religious institutions, as capitalism started to thrive they increasingly attracted funds from wealthy businesspeople—especially as they became centers of the sort of enlightenment thinking that put them increasingly at odds with the teachings of the church. That spirit of inquiry, often backed with money from philanthropists, drove impressive advances in science, especially medicine.

Philanthropists were involved in the founding of the Royal Society in 1660, which remains Britain's foremost scientific society. In 1687 the English College of Physicians resolved by unanimous vote "that all members of the College, whether fellows, candidates, or licenciates, shou'd give their advice gratis to all their sick neighbouring poor, when desir'd, within the City of London, or seven miles round." (This outpouring of medical beneficence may be the earliest example of cynically motivated corporate social responsibility—the physicians needed to win back business that was being eroded by competition from apothecaries.) The Royal Society for the Encouragement of Arts, Manufactures and Commerce was founded in 1754 with a focus on useful results— offering prizes for practical achievements that were the forerunners of today's X Prizes.

In eighteenth-century Britain, the royal physician John Radcliffe left the bulk of his estate to University College, Oxford, to pay for a science library (the Radcliffe Camera that is now part of the Bodleian Library) as well as the Radcliffe Infirmary and the Radcliffe Observatory. Philanthropists also funded new hospitals in this period to investigate specific diseases. Historically, hospitals had largely provided shelter and nourishment, but new institutions such as the Lock Hospital, which opened in 1746 and specialized in venereal disease, were inspired by a new interest in finding scientific cures. Indeed, the historian Benjamin Kirkman Gray describes the discovery of the importance of hygiene, and how to reveal dirt by putting whitewash on the walls of hospitals, as arguably "the most hopeful fact in the philanthropic history of the [eighteenth] century."

In 1829, British scientist James Smithson, who had never visited the United States, left $500,000 for the "increase and diffusion" of knowledge in America. The innovative public-private partnership that Congress created to make use of this gift is known today as the Smithsonian Institution. In 1865, Ezra Cornell, who made his fortune in the newly booming telegraph business, endowed the Ithaca, New York, university that bears his name. In the early twentieth century, J. D. Rockefeller, Andrew Carnegie, and Andrew Mellon each endowed universities; Rockefeller University in New York City remains one of the world's leading centers of medical research.

THE ATTRACTION OF giving to higher education is fairly straightforward. It is a way for philanthrocapitalists to directly invest in raising human capital, and one they personally know has a proven record of spectacular success—if, that is, the gift is to one's alma mater. Giving to support research, likewise, is a direct investment in generating knowledge that often increases the likelihood of solving the problems facing humanity. Even if this is not always the most innovative way to give, it seems like a safe bet to ensure the money is not wasted—which may be why making a big gift to higher education is the way many get started in serious philanthrocapitalism. Currently, education makes up nearly a quarter of foundation giving in the United States; much of it goes to higher education.

Even so, such giving—or at least some aspects of it—has a growing number of critics. "I love Yale," author and actor Ben Stein writes in a 2005 *New York Times* article, "Three Cheers (and a Big Question) for Yale." Yet Stein was having doubts about whether it was worth giving money to his alma mater considering that it already had a $13 billion endowment, which was growing at a remarkable 20 percent a year, thanks not least to its supersmart, super-well-paid investment managers. "Is it possible that giving to Yale right now is a bit like giving gifts to Goldman Sachs or Brown Brothers Harriman?" he mused, ". . . they really don't need my money, and other people do."

Giving to a top university is, like giving to a grand artistic institution, open to accusations of self-interest—whether it be the naming rights for a library, residence hall, or professorial chair or the (nod, wink) securing of a place for a child that might not otherwise get in. Yet the culture of giving that surrounds the top American universities in particular is the envy of the world. Harvard University alone had an endowment worth nearly $35 billion in 2006, ahead of Yale, Stanford, the University of Texas system, and Princeton, each of which sat on piles of more than $15 billion. Nowadays, any university worth its salt is trying to build an endowment of its own. Both Oxford University and Cambridge University, for example, have launched £1 billion capital-raising campaigns. An army of professional fundraisers has been hired to, among other things, remind the Oxbridge alumni that they benefited from the best part of a thousand years of philanthropy and that the university's recent dependence on taxpayer support was a historic aberration.

Philanthropy has certainly powered American universities to a position of global ascendancy, especially in their ability to hire the leading academics in every field. Some critics complain that giving to top U.S. universities has simply resulted in a "brain drain" to America by inflating academic salaries, without any evidence of an increase in the quality of their intellectual output. On the other hand, in the long run, a rise in academic salaries ought to increase the quality of people choosing to work in universities and research relative to other career options, raising the quality of what goes on in the world's ivory towers.

For the philanthrocapitalist, there are different degrees of innovation and risk-taking to consider when giving to academia. Funding a new building is the least risky, though perhaps also has the lowest expected return on the investment. However, calculating the upside of such a donation is not straightforward. For example, much of the money given to Stanford University by John Arrillaga has gone to build sports facilities, including a magnificent stadium. (The Silicon Valley real estate tycoon had won his place at Stanford through a basketball scholarship.) Some might question whether this is really a gift to academia, as opposed to recreation. Yet there is strong evidence that the vitality of an American university's sports teams is highly correlated with its ability to raise funds across the board: apparently, people like giving to winners.

Giving to support a particular field of academic inquiry, by establishing a professorship or a research center, is riskier, but may have a far higher potential return on the philanthropic investment. That is particularly true of funding blue-sky research in controversial or new areas, which other more risk-averse sources of research funding tend to ignore (especially government).

For the philanthrocapitalist, investing in the generation of good new ideas is a natural and obvious cause. The tricky question is whether a university is the best bet when it comes to out-of-the-box thinking. The problem is well described in a 2007 article in the journal *Innovations* by former Harvard president Summers. "Universities are curious institutions. On the one hand, they have a responsibility for what is most cutting edge in the education of youth and the creation of new ideas—on the other hand they're probably more ossified in their structures and their rules than almost any other institution in our society."

Yet few philanthrocapitalists are willing to give a lot to a university without having at least some influence over how their money will be spent. As Whitehead discovered, however great the need to give their ivory towers an upgrade, university academics can be terribly sniffy about the strings attached to a gift. And they can be even sniffier about the donor. Some dons at Oxford University fought fiercely against taking Saïd's money, for example, citing his alleged role in the arms trade. Nor were left-leaning members of the university thrilled by the endowment of the Rupert Murdoch Professorship of Language and Communication by the eponymous donor.

Summers recalls that there was fierce opposition within Harvard to his efforts to bring in new money and create new collaborative institutions inside the university, which can scare off some would-be donors. "There was often a sense in the Public Health School that they should have a monopoly over consideration of these issues and that there were no structural changes necessary," Summers says. He managed to convince Larry Ellison, the billionaire founder of Oracle and a reputedly reluctant philanthropist, to donate $115 million to create the Ellison Institute for World Health. But when Summers was forced out in 2006—having offended too many academics by his attempts to shake the university out of its ossified ways, as well as by commenting unwisely about the scientific abilities of women—Ellison withdrew his offer, saying he had lost confidence in the university's ability to spend the money without Summers at the helm.

Probably the greatest example of philanthrocapitalistic giving to higher education is by the obsessively secretive Irish American billionaire Chuck Feeney, who demonstrated how the principles of leverage can be applied to funding academic research. New Jersey–born Feeney set about his philanthropy with the same mixture of opportunism and long-term strategy that enabled him to build two hugely successful businesses: the global airport retailer Duty Free Shoppers and the private-equity firm General Atlantic. Since 1982, Feeney has given billions of dollars through his Atlantic Philanthropies to causes such as researching aging, improving public health, supporting disadvantaged youths, and reconciliation and human rights, mostly in the United States, South Africa, Vietnam, and above all, Ireland. But he has mostly invested in higher education, starting with his alma mater, Cornell University, which over the years has benefited to the tune of more than $600 million. He has also given to Columbia University, though his insistence on anonymity nearly caused the university to turn the money down, as it was suspicious that the gift might be from a dubious source.

That was fairly traditional academic giving, but he adopted a more strategic approach in the 1990s, when he started to give substantial sums to higher education in Ireland, starting with the University of Limerick. Eventually, all seven universities in the Republic received substantial funding from Atlantic Philanthropies, as did the two in Northern Ireland. As Conor O'Clery reports in his biography, *The Billionaire Who Wasn't: How Chuck Feeney Secretly Made and Gave Away a Fortune*, 1997 was to prove a turning point. By then, the experience of his initial giving had convinced Feeney that Irish higher education needed to get serious about postgraduate research in order to rise to the next level. The philanthropist entered into direct negotiations with a sovereign government for the first time, proposing to the Irish government a matching deal where, according to Atlantic's then head John Healy, "we put some money on the table, and forced them to put some money on the table." Eventually, a public-private-partnership research fund of IR£150 million, half of which was secretly donated by Atlantic, was announced.

Doing deals with government may sometimes be essential if philanthropists are to achieve the leverage they dream of, but governments can be difficult partners. Despite Irish government promises that its commitment was irreversible, after the 2002 election, a new minister announced a "pause" in the government's payments. "As far as I was concerned we had a partnership with the government, and this is not a way to deal with partners," recalls Healy. "We immediately told the universities and the Higher Education Authority that if the money is not flowing from the government it is not flowing from us. So we had a pause too." That did the trick. After a meeting between Feeney and then-Taoiseach Bertie Ahern, the government soon backed down. To succeed, philanthrocapitalists sometimes have to be as tough in their philanthropic dealings with beneficiaries as they would be in business.

All told, Atlantic donated €178 million of the €605 million that the first three cycles of the program cost, before easing itself out. In 2006, the Irish government announced a €1.25 billion investment in postgraduate education over the following five years. According to Thomas Mitchell, ex-head of Trinity College Dublin, "It was Chuck's biggest legacy. It revolutionized research in Ireland. It was the perfect example of leverage. They put money on the table and said to the government, 'You have got to perform.' It was a model of how a foundation can combine with government and use its leverage to change policy. This was social change in a very significant way."

Feeney also "leveraged cooperation." When he started to give to Irish universities, he called in his grateful beneficiaries at Cornell to act as advisers, a model he was to repeat elsewhere, ultimately creating a world network of universities. "American, Irish, Australian and later South African and Vietnamese university heads, academics and scientists found themselves urged on by Feeney and Atlantic Philanthropies to cooperate and help each other," O'Clery writes.

THE ANCIENT GREEKS would have applauded the continuing popularity of giving to the arts—which in America, currently accounts for a hefty 14 percent of total foundation giving. Ancient Greek philanthropy was not necessarily targeted at the needs of the poor. Most philanthropy worked through the performance of liturgies (*leitourgia*): public duties, such as sending a sports team to a tournament or funding a chorus— activities that would not be unfamiliar to many of today's philanthropists. Indeed, the Ancient Greeks would wonder why sponsoring a sports team is no longer counted as philanthropy. After all, owning a soccer or baseball team is a good way of earning personal and civic prestige while in many cases losing a lot of the owner's money.

So too the Romans. Gaius Maecenas is the most celebrated Roman donor because of his support for the poets Virgil and Horace. Indeed, his name is now synonymous with patronage of the arts (literally so in

French, where *mécène* is the word for "donor" or "sponsor"). Maecenas was a political associate of Caesar Augustus, the first emperor of Rome, and saw the value of art and literature in guiding public opinion through the political transition from republic to empire.

Today, most of the giving to the arts goes to the big beasts, such as New York's Museum of Modern Art, rather than to grassroots and community arts organizations where the need is arguably greater and the impact more clear. Such giving is more open to charges of self-interest—social status, best seats in the house, and so on—than donating to the poor, especially abroad. Collecting works of art, with a view to later leaving them to the nation, can be an enjoyable way for a wealthy person to dispose of a fortune—a lot more fun, for most people, than trying to help out in the poverty-stricken corners of the world.

Bill Gates, for one, is unimpressed. "I have no interest in giving to opera houses," he says. There are some signs that this philosophy is taking hold among the newer philanthrocapitalists, who see more pressing needs for their money. Many an arts organization is growing increasingly worried about its future, and complaining of being strapped for cash. In 2007, the influential Americans for the Arts National Arts Policy Roundtable issued an alarmist report, *The Future of Private Sector Giving to the Arts in America,* which claimed that, since 1992, philanthropic giving to the arts had declined by the equivalent of $8 billion a year.

Of course, there are exceptions to this gloomy trend in the arts. Poetry, for instance. In 2002, pharmaceutical heiress Ruth Lilly left a $100 million bequest to *Poetry* magazine, published by the Modern Poetry Association, which has since been reorganized as the Poetry Foundation. However, whilst the foundation has been applauded for its efforts to take poetry to the masses, such as through its Poetry Out Loud high school recitation competition, it has also been accused of favoring popular poetry over good poetry. In other areas, philanthrocapitalists might resolve this debate with metrics, but what does it really mean for society to have a sharp increase in the iambic pentameter?

Many arts philanthropists can defend themselves on the grounds that they have weighed the benefit of giving to the arts against other alternatives. They see the arts as part of a portfolio of investments in a better world. Indeed, like handing a check to your alma mater, giving to the arts may be a sort of "gateway drug" that gets wealthy people hooked on giving, later to move on to the harder forms of philanthropy.

Broad, for one, says that although he has given more to school reform and scientific research, giving to the arts is also essential for a healthy society. "I have been involved in the arts for many years. I've got a great deal out of it. I believe the American public needs a broader art education—to have a productive, inventive, creative populace, the arts have a role to play." Broad has backed up this desire to make art accessible to the public with his own money, especially in his adopted hometown, Los Angeles, where he has donated $50 million to build the Broad Contemporary Arts Museum at the Los Angeles County Museum of Art.

Sandy Weill, the billionaire former boss of Citigroup, gives generously to the arts, notably as chairman of New York's Carnegie Hall, but also supports hospitals and an influential educational initiative, the National Academy Foundation, which encourages urban school children to consider business careers. John Studzinski, a London-based financier, is a big supporter of the arts, but also gives to homelessness charities and Human Rights Watch. Lord David Sainsbury, of the British grocery dynasty, has probably given away more money than any living Briton. Much of it has gone to "tangible" social projects, but he has also dedicated a healthy slice to the arts. Critics may want to deride all this as selfish vanity, but perhaps the decisions of these serial philanthropists about how they allocate their giving portfolio deserve a bit more respect.

Any judgment on whether giving to the arts is a good use of a philanthrocapitalist's money must also take into account what role the state is playing, which varies widely from one country to the next. Perhaps an American philanthrocapitalist has greater justification for giving to the arts than, say, a German. According to economist Tyler Cowen, America's direct government subsidies to the arts are limited to the $120 million that the National Endowment for the Arts spends every year. At fifty cents per American per year, he says, it is peanuts compared with the $80 that every German contributes to state-funded arts.

One test for the philanthrocapitalist considering supporting the arts is "what difference will the money make?" Will the gift be going to a society seriously deficient in the arts or some part of the arts, as it was in America when Andrew Mellon gave his collection of great paintings to initiate the National Gallery? Or will it merely add another opera house to a country awash in them? Will the money encourage new artists or artistic innovation, or merely gild an already well-gilded institution of the arts establishment? And will the money be used in a way that actually applies the philanthropist's business talents to improve the effectiveness of the art?

Broad presents his plan to lend his art collection to needy museums around the world as an innovative new model for philanthropic art collectors, far more impactful than simply giving the collection to a museum. The goal, he says, is to "have the broadest possible public view what we have." He was worried that if he gave the collection to one or several museums, "ninety percent or so would be in storage all the time." The Broad Art Foundation will pay for staffing, insurance, storage, and conservation of the works. Some of Studzinski's giving, too, is genuinely entrepreneurial: in 2001, he created the Genesis Foundation to support promising young artists who lack the resources to pursue their vocation.

Once again, Carnegie may have invented a formula that today's philanthrocapitalists could use. He gave money to support theaters in many towns that needed them. Yet the building for which he is most famous, New York's Carnegie Hall, he created as a for-profit business, not as a philanthropic project. New York already had an abundance of theaters and music halls, so the only case to be made for constructing Carnegie Hall (which his wife begged him to build) was that there would be enough paying customers to keep it afloat.

In the end, there were not enough. We'll never know if Carnegie would have been happy to see the no-longer-viable concert hall close, but today Carnegie Hall, now much loved the world over, is sustained by the philanthropy of some of the wealthiest people in New York. And if some of them do not care a damn about world suffering and are giving just to show off, as critics allege, the arts are probably a better cause than spending on selfish luxuries such as yachts or space flights.

## CHAPTER 9

# The Return of the Living Dead

"I CALL IT PHILANTHROPY 3.0," SAYS Judith Rodin, who has nearly $4 billion to give away, though none of it is hers. Since taking over as head of the venerable Rockefeller Foundation in 2005, Rodin has become the most prominent member of a group of foundation managers determined to use the techniques of philanthrocapitalism to reinvigorate the giving away of fortunes made by long-dead tycoons. She wants the Rockefeller Foundation to be a leading example of philanthropy in the twenty-first century, just as it was twice in the twentieth century. Philanthropy 1.0, following the creation of the foundation in 1913, was all about pioneering systematic solutions to social problems, an approach J. D. Rockefeller called "scientific philanthropy." Philanthropy 2.0, after 1945, focused on fighting poverty in the developing world.

Rodin and her fellow reformers are trying to address an increasingly widespread belief: that the lack of a living donor to keep the "philanthrocrats" who manage the old foundations on their toes has undermined the foundations' effectiveness. Without a founding spirit to guide them, say the critics, these foundations were just going through the motions, sticking to what they had always done and failing to innovate or respond to a changing world.

"I am not a 'steady as it goes' sort of person," says Rodin, who was previously shaking things up in academia and was at one point the world's highest-paid university president, at the University of Pennsylvania. Appointing such "outsiders" is an emerging trend among the old foundations. Perhaps inspired (or threatened) by the Rockefeller Foundation's lead, the Ford Foundation, still second in size only to the Gates Foundation, in 2007 chose "a dark horse candidate with little experience of institutional philanthropy as its new president," in the words of the *New York Times*. The outsider in question, Luis Ubiñas, reassuringly uttered the usual platitudes about not wanting change for change's sake, but in picking an executive from the consulting firm McKinsey, the Ford Foundation seemed to be sending a clear signal.

This was no doubt received with some trepidation by the three hundred or so staff at the Ford Foundation, given the precedent set by Rodin. She has changed the Rockefeller Foundation's strategy, shaken up its internal structures, and shed a large proportion of its 160-strong staff—many of whom complained loudly about "Judy Come Lately" on the way out.

The language of philanthrocapitalism comes easily to Rodin's lips. In today's world, she says, philanthropic "resources need to be deployed more strategically. Nobody, even Gates with the Buffett money, has enough. So we need leverage, strategic partnerships, focus." Impact is the goal. She has adopted a "portfolio approach," experimenting with lots of different ideas that, if successful, might be scaled up by other institutions including governments. "The big challenges of the twenty-first century require greater nimbleness," she says. "We need to go at problems with the full range of artillery. The challenge is not to identify the right problems but to identify the right solutions. And also to build in exit strategies." To leverage the foundation's money as much as possible, Rodin intends to focus on finding ways to remove bottlenecks to release a massive amount of good.

One bottleneck was the planning process in New Orleans after Hurricane Katrina devastated the city in 2005. When the political process that was supposed to lead the rebuilding effort stalled, Rodin got involved. "We funded the planning process and hired a community development person who lives down there," she recalls. "The process had stalled due to politics—so this was a very high-risk thing for us to do. The mayor and the city council weren't talking to each other. There was a history of fractiousness." The process involved things that, Rodin says, the "old Rockefeller Foundation" would not have considered. "We built in an exit strategy—with the program officer becoming chief executive of a new local body in New Orleans and our funding ceasing after a year or so. The goal was to achieve impact early and quickly."

A second new initiative was to get into bed with the leading new philanthropist, partnering with the Gates Foundation in its ambitious long-
term project to end hunger by boosting agricultural production in Africa.
The Alliance for Green Revolution in Africa will tackle issues including
"seeds, soil, output markets, water, politics," says Rodin, contrasting this
open-ended commitment with the tightly defined, time-limited engagement in New Orleans.

She has also copied the new philanthropists in focusing on innovation, not least through a series of partnerships with some of the leading
firms pioneering ways to use the Internet and open source technologies.
These include InnoCentive, a firm in which Omidyar Network has invested. "Innovators have been working according to market forces, working for those who can pay. We want to tilt the innovation cycle towards
the developing world," she says.

Another big idea was to get involved in what Rodin regards as one of
the most neglected major issues facing American society: economic insecurity. Her aim is to reframe questions to allow progress in areas where
the current way the questions are put results in paralysis. "Politicians are
currently very siloed on issues—health care, pensions, social security—
whereas the person at the dinner table is thinking broadly about insecurity," says Rodin, who quickly decided to start work on an index of
economic insecurity. The foundation also started to explore ways of working with commercial vendors and trade unions to develop portable pension and health care products. Again signaling change from the
foundation's traditional liberal sympathies, Rodin insists that "we want to
look across the political spectrum, including working with very conservative think tanks."

Rodin arrived at an organization that was widely agreed to be a shadow
of its old self. "The fact is, we aren't the largest and richest foundation any-
more, so we are forced to be more creative and aggressive, because we
could become marginal in our impact," says Rodin. "We are the fifteenth-
largest foundation; we were the largest, but we still have the brand name."

Rodin says she was alarmed to find that the Rockefeller Foundation
had "never had an internal research and evaluation function," so she
immediately launched a three-pronged process to develop a strategy.
This involved creating internal task forces; hiring consultants; and seeking the advice of big hitters, including former U.S. Treasury secretaries
Robert Rubin and Larry Summers.

"As an institution we were too self-satisfied, a little too internally focused. Tough questions were not asked critically, or answers sought too aggressively. There had been a loss of emphasis on impact," says Rodin. The process also revealed the foundation's high cost structure relative to those of its peers, cumbersome decision making, and a culture that did not expect high performance nor reward it.

## OLD MAN ROCKEFELLER'S GIFT

The size of the fortune amassed by the world's first billionaire, through shrewd and aggressive investment in the booming oil industry of the late nineteenth century, set him apart from ordinary almsgivers. "Your fortune is rolling up, rolling up like an avalanche!" wrote his philanthropic adviser Frederick T. Gates (no relation of Bill) in 1896. "You must distribute it faster than it grows! If you do not, it will crush you and your children and your children's children!"

It was this that led Rockefeller to revive and upgrade the Tudor innovation of the charitable trust or foundation. Trusts were a legal mechanism that had been used since the Middle Ages to found religious institutions and associated schools, hospitals, and colleges. Many of these medieval foundations, such as Christ's Hospital in London, were near collapse because they had never been properly endowed. Tudor philanthropists not only shored up the finances of these medieval trusts but also founded many schools and almshouses themselves (seven of the nine great private schools of England were founded or refounded in this period). The philanthropists also adapted this mechanism as a way to create a perpetual charitable legacy while ensuring that the money would be used only for the donor's intended purpose, even after death. It was this mechanism that Rockefeller revived in 1901 with the creation of the Rockefeller Institute for Medical Research (now Rockefeller University).

In 1904, the pioneer of investigative journalism (or "muckraking," as it was known at the time), Ida Tarbell, published her sledgehammer attack on Rockefeller, *The History of the Standard Oil Company*, which alleged that his fortune was based on "fraud, deceit, special privilege, gross illegality, bribery, coercion, corruption, intimidation, espionage or outright terror." Tarbell acknowledged Rockefeller's generosity, although she gave him no credit for it. "Is it too much to hope that even Mr. Rockefeller will

Rodin is keen to promote greater transparency about the foundation's activities. It has partnered with the charitable arms of Salesforce.com and Google, among others, to develop ways of tracking and publishing online data about the performance of its grants and grantees.

"We need to be articulate about what we want to achieve. Maybe we should have an impact curve, with impact on the $y$ axis and time on the $x$

see, at last, that what we need in society is not charity but fair play?" she asked.

This public clamor to tame the robber barons was harnessed by Presidents Theodore Roosevelt and William Taft, who attacked the industrial power of the "malefactors of great wealth" by introducing tough antitrust legislation that resulted in the breakup of the big monopolies such as Rockefeller's Standard Oil, which was dissolved in 1911. Roosevelt probably strengthened American capitalism by subjecting its biggest businesses to greater competitive pressure, but the trust-busters also nearly strangled the Rockefeller Foundation at birth, refusing a federal charter for its foundation. In the end, Rockefeller instead created the foundation under New York state law in 1913.

Early foundation program applied Rockefeller's philosophy of scientific philanthropy to address diseases such as hookworm and yellow fever. More controversially, the foundation also backed the reform of medical education in the United States (which had begun with funding from Andrew Carnegie) led by Abraham Flexner. Supporters see this program as the basis of America's leading position today in the world in medical research and education. Critics say it favored the male, white, moneyed elite in medicine at the expense of women, blacks, and the poor, who could no longer afford to participate.

As time went by, the Rockefeller Foundation increasingly focused its attention on problems of the developing world, which were relatively neglected by state funding. In doing so, it scored notable successes, particularly in supporting the green revolution in agriculture, beginning in the 1940s, that helped Asia avoid a Malthusian nightmare of rising hunger on the back of a rising population. By increasing the productivity of basic agriculture, the foundation helped to save (it is generally agreed) at least a billion lives.

axis. Obviously, the green revolution will take at least twenty years, with low impact at first and no exit planned now. New Orleans is quick impact, early exit."

As reformers often do, Rodin has been careful to describe her revolution as returning the foundation to its roots. Hence her frequent references to "scientific philanthropy." The Rockefeller Foundation has traditionally been all about results, she says. Old man Rockefeller was extremely serious about what he called the "business of beneficence." He was not "putting Band-Aids on big weeping wounds. He hired experts and paid them really well," says Rodin. "Impact is what we are all about historically, and I needed to reassert that as a criterion for everything we do."

A large contingent of Rockefeller Foundation alumni have been upset

## TOP TEN U.S. FOUNDATIONS (BY ASSETS), WITH ANNUAL GIVING

| FOUNDATION (DATE OF CREATION) | ASSETS (2006) IN MILLIONS OF DOLLARS | GIVING (2006) IN MILLIONS OF DOLLARS |
|---|---|---|
| 1   Bill and Melinda Gates Foundation (2000) | $33,120m | $1,563m |
| 2   Ford Foundation (1936) | $13,660m | $581m* |
| 3   J. Paul Getty Trust (1982) | $10,133m | n/a |
| 4   Robert Wood Johnson Foundation (1968) | $10,095m | $368m |
| 5   William and Flora Hewlett Foundation (1966) | $8,521m | $212m |
| 6   W. K. Kellogg Foundation (1934) | $8,403m* | $303m* |
| 7   Lilly Endowment (1937) | $7,602m | $352m |
| 8   David and Lucile Packard Foundation (1964) | $6,351m | $238m |
| 9   John D. and Catherine T. MacArthur Foundation (1978) | $6,178m | $217m |
| 10  Andrew W. Mellon Foundation (1969) | $6,131m | $177m |

*2007

SOURCE: Foundation Center.

that their old home is being torn down. Many of those who have left during Rodin's reign have gone on to influential positions elsewhere, and some have been only too happy to brief against her. They may have been behind a hostile report in medical journal the *Lancet* that asked if the Rockefeller Foundation planned to "reduce or even withdraw its long-standing commitments to public health," prompting Rodin to issue a formal denial.

Rodin's outspoken embrace of the language and methods of the new philanthropists has irritated many of her peers at the established foundations. Some suspect that she is all talk and that she will struggle to deliver the results that her fighting words demand. Expect plenty of schadenfreude if she fails. But many people hope she will succeed, not just for the sake of the Rockefeller Foundation but because it would inspire similar changes at other established foundations, including some that are far bigger (see "Top ten U.S. foundations" table).

THE SOUND OF a foundation blowing its own trumpet is presumably sweet music to the ears of Joel L. Fleishman. After all, the subtitle of his 2007 book, *The Foundation: A Great American Secret*, reflects his belief that the many great achievements of philanthropy are largely unknown to the public, not least because foundations do so little to tell anyone about them. Fleishman has also published a collection of one hundred case studies of ways in which foundations have changed the world.

Nonetheless, Fleishman has a great deal of sympathy for Rodin's agenda of change; indeed, he has been a valuable source of advice for her. As he points out in the book, if philanthropy has been disappointingly quiet about its successes, it is positively Trappist about its failures. By one count, only four foundations have ever admitted a failure. Few ever publish their full evaluations. Yet, writes Fleishman, "the foundation sector as a whole, as great as its social contribution is now and has been for most of its history, seriously underperforms its potential with respect both to the social benefit it might otherwise have conferred if it were not underperforming, and also to the mission that its freedom from substantial government and social control is designed to fulfill." Fleishman is not some disenchanted spoiler; he used to manage the American arm of Chuck Feeney's Atlantic Philanthropies and is well respected within the giving industry.

The same message was delivered in more robust language by Harvard Business School professor Michael E. Porter and his colleague Mark Kramer in 1999. The *Harvard Business Review*, which had just started to take an interest in the nonprofit world, delivered a broadside in Porter and Kramer's article "Philanthropy's New Agenda: Creating Value." Whilst what the press typically regard as foundation scandals tends to be about pay and perks of foundation employees, "the real scandal is how much money is pissed away on activities that have no real impact," Porter summarized later. "Billions are wasted on ineffective philanthropy."

In the history of American foundations there have certainly been some ghastly blunders. The Rockefeller Foundation and the Carnegie Institution ran eugenics programs in Germany from the start of twentieth century into the Nazi era of the 1930s. The Rockefeller Foundation also supported unethical syphilis experimentation in Alabama, which took place without the informed consent of participants from 1932 to 1972.

From time to time, the media report on some scandal involving philanthrocrats. In 2006, for example, Barry Munitz, the chief executive of the John Paul Getty Trust, a big supporter of the arts, resigned abruptly following outcry over his $1 million salary, his expenses, and the foundation's gift to him of a Porsche. The curator of the Getty Trust's antiquities division then found herself accused in an Italian court of helping antiques dealer Robert Hecht illegally export to America priceless ancient artworks.

What troubles Fleishman, Porter, and Kramer are not occasional lapses of judgment, however appalling, but a series of more endemic failings. They are especially critical of the lack of strategic thinking by foundations, and of any meaningful focus on impact.

One reflection of this has been too much unstrategic funding, known in the trade as "spray and pray." The Ford Foundation gives out two thousand grants every year—admittedly whittled down from around forty-four thousand applications. Most grants from U.S. foundations are for eighteen months or less, and the median grant is worth $50,000—which means that charities are constantly competing for funding rather than getting on with their core business. As Thomas Tierney of Bridgespan, a consultancy that works with philanthropists and NGOs, asks: "How many social problems can be solved with $50k? Over eighteen months? Not many." In practice, says Tierney, often at foundations "there is naivety mingled with wishful thinking—a rhetoric-versus-reality gap. You find great mission statements, photos, and so on, all very heart-warming but far from reality."

Much of the philanthropic old guard resists such criticisms. Susan Berresford, who ran the Ford Foundation from 1996 to 2008, retired with a well-deserved reputation as old philanthropy's leading diplomat, with a fine record of making her industry's case in Washington, D.C. Most of her valedictory annual report was devoted to proudly listing many examples of good work by the foundation, which has given away over $13 billion since it was created by Edsel and Henry Ford in 1936. The Ford Foundation, she pointed out, had been one of the first backers of Muhammad Yunus of the Grameen microcredit bank. Not only did Ford have a record of effectively supporting a diverse range of projects, but for more than fifty years it had also demonstrated an ability to be a "long-term and flexible partner with innovative leaders of thought and action," she wrote.

Fleishman, Porter, and Kramer are unrepentant. They were all involved in the 2001 creation of the Center for Effective Philanthropy (CEP), which seeks to help foundations improve their performance. The CEP's most notable innovation has been to ask the recipients of foundation grants—the charities who actually do the work—what they think of their donors. Whilst this does not indicate whether foundations achieve much impact, listening to those whose work they fund is certainly revealing. All too often, these "Grantee Perception Reports" are littered with complaints about what Fleishman calls the "besetting sins" of foundations: arrogance, discourtesy, inaccessibility, arbitrariness, failure to communicate (dragging out the grant-making process, slow payment), and foundation attention deficit disorder (short-term behavior, faddism, and herd mentality).

Until the CEP came along, foundations could kid themselves that nothing was wrong, because without the confidential mechanism for communication offered by the grantee reports, grantees dared not say anything critical. "The CEP has given grantees a voice against foundations," says Fleishman. "It takes a great deal of courage to ruffle the feathers of the goose whose life mission is to lay golden eggs for society." Not surprisingly, the grantee reports prompted some pushback from foundations that felt the criticisms were unjustified. Yet by 2007, seven of the ten biggest foundations had agreed to commission a Grantee

Perception Report. A few foundations have even made their reports public. The next challenge is to create transparency about performance and a meaningful debate about the impact of the money that foundations give away.

New thinking within the established philanthropy industry has also started to spread across the sector with the help of trade bodies such as the Council on Foundations and Foundation Center. There is not necessarily a consensus on what needs to be done—the liberal National Committee for Responsive Philanthropy has called for more regulation of ineffective and self-serving philanthropy, while the conservative Philanthropy Roundtable wants minimal government intervention in the sector—but there is a lively debate.

In September 2007, several large established foundations announced a significant philanthropic innovation designed to increase their effectiveness. The Edna McConnell Clark Foundation created a growth fund to invest in growing established nonprofits, putting up the first $39 million of what it hopes will become a $120 million fund by June 2008. The Robert Wood Johnson Foundation and the Gates Foundation joined this effort, contributing a further $49 million. The first beneficiary was the Nurse-Family Partnership, which was raising $50 million to finance its growth from 96 sites helping 13,000 families to 950 sites helping 100,000 families by 2017. The Nurse-Family Partnership's intention was at the same time to leverage the philanthropic funds by increasing the support it gets from government from $52 million a year to $360 million.

OUTSIDE AMERICA, ALTHOUGH the debate about the performance and accountability of "old philanthropy" has not reached the same intensity, similar criticisms of foundation performance are starting to be heard. The list of established European charitable trusts is dominated by the Wellcome Trust in Britain, which could easily hold its own with the big U.S. foundations, in terms of resources at least (its endowment is worth nearly $30 billion and it spends around $1 billion a year). Perhaps inevitably, the man who gave away this huge chunk of cash was not a Briton but an American. Henry Wellcome was born in a log cabin in Wisconsin but built up his pharmaceutical empire in Britain by pioneering techniques such as the first mass production of insulin. Having supported medical research throughout his life, he left his fortune to his eponymous foundation to continue this work after his death in 1936.

The scale of the Wellcome Trust's giving to medical research makes it one of the most significant areas in Britain where the contribution of philanthropy rivals that of the state. In this respect, philanthropy plays a bigger role than in America, where the funding of early-stage research is largely provided by the governmental National Institutes of Health. The Wellcome Trust claims as its greatest achievement ensuring that the human DNA sequence is publicly available for anyone to use, rather than the intellectual property of a private company. It did this by partnering with the U.S. government in bankrolling the $3 billion Human Genome Project (HGP). Indeed, when Craig Venter's private company, Celera, announced its plan in 1998 to beat the HGP in the race to map the human genome, it was the Wellcome Trust that dissuaded the National Institutes of Health from cutting a deal with the commercial upstart by pumping more cash into the project. This was certainly big strategic philanthropy. But arguably, it was an exception to the more lackluster norm at the trust, which, for all its resources, is seen by its critics as inflexible and bureaucratic, failing to match the impact on global health issues, for example, of the big American foundations.

According to research by Watson Wyatt Investment Consulting and the London Business School, European foundations tend to give away a smaller share of their endowments than their American peers. This problem is exacerbated by accounting rules that often obscure the real value of foundation assets. In Germany, the Bertelsmann and Bosch foundations, for example, hugely understate the value of their controlling shareholdings in the giant companies that share their names. At market value, their endowments might rival that of Wellcome Trust, though they are giving far less away than their British peer. Moreover, European foundation giving tends towards the conservative, risk-averse, "spray and pray" approach. The second-largest U.K. foundation, Garfield Weston (founded not by an American but a Canadian), for example, reports that 84 percent of its grants are for £20,000 or less. "European foundations are still too classical, not thinking about impact," says Luc Tayart de Borms, managing director of the King Baudoin Foundation in Belgium.

A number of the largest foundations in Europe are Italian, created by the privatization of banks in the 1990s, but none of them has set the world alight. In a sense they have come full circle: the Siena Foundation Montei dei Paschi di Siena, for example, is the descendant of the first *monte di pietà* from the Renaissance. So perhaps it will start to draw on its historical inspiration and rediscover the spirit of philanthrocapitalism.

Reform has started to creep across the Atlantic, through a group of progressive foundations from the United States and Britain that meet under the name Woburn Park Collective. The formal U.K. donors club, the Association of Charitable Trusts, is a model of British reserve, but philanthropy insiders think the association has been nudging the sleepy U.K. foundation sector from its torpor—all very discreetly of course. In Europe, Tayart de Borms is part of a new generation of philanthropists and foundation professionals that has started lobbying for a Europe-wide law on foundations to sweep away regulations that have impeded the development of the sector in many countries. As he says, "foundations need a more modern legal and fiscal environment if they are to live up to their potential to create real value."

THE ROOT CAUSE of the ineffectiveness of many established foundations is that the original donor is no longer around. If a living donor does not like what the philanthrocrat managers are doing, the solution is straightforward: fire them. The billionaire financier and philanthropist George Soros, for example, freely admits that his Open Society Institute in Russia ran out of control in 1991, saying, "I had to organize a putsch within the foundation to regain control. Unfortunately the people who helped me in the putsch also got out of control, so I had to organize a second putsch to remove them."

But you can't putsch if you're pushing up the daisies. Hence, as Martin Morse Wooster, author of *Great Philanthropic Mistakes*, explains, "Foundations lack the self-corrective mechanisms the market provides. To be successful, artists, inventors, and entrepreneurs have to create products that please an audience . . . Philanthropists do not have customers to please, which gives foundation presidents the opportunity to squander a donor's legacy." In designing a legacy, the donor therefore faces a problem: how to ensure that those giving away his money after his death work hard and do not pursue an agenda that is more their own than his.

Many philanthropists prefer to avoid the problem by giving their own money away while they are alive, rather than trusting it to their descendants or professionals. Yet not everyone agrees that setting up a perpetual foundation is such a bad idea. The Tudor philanthropists who originated the concept were influenced by their own experience of having to shore up crumbling medieval foundations that had been underendowed by their founders. The debate over whether it is better to give now or later is likely to rumble on forever (see "A Bridge Too Far?" box).

Even those who want to oversee the distribution of their entire fortune during their lifetime can find (like Carnegie) that they run out of time, perhaps because their fortunes grow faster than they can give money away. Often there is no alternative but to entrust such funds to future generations to manage.

Some dead donors must take some responsibility for the failure of their foundation and its managers to stay focused. As Peter Frumkin argues in *Strategic Giving: The Art and Science of Philanthropy*, too many foundations have been set up with vague missions and unclear goals. The Carnegie Corporation of New York, for example, is tasked "to promote the advancement and diffusion of knowledge and understanding," while the Rockefeller Foundation's role is "to identify, and address at their source, the causes of human suffering." Hardly much of a steer.

Even after appointing a committee to figure out its mission after the death of its founders, the Ford Foundation found itself committed to the "advancement of human welfare." The extent to which successive generations of Ford Foundation managers ought to do things of which the founder would have approved has been the subject of prolonged controversy. Henry Ford II, grandson of the Henry Ford who started the foundation, deliberately relinquished control after his grandfather's death in 1947 to prove that he was sincere about its humanitarian mission (although he did keep a seat on the board).

With a team of experts in charge, the Ford Foundation became increasingly associated with liberal causes that right-wing critics of the foundation's new managers plausibly claimed would have had (nasty) old man Ford spinning in his grave. One initiative, for example, was pushing voter registration in Cleveland, which secured the election of the Democrat Carl Stokes, the first African American mayor of a major U.S. city.

Have today's philanthrocapitalists learned these lessons? George

Soros says that he is thinking about "how to keep the foundation risk-taking after my death"—when he is no longer able to putsch out unacceptable managers. Warren Buffett had intended for his wife, Susan, to give away his fortune if he died without doing so. But when she died first, he decided to entrust the job to his friend Bill Gates.

Of course, the effectiveness problems of many foundations are not simply a matter of "live donors, good; dead donors, bad." Media billionaire Walter H. Annenberg established his eponymous foundation in 1989, well before his death in 2002. Yet it was responsible for "one of

---

## A BRIDGE TOO FAR?

Even if a donor is clear about his or her intentions and the trustees stick to these goals, the result can still be unsatisfactory. This is illustrated by some of the world's oldest trusts, such as the City Bridge Trust, whose origins go back to the eleventh century and which owns and manages most of London's bridges. Even with its existing liabilities, the trust found that it had surplus cash that it was unable to use because the terms of the trust were too narrow. In 1995, the trustees decided that this was an unnecessary waste of resources and appealed to the courts for an amendment to its articles that would allow it to allocate some of its funds to local charitable causes. The British courts agreed, under a provision called cy pres (from French, meaning "as near as possible").

The government, too, can get involved in restructuring outdated or redundant trusts in the public interest. This happened to the Panacea Society, which was founded in Bedford, England, in 1918 to further the mission of the nineteenth-century prophetess Joanna Southcott. The society was led by Mabel Barltrop, who claimed to be Shiloh, the child of the prophetess (no matter that Southcott had died more than one hundred years previously). The society guards an "ark" of prophecies that will only be opened in the presence of twenty-four bishops and had amassed considerable assets (including a purpose-built building with twenty-four bedrooms—you can't expect bishops to double up—and a dedicated ark-opening room). The foundation was sitting on a large endowment (now valued at £22 million) that was not being used to benefit the public. In 2001, the British regulator, the Charities Commission, stepped in and forced the Panaceans to start spending some of their money on good causes in Bedford.

the major failures in foundation history," according to Fleishman. The goal of the $500 million Annenberg Challenge was to reform public education in the United States. From 1993 to 2000 the Annenberg Foundation supported improvements in over two thousand schools serving more than 1.5 million children across the country. Annenberg tried using a range of grants at the national, city, and local levels to drive change in America's public schools, but the program was piecemeal and lacked any overall vision.

An independent evaluation of the challenge in 2000 observed that, in

---

But how far should such a policy be taken? One British trust, the National Fund, sits on an endowment of £200 million and appears to have made no grants since it was founded by an anonymous donor in 1928 with the goal of paying off the national debt. It may be a rather pointless and unrealistic mission, but it is not self-evident that the public interest in putting this cash to use overrides the rights of the original benefactor.

Although cy pres exists in American law, U.S. courts have been much less willing than their British counterparts to meddle with the goals of foundations (whilst continental European law tends to be much more protective of the interests of dead donors). This may partly reflect the fact that American foundations are mere striplings compared with some of their elderly British counterparts. There is also the precedent established by the 1819 Supreme Court ruling in the Dartmouth College case. Here, the court ruled against the (publicly popular) decision of the New Hampshire governor to take this private trust into public ownership on the grounds that "legislative perceptions of the public good cannot overcome the rights of individuals expressed in contracts."

U.S. legislators have, however, made provision for the public interest through the requirement that foundations should pay out at least 5 percent of the value of their assets each year. This is intended to ensure that society derives some annual benefit from the generous tax breaks it gives to foundations, rather than subsidizing their hoarding of wealth. Perhaps legislators elsewhere should follow suit, although some donors complain that this imposes an artificial straitjacket on their giving, forcing them to distribute money too quickly.

order to avoid confrontation, Annenberg failed to choose between two opposing theories on school reform: privatization and stronger central control of schools. As a result, the initiative lacked a coherent strategy and alienated supporters on both sides. The program also relied on making grants to intermediary organizations rather than working directly with schools and public education bodies themselves, so there were no real advocates for change within the organizations on which the whole initiative relied: schools and education boards.

Without an idea of how it was going to change the school system, and with resources fairly thinly spread, the challenge never met its lofty goal. The faint praise of the Annenberg Foundation's own midterm evaluation of 1999, which claimed it was leaving "small yet encouraging footprints," is perhaps the most damning judgment on his half a billion dollars.

THERE IS ONE aspect of philanthrocapitalism in which some older foundations are innovating faster than most of the new-generation ones. That is, how to invest the endowment's assets in ways that not only generate cash to fund grant making but also contribute directly to the achievement of the social goals the foundation is pursuing through its grant making. This is known as "mission-related investing" (MRI).

In its "lite" form, MRI means adopting an ethical investment policy to screen out inappropriate companies from the foundation's investment portfolio. A more activist approach involves pushing company management to behave more ethically. Hard-core MRI involves investing directly in projects that address a specific social goal of the foundation.

How ethical is ethical enough is much debated. The refusal of the Gates Foundation to engage in screening (except for tobacco companies) resulted in its coming under fire in 2007. Two articles in the *Los Angeles Times* accused the foundation of profiting from investments in companies whose activities contribute to the very problems it is trying to solve (poverty, debt, disease, and so on). The newspaper calculated that some 41 percent of the Gates Foundation portfolio was invested in companies— ranging from oil major ExxonMobil to drug giant Abbott Laboratories— that "countered the foundation's charitable goals or socially concerned philosophy." This prompted an avalanche of media comment along the lines of "giving with one hand, taking with the other."

Bill Gates was unimpressed and categorically denied the charges. His foundation does not own big-enough stakes in companies to influence their behavior through shareholder activism, he argues, and changes in its investment practices would have little or no impact on the suffering identified by the *LA Times*. Far better, he says, that the foundation concentrate on using its expertise and its money to change the things it can influence, rather then engage in impotent protests against corporate behavior.

At least he is consistent. He says he does not believe the foundation is making any difference in the one notable area where it does refuse to invest on principle: the tobacco industry. "How many lives do I want credit for, for the fact that we don't own tobacco?" he asks. "Don't put anything down for that . . . You know that the tobacco companies didn't say, 'Oh no, the Gates Foundation won't buy our shares. Let's make candy.' "

Yet some new philanthropists are more sympathetic to ethical investing. Jeff Skoll, for example. During the filming of *Fast Food Nation*, which highlighted problems in the social impact of big food companies, Skoll started to think about ethical investing. "We had shares in Coca-Cola, Burger King, and so on. I asked myself, how do I reconcile owning shares in them with making the movie?" Since then, he has tried to manage his investment portfolio in a way that better supports his philanthropic mission.

To help foundations go beyond screening to engage in active ethical shareholding, Rockefeller Philanthropy Advisors now publishes an annual *Proxy Season Preview* to guide foundations on how to use their voting power in the companies in which they invest to push for more socially and environmentally responsible corporate practices.

As for hard-core MRI, which currently accounts for around 3 percent of the assets of large American foundations, the Ford Foundation has a program of lending rather than just giving to nonprofits and the MacArthur Foundation has provided a loan guarantee on commercial terms for a social investment project in Chicago. The F. B. Heron Foundation (a relative tiddler in the foundation pond with assets of $300 million) has probably gone furthest, investing more than 18 percent of its assets in financial institutions with a social purpose, such as community-development banks and credit unions.

---

## PAY NOW OR PAY LATER?

The great American polymath Benjamin Franklin is usually credited with pioneering the idea that investing your money to give away tomorrow may be more beneficial than giving it away today. Near the end of his life he decided to switch the bequest in his will from a $9,000 grant for a navigation scheme to two grants of $4,500 to be invested for the benefit of the people of Boston and Philadelphia in the future. He estimated that within two hundred years these gifts would be worth $9 million each. However, in 1990, when the investments matured, Boston had accrued only $5 million and Philadelphia $2.25 million.

Franklin might have some cause to grumble about the stewardship of his money over this period, but even if he had hit his targets, are the benefits of $9 million to spend on good works today greater than what he could have achieved with $4,500 in 1790? Obviously inflation has to be taken into account—$4,500 would have bought a lot more in 1790 than in 1990.

"Permanent endowments tend to lessen the amount available for immediate needs; and our immediate needs are too plain and too urgent to allow us to do the work of future generations," argued Julius Rosenwald. In the early twentieth century, his foundation spent much of the fortune he made from his ownership of retailer Sears, Roebuck and Co. on the provision of

---

Great claims are made for MRI. One report from McKinsey argues that this type of investment can earn the same risk-adjusted returns as mainstream investments. Well, maybe. On the other hand, many MRIs, such as the Ford Foundation loans to nonprofits, are explicitly given at below market rates. It may be worthwhile for a foundation such as Ford to accept a slightly lower return on investment in return for philanthropic impact, but foundations need to be clear what effect this will have on their future giving potential. If they accept a lower rate of return on MRI, they will have less money to give away than they would if they had invested to maximize the financial return. Without great care when balancing hard-to-measure social impact against the cost of the lower financial returns, MRI could lead to the worst of all worlds—poor investment returns that diminish the future giving capacity of the foundation and less impact from its programs.

schooling to African Americans in the American South. Rosenwald made it clear that the money should be put to good use as soon as possible, not hoarded in perpetuity, and accordingly the Rosenwald Fund had used up its endowment within sixteen years of his death.

The free market philanthropist John M. Olin made a similar decision, although he appears to have been motivated mainly by fear that the foundation could lose its way in the future without his guiding hand. After his decision in 1975, the Olin Foundation still took thirty years to give away all his money, which highlights the practical problems of spending huge fortunes quickly.

In one notable case the decision to give away all a foundation's money has been made not by the "donor" but by the trustees. Cynics might argue that the Princess Diana Memorial Fund opted to spend its funds because it lost a large chunk of capital in a legal dispute. The hope was that distributing the remaining cash quickly would help salvage the fund's reputation after it had threatened to renege on grants promised to some of the late princess's favorite causes.

Putting an end date on a foundation is a rarity historically. It is too early to tell whether today's philanthrocapitalists will take a different approach, or succumb to the lure of a sort of immortality.

Yet shareholder activism, socially responsible investing, and mission-related investing are attracting some of the brightest minds in finance and philanthropy, and the amounts of money involved are increasing, including at some leading foundations, which are convinced that it is absurd not to enlist their huge investment portfolios directly in their efforts to do good. This may be one respect in which the Gates Foundation reflects philanthropy's past, not its future.

"ROCKEFELLER—THEY ARE a great foundation. In fact I think over the decades they have probably done more good things than any foundation that I can think of." It may seem strange that Bill Gates is so enthusiastic about the achievements of a foundation whose own president thinks needs a complete turnaround. Some may also find it particularly ironic, given the widely held perception that it is the massive investment by the Gates Foundation in global health issues that has largely squeezed the Rockefeller Foundation out of this sector, despite its long and distinguished track record there.

Gates denies that he is crowding out the old foundations, but he undoubtedly presents a challenge. The Rockefeller Foundation may still be giving out $100 million per year, and the Ford Foundation $500 million, but what is their role when Gates is pumping out $3 billion a year? Partnership, up to a point—though it is clear who is wearing the trousers in the Gates-Rockefeller Alliance for a Green Revolution for Africa. Still, whilst it will be years before Judith Rodin's reform program can be properly judged, slipstreaming behind the market leader looks like a wise move.

Rodin thinks that other heads of foundations whose donors are no longer around will start to follow her lead in reform. One reason is external pressure, as the growing attention paid to philanthropy—largely because of the emergence of Gates and other newbies—will result in more scrutiny of the performance of all foundations by everyone from the media to politicians. She also expects more self-examination by foundations, not least because of a natural desire to be part of something exciting that society approves of. That is certainly part of the story at the Rockefeller Foundation. "With so much going on in philanthropy, we are asking, 'How can we capitalize on this energy?' It's not so much competitiveness as a desire to leverage what is going on. This is an exciting time in philanthropy," she says. And generation change at the top of many established foundations will also help. "A new wave of leaders is wanting to take new, smart risks. There is a chance with this kind of money to do extraordinary things," says Rodin.

Efforts to increase the transparency of foundations also have a crucial role to play in keeping philanthrocrats focused on achieving impact. One encouraging sign is a growing willingness of established foundations to be more open about their failings. As well as publishing its Grantee Perception Reports, Paul Brest, head of the William and Flora Hewlett Foundation, has asked staff to name the worst grant they made and what they learned from it. The winner is decided by a vote among the staff. The reward for failure? A free dinner for the officer who made, and learned from, the biggest mistake of the year—oh, and better due diligence for the program.

It is the competitive challenge, or at least the raising of the bar, by the new entrants to the philanthropic market that, more than anything, is putting pressure on the old foundations to change. Increasingly, they are concluding that they need to adapt or be left behind. That's philanthrocapitalism.

## CHAPTER 10

# The Good Company

"SAVE THE WORLD. IT'S NOT EASY, Googlers, so mail your ideas." In spring 2007, these words were scrawled on a white board in the offices of Google.org, in the heart of the Googleplex, as the Mountain View, California, headquarters of the Internet search giant is known. The formation of Google.org, a philanthropic division of the Google corporation, which they hoped would "eclipse" in its impact everything else the company does, had been announced in 2004 by Sergey Brin and Larry Page, the firm's cofounders, as they prepared for the firm's lucrative initial public offering of shares. The creation of this revolutionary new sort of philanthropic business unit was the most visible incarnation of the controversial shared belief of the "Google guys" that companies should be a positive force in society—a role that many people, on both the right and left, think that businesses do not, will not, cannot, and even should not play.

"I believe that a successful corporation has a responsibility that's greater than simply growing itself as large as it can be. I believe large, successful corporations have a number of resources and have an obligation to apply some of those resources to at least try to solve or ameliorate a number of the world's problems and ultimately to make the world a better place," Brin explained. "We believe strongly that in the long term, we will be better served—as shareholders and in all other ways—by a company that does good things for the world even if we forgo some short-term gains," elaborated Page.

To emphasize the point, the firm famously adopted an unofficial motto: "Don't be evil." This "serves as a reminder to all our employees to consider the consequences of our actions," Page told the Global Philanthropy Forum, which he and Brin hosted in 2007 at the Googleplex. Then he joked, "Perhaps it was a mistake—we should have said, 'Be good.'"

According to Google legend, when the pair first met in 1995, as computer science students at Stanford University, they were "not terribly fond of each other." That soon changed, and they went on to write a seminal paper together, "The Anatomy of a Large-Scale Hypertextual Web Search Engine," before founding Google, which was incorporated as a private company in September 1998.

Less than six years later, the online search firm, with its mission to "organize the world's information and make it universally accessible and useful," sold its shares to the public, instantly making the American-born Page and the Russian-born Brin billionaires several times over.

Because of Brin's and Page's controlling shareholdings in Google, Google.org largely reflects their personal philanthropic interests. Both men also do some giving outside Google, which they plan to increase as they get older (see "Those Giving Google Guys" box on page 176). Even before its IPO, Google had supported several hundred nonprofits through its Google Grants program, which awarded them credits to buy advertisements within the Google search system. When the firm went public, it endowed Google.org with 1 percent of its equity (worth about $2 billion at the end of 2007), which it planned to supplement with 1 percent of its annual profits (around $400 million in 2007) and 1 percent of its employees' working time.

The Google guys got the idea for this "1 percent solution" from another Silicon Valley philanthrocapitalist, Marc Benioff, the founder of Salesforce.com, an on-demand software company. Benioff, a reknowned salesman who made his name at Oracle, is evangelical about the need for companies to practice "integrated philanthropy" and has written two books about it, *Compassionate Capitalism* and *The Business of Changing the World*.

Initially, the plan was to use the Google 1 percent to create a traditional corporate charitable foundation. But the Google Foundation that they had formed in 2004 soon evolved into Google.org, which—much like Omidyar Network—can be involved in both nonprofit and for-profit activities and is also free to engage in political lobbying and campaigning, something forbidden to traditional (tax-exempt) foundations.

There is a crucial difference, however: although Omidyar Network can make for-profit investments, its ultimate goal is to give everything away, whereas Google.org is an arm of a for-profit public company whose shareholders expect a financial return, albeit one whose founders retain a controlling stake.

After a long search, Brin and Page found someone to run Google.org whom they considered a perfect fit: Larry Brilliant, a public health expert who studied under a Hindu guru in a Himalayan monastery, worked as a Silicon Valley entrepreneur, and was once doctor to the Grateful Dead. He has become a philanthrocapitalism enthusiast, enjoying seeing the new rich "fighting not over whether to do good, but how to do good, and which good is the goodest." Brilliant describes Google.org, with its tremendous freedom to "play with all the keys on the keyboard" by pursuing everything from nonprofit to for-profit to politics, as, "in effect, a philanthropic hedge fund." Yet his experience is likely to make him a stabilizing influence on his young backers: "These kids, by dint of how fast they got rich, expect fast results. If I had a dollar for every time people said they wanted quick wins, I would be able to buy you a free lunch," he says.

Brilliant believes focus is crucial to be effective. "We would become a diffuse, unfocused, and ultimately unsuccessful organization if we staffed up to do all the different things suggested to us," he says. In January 2008, Google.org announced that it would concentrate on five key initiatives. Two reflect the passion of the two Google founders to develop cost-effective alternative energy to replace carbon fuels: Google.org has invested $10 million in RechargeIT.org, a project to accelerate the adoption of hybrid electric vehicles; and it announced a multimillion-dollar research and development program, RE<C, to find ways to produce renewable energy (RE) at a lower cost per gigawatt than electricity from coal-powered (C) plants. Google.org's economic development initiative will promote middle-class jobs in developing countries, to which end it has backed various nonprofits, including TechnoServe, which holds a popular "Believe Begin Become" business-plan competition in Africa to identify good ideas and help them secure funding.

Brilliant stressed the importance of focusing on things that related to the core strengths of Google.com, notably its technological and engineering abilities, its global reach, and its deep understanding of the power of information to change the world. The last of these inspired the organization's fourth and fifth initiatives: improving public services in developing countries by providing much better information about service quality to those who run them and those who use them; and, a long-time personal interest of Brilliant, developing an early-warning and rapid-response infrastructure for global pandemics and other catastrophes. Google.org has seeded Innovative Support to Emergencies Diseases and Disasters (InSTEDD), a nonprofit that is working to better connect the best brains in the technology industry with those responsible for monitoring and responding to such crises.

Brilliant stresses that doing good is not limited within the company to Google.org. Most people choose to work for Google because they want to change the world, he says. Every "Googler" is encouraged to spend some work time "doing good." But the difference at Google.org, Brilliant says, is that "we are trying to take a businesslike approach to the biggest problems in the world without worrying about making a profit."

HAVING BEEN ABLE TO build philanthropy into its organizational structure from the start of its life as a public company, Google has arguably gone further than any other firm in philanthrocapitalistic innovation. For most firms, like tycoons, philanthropy comes later in life, if at all. Yet in recent years big business has taken a growing interest in finding ways to do good by tackling society's big problems. Although some of this interest has been expressed through charitable foundations established by companies, much of it has been broader and has taken place not through creating new divisions like Google.org but under the banner of "corporate social responsibility" or "corporate citizenship." Increasingly, it is also being driven by the belief that doing good can be profitable, or at least boost the firm's reputation so that it can more easily recruit the best talent. In 2008, in a speech to fellow business leaders and philanthrocapitalists at the World Economic Forum in Davos, Bill Gates called this new approach "creative capitalism," which he says is an attempt to "stretch the reach of market forces so that more people can make a profit, or gain recognition, doing work that eases the world's inequities."

There are already several prominent examples of this "stretch." Like Google, General Electric, led by chief executive Jeffrey Immelt, has embraced environmental sustainability as a crusade under the banner of "Ecomagination." Environmentalism has also been championed by oil giant BP, with its "Beyond Petroleum" campaign, and by retail giant

## THOSE GIVING GOOGLE GUYS

The Google guys are big innovators in corporate giving, but what about their personal philanthropy? So far, there is not much to report—a fact that has been commented on disapprovingly in private by some prominent donors. Sergey Brin has said that he intends to do a lot of giving directly from his fortune, but mostly later in life, "in a few years, when I feel I'm more educated." As yet, Brin says, "I don't think it's something I have had time to become an expert at." Currently, what he describes as his "modest" giving is limited to a few charities that have supported him and his family, such as the Hebrew Immigration Aid Society (HIAS), which helped them emigrate from the Soviet Union to America when Brin was six and is currently creating a digital record of Jewish immigrant archives. Larry Page, meanwhile, has reportedly made donations to the X Prize Foundation and in 2007 hosted a gala in the Googleplex to encourage other wealthy donors to follow suit.

Both Google guys are active participants in the elite global gatherings where philanthrocapitalists rub shoulders with politicians and other influential folks. These include the World Economic Forum in Davos, the Clinton Global Initiative, and Technology, Entertainment, and Design (TED), a conference at which luminaries such as Bill Clinton and Bono are awarded prizes to help them achieve a "wish to change the world." At Davos in 2006, where Google made headlines mostly for the superior quality of the wine served at its party, Page gave a talk about space flight, one of his great passions. Indeed, in the main building of the Googleplex hangs a replica of SpaceShipOne, the privately developed spacecraft that won the first prize—of $10 million—ever awarded by the X Prize Foundation.

In Davos in 2007, both Google guys spoke in favor of offsetting carbon emissions in order to combat climate change. They certainly take steps to "offset" the carbon emitted during flights of the Google corporate jet, which was the subject of a rare dispute between the two tycoons, who had a falling out about the size of the beds to be fitted on the Boeing 767. After Google's (older) chief executive, Eric Schmidt, described the jet as "a party airplane," Page told the Wall Street Journal that "part of the equation for this sort of machinery is to be able to take large numbers of people to places such as Africa. I think that can only be good for the world." Well, maybe. Bill Clinton, among others, has been transported to Africa aboard the Google jet, presumably to do good works rather than party.

Wal-Mart. Internet-infrastructure firm Cisco has a long record of trying to close the "digital divide" by providing education in information technology in developing countries. Shell has launched a foundation that focuses on creating new small- and medium-size businesses in the developing world. A. G. Lafley, boss of Procter & Gamble, has promised to help eliminate maternal and neonatal tetanus by providing forty-five million vaccines in the developing world, under the banner of the company's Pampers brand.

This growing interest in corporate giving raises many questions, not least about the balance between a firm's duty to its shareholders to make a profit and its responsibility to society to do good. (Even Google has been accused of ethical lapses, such as compromising with the government of China in order to gain market access.) Should companies be aiming for anything but profitability? Does a company deserve credit from the public if its giving is part of a strategy to maximize its profits or only if it makes the firm worse off? Do companies have particular capabilities that can be used to solve societal problems that even wealthy individuals or governments cannot? Beyond their role in making their founders wealthy enough to give, are companies an integral part of philanthrocapitalism? Certainly, the scale and power of big companies means that they have the potential to be an important force for good. However, the need to make a profit will constrain the ways in which they can do so in ways that their nonprofit-driven partners in any cause need to understand, or risk disappointment.

To antibusiness activists, corporate philanthropy and corporate social responsibility are superficial at best, an attempt to disguise the ugly underlying reality of big business today. In his 2007 book, *Supercapitalism*, Robert B. Reich, a professor at the University of California, Berkeley (and labor secretary in Bill Clinton's cabinet), writes that corporate social responsibility is "as meaningful as cotton candy. The more you try to bite into it the faster it dissolves." It is not that company bosses are evil, or even less ethical than everyone else, says Reich, but in today's supercompetitive globalized capitalism few firms can afford to be socially responsible, at least not to any significant extent: "Corporations were never set up to be charitable institutions and are less able to operate in that sphere now," he says, pointing out that the sums spent by business on "doing good" are dwarfed by what firms spend lobbying politicians to promote their narrow interests, often against the public interest. For Reich, the only meaningful answer to society's problems, and the way to ensure that firms do more social good than harm, is politics—better government, better regulation—not corporate giving.

Reich's disdain for corporate social responsibility, but not his enthusiasm for more government, was shared by the late, great free market economist Milton Friedman, who famously argued in 1970 that "there is one and only one social responsibility of business—to use its resources and engage in activities designed to increase its profits, so long as it stays within the rules of the game." He believed that in these circumstances—that is, engaging in open and free competition without deception or fraud—generating higher profits was a reflection of the benefit that business generated for society. Anything else, he might have said, is cotton candy.

Increasingly, however, even some of those business leaders who are sympathetic to Friedman think he failed to recognize the positive profit-making possibilities that can arise from participating in solving society's biggest problems. As for Reich, they say, perhaps he simply doesn't understand business.

According to Michael E. Porter and Mark Kramer, two of the leading academic observers of philanthrocapitalism, firms looking to maximize long-run profits should use their philanthropic efforts to "improve their competitive context"—that is, "the quality of the business environment in the locations where they operate." Particularly in countries with weak or ineffective governance and infrastructure, firms have a chance to enhance their long-term prospects by using philanthropy (broadly defined) to build a sustainable business environment.

Porter and Kramer would surely applaud G.E.'s use of Ecomagination as a way to make a lot of money in the long run; even in the two years after Immelt launched the crusade, it generated revenues of $12 billion, which G.E. expects to rise to $20 billion by 2010. G.E. has joined with other big companies and NGOs to form the U.S. Climate Action Partnership to lobby for national legislation in America to cap carbon emissions. This would help create a market for its Ecomagination products. Other big companies in industries such as aluminum and electricity generation have also lobbied in favor of carbon regulation. Though it would increase their costs, the existence of a system of carbon regulation with broad public support would make the business conditions in which they will operate in future more predictable, reducing the risk

involved when they make multibillion-dollar investments in new operations that may take years to build and decades to generate profit.

Likewise, Benioff is clear that one of the goals of Salesforce.com's philanthropy is to attract the best talent. Surveys show that college graduates, in particular, increasingly want to work for a company that shares
their values and commitment to a better world. Benioff is adamant that
he has been able to recruit better employees because of his firm's philanthropic commitment, and that having lots of employees who are motivated by this sense of mission makes Salesforce.com a more successful
business.

Yet Porter and Kramer readily concede that reality is often a long way
from their ideal. Frequently, "philanthropy is used as a form of public
relations or advertising, promoting a company's image through high-
profile sponsorships," they note in "The Competitive Advantage of
Corporate Philanthropy," an article in the *Harvard Business Review* in
2002.

As with philanthropy in general, they argue, this lack of rigor and seriousness amounts to a huge lost opportunity. Company management
should instead be clear as to how their firm's philanthropic activity con-
nects to its core strategy for making money, otherwise it may not achieve
much impact; and even if it does, there is a high probability that it will
be the first thing to be cut if times get hard. The best approach, say
Porter and Kramer, is for management to treat their firm's philanthropy
as akin to spending on research and development: an investment in the
future. Just as well-run companies know they cut back on R&D at their
peril, even if the impact is only felt in the long run, so they will be reluctant to reduce their philanthropy if they believe that it has long-term
bottom-line benefits.

Reich concedes that there are activities taking place under the banner
of corporate social responsibility or corporate philanthropy that are both
good for society and profitable for the companies that do them. Indeed,
that is why he is underwhelmed by them. "All these steps may be worthwhile but they are not undertaken because they are socially responsible," he writes. They are done to reduce costs or boost profits in other
ways. "To credit these corporations with being 'socially responsible' is to
stretch the term to mean anything a company might do to increase profits if, in doing so, it also happens to have some beneficent impact on the
rest of society."

Reich misses the point, however, about the difficult choices that companies face. Many executives are so focused on dealing with short-term pressures for bigger profits that they do not devote sufficient time to thinking about what is in their long-term-profit-maximizing, enlightened self-interest. Even if they do think about it, it is all too rare that an executive is willing to incur the short-run costs (such as that R&D–like philanthropy) necessary to achieve that more profitable long-term goal. Spending on lobbying against change that may impose a short-term cost is often the reflex reaction. Corporate "doing well by doing good" may provide a win-win for the firm and society, but it is a win that too few firms even attempt—which is why those firms that do try surely deserve the public's encouragement.

This enlightened self-interest case for business to engage fully in society was set out by Klaus Schwab, founder of the World Economic Forum, in the January-February 2008 issue of *Foreign Affairs*. Especially since anticapitalist protesters started to target the WEF's annual meetings in the 1990s, Schwab has thought hard about the need for business to engage more constructively in society—and has led by example in opening up the WEF to more diverse opinions, including from some of the people who would once have supported the activists on the other side of the Davos security fence. In his article "Global Corporate Citizenship," he calls on international business leaders to "fully commit to sustainable development and address paramount global challenges," including climate change, the provision of public health care, energy conservation, and the management of resources, particularly water, as part of a long-term profit-maximization strategy.

Schwab argues that the emergence of global corporate citizenship is the "inevitable result" of several factors. One is the weakness of government: Schwab would reject Reich's big-government prescriptions because the role of the nation-state is declining and global governance institutions (such as the U.N. and World Trade Organization) are inadequate to address global challenges. He also points to the increasing effectiveness of firms, not least through their mastery of technology. There are things that companies, particularly big multinational firms, can do better than anyone to help solve society's problems, he says. This has brought about what he calls a "fundamental shift in the global power equation": as state power has declined, the influence of corporations on communities, on the lives of citizens, and on the environment has sharply increased.

Schwab takes a broad view of citizenship that extends well beyond traditional giving through a corporate foundation. In his opinion, there are five different sorts of engagement between a firm and society: corporate governance (which can include ethical rules, such as on corruption); corporate philanthropy (giving money and time); corporate social responsibility (how a firm responds to the concerns of its stakeholders); corporate social entrepreneurship (transforming socially or environmentally responsible ideas into products or services); and global corporate citizenship (engagement at a macro level on issues of importance to the world).

When engaging in global corporate citizenship, companies should "get involved in areas and in ways in which they can contribute meaningfully," Schwab argues. This they can do through "thought leadership" or through concrete action, or both. Echoing Porter and Kramer, he writes that "global corporate citizenship can be considered a long-term investment. Since companies depend on global development, which in turn relies on stability and increased prosperity, it is in their direct interest to help improve the state of the world."

Yet a 2007 survey by McKinsey found that fewer than half the executives in America believed that they or their peers should take the lead in shaping the debate on major issues such as education, health care, and foreign policy. Only one in seven respondents believed that they were playing that role—and most of them said they were motivated primarily by personal reasons and were acting as private citizens.

Why are many corporate executives shirking their responsibility to build successful companies and at the same time shaping the world? One reason, Schwab agrees, is that the pursuit of short-term profits at the expense of the long-term best interests of the firm may lead to "corporate attention deficit disorder, whereby companies lose focus on the big picture." Another possibility (ignoring greed and incompetence) is that "corporate leaders may also be overwhelmed by the sheer magnitude and complexity of global challenges and the expectations of the public for them to assume partial responsibility for all the deficiencies of the global system." Schwab concludes that "this mindset must be changed" if corporations are to maximize their profitability and their contribution to society.

WHAT IS BEYOND dispute is that there is a long history of social engagement by companies, and that when companies ignore the big issues of

society, they can live to regret it. Today's growing interest by big companies in philanthropic activities reflects a rediscovery of a historic tradition that was lost, not least, in the 1980s and 1990s, when the focus was
too often on maximizing short-term shareholder value.

Much of the pioneering early corporate philanthropy took place in
Europe, long before it reached America, and was directed by companies
towards their own employees, through a mixture of idealism and the
self-interested belief that better-looked-after workers would be more
productive. A nineteenth-century Yorkshire textile magnate, Titus Salt,
one of the first industrialist-philanthropists, donated the hospital, almshouses, institute, bathhouses, and churches that became the town of
Saltaire, essentially creating a public-services sector for a population
that had none. Later, enlightened factory owners such as the confec-
tionery-making Cadbury and Rowntree dynasties began providing decent housing for their workers in model villages. George Cadbury took
over the family chocolate company from his father in 1861 and, with
his brother Richard, built a new factory at Bournville in 1879. Their
vision was "a factory in a garden" with decent, affordable housing for
the workers.

Soap magnate Lord Leverhulme, founder of what is now Unilever,
also joined in this Victorian tradition. He bought a site and built his own
factory, with decent housing for his workers at reasonable rents. He
would provide them with schools, a library, institutes, and public buildings that they could use to improve themselves as he had done. In return,
he hoped, they were to prove themselves worthy of all this by following a
life characterized by sobriety, thrift, and the desire for self-improvement.
Leverhulme's model village Port Sunlight, near Liverpool, was founded
in 1889 and was a "neat and cheerful" place that fulfilled his desire to
share his profits with his workers and combined with his interests in
housing reform. Port Sunlight remained exclusively for Unilever employees until the 1980s, when it was opened up to private buyers.

Still more radical was Robert Owen, the father of the cooperative
movement. After successfully running mills in Manchester, Owen and
his philanthropist-investor partners acquired a factory at New Lanark in
Scotland in 1800, which he managed according to his own principles:
limits on working age, educational programs for children and adults, and
a company store to sell basic goods to the workers at little more than cost.
It made money too. As New Lanark's reputation grew, Owen traveled to

the United States in 1824, where he addressed Congress and established a model community called New Harmony in Indiana. Whether it was the people it attracted or the limitations of the communal system that Owen devised, New Harmony was a dismal failure that closed in 1829, when its wealthy philanthropic backer, William MacLure, cut off funding.

In the mid-twentieth century a bold step was taken by the British retail firm John Lewis when the founder's son, John Spedan Lewis, shared out the ownership of the firm among its employees. He explained the decision in the book *Partnership for All* in 1948, rejecting Owenite idealism but seeing this as the best way forward for capitalism. Although the firm remains a partnership today, Spedan Lewis's ideas have not transformed capitalism as he had hoped.

During the twentieth century, similar instincts of responsibility for employees led to the development of company pensions to provide for workers in retirement—and, later, in America to the emergence of a health care system largely paid for by companies. This was somewhat accidental, as U.S. companies started to pay for the bulk of their employees' health care as a way to get around limits on pay increases imposed in the war against inflation by President Richard Nixon.

Whilst it is plausible to see the benefits provided by companies to workers as narrowly self-interested rather than truly philanthropic, by the mid-twentieth century companies in America were playing a crucial role in addressing some big social issues of the day. There was an informal social contract in place between business and society in which leading company bosses, such as General Motors chief executive Charles Wilson, regarded themselves as "corporate statesmen." It was Wilson who famously observed that what was good for General Motors was good for America, and vice versa. These corporate statesmen testified frequently before Congress on all sorts of social issues.

Much of this activity was coordinated by the Committee for Economic Development, a business-led organization with a broad, progressive social agenda. It campaigned, among other things, for the Full Employment Act and for the Marshall Plan that directed millions of American dollars to revive foreign economies devastated by the Second World War.

At the same moment that this old social contract was being torn up, not least by globalization and the intensification of competition that came with it, from the 1970s on, corporate leaders were challenged by new demands from consumers and citizens who felt that businesses had a broader social responsibility beyond treating their workers well. At first, firms resisted these demands, and came to regret it.

In 1969, a consumer boycott of Barclays bank began in Britain over its involvement with the apartheid regime in South Africa. It took a while for Barclays to catch on, so that by the time it sold its South African operations in 1986, it had seen its share of the British student banking market fall from 27 percent to 15 percent. In the same way, in 1977, a consumer boycott began against food multinational Nestlé, starting in America and swiftly spreading throughout Europe. It was alleged that the firm's infant milk formula, a substitute for breast milk, caused death and sickness in babies in developing countries. The boycott rumbles on to this day, despite Nestlé's insistence that it is innocent and has not only complied fully with World Health Organization standards but had also investigated any substantiated claims made by those who believe there have been breaches of standards, taking disciplinary action against any offenders.

As the consumer movement grew in the 1990s, sporting goods giant Nike was embarrassed by media reports about labor abuses by its Indonesian suppliers that led to calls for a consumer boycott. Yet it was not until 1998 that Nike started to engage with the issue. The firm is now committed to working with its suppliers to improve the treatment of the two thirds of a million employees in its supply chain. Having established a comprehensive set of environmental, health, safety, and labor standards, Nike now has seventy-five full-time employees inspecting factories and working with suppliers. It conducts unannounced factory audits in partnership with a nonprofit called the Fair Labor Association. A typical garment factory working in Nike's supply chain can expect to be visited by inspectors around twenty-five times a year.

Today, a growing number of firms realize that to be successful they must be ahead of public opinion, not behind it. But this is still far from the norm. In 2007, a survey of the Global 2000 companies by Integrity Interactive, a risk consultancy, found that 78 percent did not require suppliers to enforce a code of conduct and that only 42 percent regularly assessed ethics risk in their supply chain.

The inactive firms are making a mistake. Nike's reputation with the broader public has yet to fully recover, and the same is true of Nestlé, Barclays, and others. A good reputation is of immense value to a company; it is easily lost and extremely difficult to regain. Beyond that, corporate bad behavior may provoke a political reaction, such as new laws, the cost of which will far outweigh any short-term benefits from the behavior. Bosses who do not ensure they understand and actively manage the risks and opportunities presented by the big issues shaping society are guilty not just of a lack of social conscience but also of a reckless negligence in the management of their firms.

ROYAL DUTCH SHELL was once one of the most unpopular companies in one of the industries most reviled by consumer activists: oil. "Shell to hell" became a popular slogan of antiglobalization activists when, in 1995, the Anglo-Dutch corporation was in the center of two storms over its role in society. First, it was the target of campaigns by environmentalists over its plans to dump a defunct oil rig in the North Sea off Brent Spar. Then it was widely vilified for standing by as the government of Nigeria, with which it was close, executed the writer, environmentalist, and human rights activist Ken Saro-Wiwa. Yet out of this crisis grew a concerted effort to rebuild its reputation, not least by creating a charitable foundation with an important new twist on the traditional model.

Around $12 billion a year is given away by corporate foundations, mostly in America. Sadly, most corporate foundations are unfocused, often handing out money at the whim of the chief executive, who may use gifts to oil the wheels of a business relationship or favor his or her own pet cause. According to Charles Moore of the Committee Encouraging Corporate Philanthropy, what companies should be doing is forming a philanthropic strategy that is "aligned with their for-profit strategy." This is exactly what Shell believes it has done.

"The international development community, donors, NGOs, and foundations created by rich people are stuffed full of issue experts who don't know how to solve problems or produce scaleable solutions," says Shell Foundation director Kurt Hoffman. "They largely lack the tools, drivers, and efficiency incentives that business uses to solve problems en route to making a profit."

The Shell Foundation attempts to go beyond both the PR-focused corporate social responsibility of many companies, which delivers little in social impact, and also the well-intentioned charitable approaches that never reach any scale because they are not commercially viable. Launched in 2000, with an initial endowment of $250 million, the foundation is committed to finding business-based solutions to poverty, not just because it thinks this is the best way of helping the poor but because it thinks it is the best way for a corporation to help the poor, says Hoffman. "The old crop of NGOs and donors, and the new generation of guilty artists and rich offspring of rich people, have only money—the least valuable social-change asset—to bring to the table. They have no business acumen at all and worry about solving the ego-assuaging visible consequences of poverty rather than tackling its causes."

The Shell Foundation's biggest success so far has been in creating an investment fund for small and medium-size enterprises in Africa targeting "high-risk, pro-poor" companies that cannot get funding elsewhere. So far, so familiar, but what is different about the Shell Foundation approach is that it has converted a successful pilot into a commercially viable investment vehicle. Having covered the foundation's setup costs with $12 million of its own capital, Shell had already levered in $100 million of commercial investment by early 2008 and claimed to be well on the way to $250 million. "Essentially we have created a new pro-poor investment 'asset class' and proven it can deliver commercial returns," says Hoffman. If he is right, then, as Muhammad Yunus and Grameen bank did by turning microfinance into an asset class, Shell may have kicked off a multibillion-dollar investment in ending poverty.

Of course, Shell benefits from this success. An increase in small and medium enterprises in Africa could improve supply chains for the company's African operations, making it easier to do business, which is good for long-term profitability. Successful Shell Foundation programs also make a direct contribution to the success of the company since they are an attractive part of Shell's offer when negotiating with governments. Working on foundation projects may boost Shell staff morale too. And it is good for the company's once-tainted reputation.

Hoffman is certain that the secret of the Shell Foundation's success is access to the expertise its parent company has in finance, marketing, logistics, and such (he calls himself a "cynical old development fart" but recruits staff with business experience). He is bemused, therefore, by the behavior of so many of today's philanthrocapitalists, who have renounced business and taken up philanthropy full time. "They have money and they have general business acumen, but they are cut off from the vast storehouse of expertise and knowledge that resides in the companies they no longer run," he says. The Google guys are doing their philanthropy within their business, but what if Bill Gates had done his within Microsoft instead of launching his own separate foundation?

"AT WAL-MART WE didn't watch Katrina; we experienced it." In October 2005, Lee Scott, the chief executive of the giant low-cost retailer, gave a speech to staff in its Bentonville headquarters that in many ways captured the new approach that big business claims to be taking to its role in society. That August, the hurricane that had devastated New Orleans and its neighborhood, had left Wal-Mart stores underwater and robbed some if its workers (which it calls its "associates") of their savings, and in a few tragic cases, their lives. Whilst the American government struggled to get its act together, Wal-Mart had moved decisively. Asked by government, relief agencies, and communities to help, it did so not by dropping some corporate dollars on a few favored charities but by using its logistical expertise to ship water and food quickly to the disaster area, including more than one hundred truckloads of free merchandise. Wal-Mart also used its customer databases to identify the most demanded products after a hurricane and sent in large quantities of strawberry Pop-Tarts as a result.

"Katrina asked this critical question," said Scott. "What would it take for Wal-Mart to be that company, at our best, all the time? What if we used our size and our resources to make this country and this earth an even better place for all of us: our customers, associates, our children, and generations unborn? What would that mean? Could we do it? Is this consistent with our business model? What if the very things people criticize us for—our size and reach—became a trusted friend and ally to all, just as it did in Katrina?"

Strictly speaking, this was not an entirely new thought. Despite giving away around $300 million a year—more than any other firm—to support communities around the world where it operates, and despite its employees donating over a million working hours to charity, Wal-Mart has been the subject of growing criticism for years. Indeed, in 2005, the National Committee for Responsive Philanthropy criticized

Wal-Mart's corporate philanthropy for being PR driven, focused entirely in places it has businesses and using scattershot small grants rather than trying to make a real difference.

One concern is the retailer's sheer size, which has arguably made it too powerful and deaf to criticism. It has 176 million customers in fourteen countries. As Scott says, "If we were a country, we would be the twentieth largest in the world. If we were a city, we would be the fifth largest in America. People expect a lot of us, and they have a right to."

Critics have been particularly exercised over its opposition to trade unions and its tough employment practices, including wages that some observers consider unacceptably low. In 2004, it began a yearlong "listening process," trying to better understand its critics and its impact on society. Scott had concluded that "many of our most vocal critics do not want us to stop doing business, but they feel business needs to change—not just our company but all companies."

Scott also concluded that the company had been responding in the wrong way to its critics. He listed jobs, health care, community involvement, product sourcing, diversity, and environmental impact as "all the issues that we've been dealing with historically from a defensive posture. What became clear is that in order to build a twenty-first-century company, we need to view these same issues in a different light. In fact, they represent gateways for Wal-Mart in becoming the most competitive and innovative company in the world."

Scott had seen the environment as almost an irrelevance to Wal-Mart, beyond a "responsible recycling program" and a concern to avoid unnecessary waste. A Wal-Mart environment program "sounded more like a public relations campaign than substance to me," he recalled. Katrina changed that. "A lightbulb came on—a compact fluorescent lightbulb," Scott said, when he realized that climate change is like "Katrina in slow motion." He also concluded that "being a steward of the environment and being efficient and profitable are one and the same."

"We are a large company," he said. "For Wal-Mart to be successful and continue to grow, we must operate in a world that is healthy and successful."

Due to Wal-Mart's size and scope, Scott believed it was "uniquely positioned to have great success and impact in the world, perhaps like no company before us." He set ambitious goals: to use only renewable energy, to create zero waste, and to sell products that sustain the earth's resources and environment. Wal-Mart's workers were already the most productive in retailing in the world, he said, so "why not spend the next four decades making our trucks, refrigerators, stores, lighting, packaging, shipping—every aspect of our business—the most productive in the world? This will be good for the environment, it will save us money, and in some cases, it will actually add profits to our bottom line."

"We didn't just get needed goods to Katrina victims—we did it less expensively than anyone," Scott noted. "The environment is begging for 'Every Day Low Cost'—for the Wal-Mart business model." Among Wal-Mart's goals are commitments to improve the fuel efficiency of its truck fleet by one mile per gallon, to reduce the energy consumption of its stores by 30 percent, and to use solar panels, wind turbines, and mature trees to shade buildings to reduce its greenhouse-gas emissions. It is investing $500 million a year in new green technologies.

Perhaps of particular significance, Wal-Mart is insisting that its suppliers from China adopt green standards. One of the most important advantages of being big is that Wal-Mart can throw its weight around. When it shouts, its suppliers jump. And once they have adopted green standards, the other firms that buy from them will often get those standards too, by default.

The company plans to further cut down on waste through a 5 percent reduction in overall packaging by 2013. One example: slightly smaller packaging for one store-brand toy will use 497 fewer transport containers and save 3,800 trees and over a thousand barrels of oil. Wal-Mart's British unit, Asda, is providing leadership for the whole company by aiming to send no waste to landfills by 2010. By 2007, it had already reduced such waste by 245,000 tons compared with two years earlier.

But perhaps the company's most significant innovation will be in the products it sells. Wal-Mart is attempting to bring to the mass market the sort of socially conscious products that were once considered attractive only to those virtuous shoppers willing to pay more for "green" products. British retailer Marks and Spencer (M&S), which has long been known as a good corporate citizen, reckons that British consumers can be divided into three groups: 10 percent are passionately green and will go out of their way to find suitable purchases; 25 percent are totally uninterested; and 65 percent are willing to care if they can find easy ways to make a difference. M&S sees the 65 percent as a huge opportunity. But Wal-Mart believes that by using its scale and purchasing power it can make virtuous products affordable for everyone. "You should not need a greater income for access to seafood, cotton, forest, or paper products that are safe for your family or produced in a sustainable way," insists Scott. By 2007, the firm already had a team of two hundred people working on sourcing products that are ethically made. (It boasts that sustainability has "become a recruitment and retention tool" and offers a personal sustainability practices program to staff.)

One example is those lightbulbs. Wal-Mart estimated that its goal of selling 100 million compact fluorescent lightbulbs in the United States by end of 2007 would ultimately save consumers $3 billion from their electricity bills and reduce greenhouse-gas emissions by 20 million tons a year—equivalent to taking 700,000 cars off the road.

Another is a potentially huge new market in organic cotton goods. Wal-Mart has given a boost to small organic cotton farmers in developing countries around the world by ensuring there will be a market for what they grow. It sold 190,000 of a new range of sustainable-cotton yoga outfits in ten weeks and, because these were made using fibers grown without nasty chemicals, "saved two jumbo jets full of pesticides."

Asda already sells 250 million rolls a year of store-brand toilet paper. Wal-Mart worked with the Forestry Stewardship Council (FSC) to ensure that this was made from sustainably harvested wood. This has not added a single penny to the price of a roll, says Scott. By 2009, Wal-Mart will buy all its wild-caught seafood from fisheries approved by the Marine Stewardship Council.

Working with NGOs to label products as ethically produced has become crucial to selling to the socially conscious consumer. (This creates reputational and other risk for the NGOs, which need to be clear about whether to accept money from a corporate partner, and may find their ability to campaign impaired by suspicions that they are sleeping with the enemy.) Not everybody welcomes Wal-Mart's decision to enter these ethical markets, however. In 2006, the company's announcement that it planned to sell organic food was greeted unenthusiastically, not least by the *New York Times*, which complained that "people who think seriously about food have come to realize that 'local' is at least as important a word as 'organic.' The only thing local about Wal-Mart is its shoppers." The newspaper worried that *organic* could become "just another shill word, like 'new' or 'improved.'" Well, maybe. But it is hard to exaggerate the extent to which Wal-Mart's description of its approach to some of the world's big challenges has changed in recent years. Most people will be delighted if Wal-Mart succeeds in walking the walk as well as it now talks the talk.


PARTNERSHIPS BETWEEN BIG business, nonprofits, philanthropists, and governments are proliferating as leading firms start to be more strategic in their engagement with society.

Pfizer developed a cost-effective treatment for the prevention of trachoma, the leading cause of preventable blindness in developing countries. It donated the drugs and worked with the Edna McConnell Clark Foundation and various health organizations to create the infrastructure to prescribe and distribute them to populations that previously had little access to health care. Within a year, the incidence of trachoma was down by 50 percent in Morocco and Tanzania. The program has since been expanded aggressively by the Gates Foundation and the British government's Department for International Development, with a goal of reaching thirty million people.

Coca-Cola, which has come to realize that water conservation is critical to its future, has formed a partnership with the World Wildlife Fund to conserve seven major freshwater basins and is also working with Greenpeace. "Ten years ago you couldn't get Coca-Cola and Greenpeace in the same room," says Neville Isdell, Coca-Cola's chief executive when the partnerships began.

There has been a huge growth in corporate commitments to uphold human rights. Thirteen top firms, such as Gap, Coca-Cola, and GE, are members of the Business Leaders Initiative on Human Rights, chaired by former president of Ireland and now Elder, Mary Robinson. Its goal is to find "practical ways of applying the Universal Declaration of Human Rights within a business context."

There is also the U.N. Global Compact, a framework of ten core principles to guide business behavior in areas such as human rights, the environment, corruption, and labor standards. Announced at the World Economic Forum in 1999, and officially launched in 2000, it has since been adopted by over four thousand companies in 120 countries (see "Corporate Social Responsibility Goes Global" box). Critics object to the U.N. providing what they call "bluewash" to big business, but most observers view the compact's popularity as evidence that firms are taking these issues more seriously. However, the U.N. is considering introducing clearer guidelines on what behavior is acceptable by firms, especially in countries with questionable records on human rights. In 2007, a split opened up over these guidelines between NGOs that wanted

## CORPORATE SOCIAL RESPONSIBILITY GOES GLOBAL

It is tempting to see the global boom in corporate social responsibility (CSR) as yet another sign of multinationals exporting business practices from the rich world to the poor one. In China, for example, foreign companies have been enthusiastic members of the Global Business Coalition on HIV/AIDS, Tuberculosis, and Malaria, motivated perhaps by the opportunity to build good relations with the Chinese government by helping it tackle some of the country's looming social problems.

But this is only half the story. Across the developing world, local tycoons are equally excited about CSR. "Safety on the road, safety off the road" is the slogan of an AIDS awareness campaign in Indonesia that runs advertisements featuring a car tire and a condom. The campaign, which was initially controversial in the majority Muslim country but has since won awards reflecting its positive impact, is funded by a tire company that belongs to the Nursalim business dynasty. The force behind this project is the patriarch's daughter Cherie Nursalim, who is also an eager champion of personal philanthropy. On the other side of the world, a leading Brazilian businessman, Oded Grajew, has recruited hundreds of companies, accounting for one third of his country's GDP, to embrace social responsibility through the Ethos Institute, which he founded in 1998. In India, big firms such as the group of companies owned by Sunil Bharti Mittal are giving substantial sums to improve basic education.

Perhaps this reflects the desire of emerging-market companies to keep up with businesses in the Western world. But it is also a reflection of the fact that big corporations in developing countries tend to belong to wealthy individuals or families, rather than the institutional investors and small shareholders who own publicly listed companies in the West. This means that the line between personal and company wealth is more blurred in developing countries, which makes the distinction between corporate and personal philanthropy less important for rich people in these countries. What is clear is that social problems tend to be worse and more visible in developing countries, which makes a domestic company's failure to help all the more obvious and hard to explain away to an angry public.

to continue a constructive engagement with big business and those that preferred to "name and shame."

And Wal-Mart is not the only firm that claims to be ready when disaster strikes. The logistics firm TNT, headquartered in Amsterdam, says it always has fifty people on standby to intervene in humanitarian crises anywhere in the world within forty-eight hours. This is part of a five-year-old partnership with the U.N.'s World Food Program, under which TNT staff volunteer on secondment to the WFP and are encouraged to raise money for it, and the firm helps to improve the food supply chain in places such as Liberia and Congo. In the spirit of philanthrocapitalism, TNT measures its outputs as well as inputs. In Liberia, for example, it has increased the efficiency of the supply chain bringing food to 2,100 schools by 15 to 20 percent.

It is easy to be cynical about corporate attempts to be good, or even not to be evil. Certainly, the public should ensure that politicians properly regulate companies in areas where it is unrealistic to rely on self-regulation or good behavior. Equally, the need to make a profit limits the ability of a firm to devote its resources to solving the world's biggest problems. This is especially true of public companies with a broad base of shareholders to please; privately owned firms may have more discretion, and can sometimes be a funnel for the owner's personal philanthropy. When business conditions get tough, philanthropy can often be the first casualty, and anyone working in partnership with a business should realize that the more closely the firm's philanthropy is bound into its core profit-making strategy, the more sustainable it is likely to be.

Moreover, many good causes will not fit into a firm's core business strategy. To avoid disappointment, it is crucial that philanthropists, governments, NGOs, and others who hope that business will partner with them understand the limitations, as well as the exciting possibilities, of working to achieve good in tandem with a company.

Certainly, companies claiming to do good should be scrutinized at least as carefully as anyone else who makes such claims—especially as firms often have large public relations budgets to spend on making themselves look good. Yet there are many reasons to believe that firms pursuing their enlightened self-interest can play a significant part in tackling the world's biggest problems. Potentially they have a huge role to play in philanthrocapitalism's new division of labor.

## CHAPTER 11

# Enter the Celanthropist

BILL GATES IS SITTING IN A NEW YORK bar with Bono and a few friends when there's a knock at the door into the hotel at the back. "I open the door and there is [hip-hop legend] P Diddy—Puffy—who had heard we were all hanging out and wanted to join us," recalls Bono. "Bill is not up on hip-hop, and he sees what seems to him like a gangster. And Puffy says, 'Before I sit down, could I say something?' Bill's eyes just dart at him, and Puffy says, 'You are a motherfucker.' And Bill looks alarmed, and he says again, 'You are a motherfucker. What you are doing on immunization in Botswana? Motherfucker.'"

At this point, the billionaire realizes that he is being paid a compliment and relaxes. As Bono explains, "Puffy calls Gates 'the MacDaddy.' Jay-Z, all of the hip-hop guys, kind of adore him. Because he is not seen as a romantic figure—well, maybe romantic in the sense that Neil Armstrong is romantic, a scientist but not a poet. He gets shit done." Bono, for his part, prefers to call him "Kill Bill." "In meetings he is so direct. I'm more judo; we use our opponents' own energy to defeat them. Bill is more Mike Tyson."

Partnership is one of the features of philanthrocapitalism, but there are surely no stranger bedfellows than wealthy businesspeople and popular celebrities. Bono and Gates first met early in 2002 at the World Economic Forum—which that year, in an act of post-9/11 solidarity, was held in New York. Paul Allen, cofounder of Microsoft, had been urging a meeting with Bono for a while, but Gates says he was skeptical: "Meeting with a rock star—how much of this stuff is he really going to know?"

But the two men hit it off at once, and soon Gates agreed to give $1 million to help Bono launch a new organization that would campaign for action on AIDS, trade, and development. His only condition was that the rock star must first raise two matching donations, which he did—one from George Soros, the other from a software tycoon, Ed Scott.

This organization, called DATA, became the guiding hand behind the One campaign in America and the Make Poverty History campaign in Britain and several other countries, playing a pivotal role in securing billions of dollars of developing-country debt-reduction and new aid at the G8 summit in 2005. Indeed, some say the Gates Foundation's initial investment of $1 million, by generating an impact that arguably totaled many billions of dollars, is the greatest-ever example of philanthropic leverage. It was this that *Time* magazine marked by declaring Bono and Bill and Melinda Gates its "people of the year" for 2005, rather than Tony Blair, George W. Bush, or any of the other G8 leaders who made the pledges to double aid to Africa at the Gleneagles summit.

The investment also marked the coming of age of an increasingly important force in the world of philanthropy, the celebrity philanthropist—christened by *Time* as the "celanthropist."

Celanthropists are becoming an integral part of philanthrocapitalism—mirroring the growing importance of brands and famous personalities as a source of wealth creation in capitalism. As well as often donating large amounts of their own fortunes—today's top talent can get seriously rich—and being particularly effective at raising funds from others, the best celanthropists bring a mastery of branding, mass communication skills, and high-level access that can be invaluable to any cause. As Angelina Jolie, perhaps the most famous of all celanthropists, puts it, "People take my calls."

Yet celebrity activism has brought with it a growing cynicism—at least some of it deserved. In a fierce 2005 article titled "The Rock Star's Burden," author Paul Theroux likened Bono to the Dickens character Mrs. Jellyby, but "in a ten-gallon hat." In *Bleak House*, Theroux notes, Mrs. Jellyby talks constantly "about her adopted village of Borrioboola-Gha 'on the left bank of the River Niger,'" and "tries to save the Africans by financing them in coffee growing and encouraging schemes 'to turn pianoforte legs and establish an export trade,' all the while badgering people for money." He writes, "There are probably more annoying things than being hectored about African development by a wealthy Irish rock star in a cowboy hat, but I can't think of one at the moment," before turning his guns on Jolie and her partner in love and philanthropy, Brad Pitt. He says that seeing them "cuddling African children and lecturing the world on charity, the image that immediately sprang to my mind was Tarzan and Jane."

Theroux's cynicism seemed more than justified the following year when the singer Madonna paid a philanthropic visit to the village of Mchinji in Malawi, during which she generated headlines around the world by adopting a one-year-old boy. The child turned out not to be an orphan, as first thought. His father protested, the legality of the adoption was questioned, some human rights NGOs were outraged, and there were reports of a spat between Madonna and Jolie, who has also adopted in the developing world. If any single incident captured why many people are skeptical about the growing role of at least some celanthropists, this was it.

Yet the leading celanthropists mostly go about their philanthropy in the sort of businesslike, professional way that is the essence of philanthrocapitalism. Their influence is growing so fast that, according to a 2007 paper by Lael Brainard and Derek Chollet of the Brookings Institution, one day people may "look back on our era as the 'age of celanthropy.'"

CELEBRITIES CAN GRAB the attention of the public like nobody else, giving them a powerful pulpit from which to advocate change. The rise of celanthropy today is being driven by a revival of the sort of public policy advocacy by philanthropists that first emerged in William Wilberforce's campaign against the slave trade in the eighteenth and nineteenth centuries. This was a battle at and for the heart of capitalism, between reformers backed by philanthropists and businessmen who benefited from the slave trade. Wilberforce and his allies in the Abolition Society, including several wealthy bankers, founded the Sierra Leone Company in 1792 to resettle slaves on the west coast of Africa. Although this scheme was not a success, his lobbying of the British government to ban the slave trade ultimately ended in triumph in 1807.

A committed evangelical Christian and Member of Parliament, Wilberforce worked mostly through the churches and the press to mobilize public opinion. But by the late eighteenth century, the idea of involving famous people in promoting good causes had already been born. Thomas Coram's Foundling Hospital for disadvantaged children in London was championed by Queen Caroline. William Hogarth sat on its board and donated several of his pictures to decorate the walls. This inspired other contemporary painters to make similar gifts, leading to the creation of Britain's first art gallery. This played a valuable fundraising role: the rich and powerful were invited to visit the gallery in the hope that they would commission from the artists whose work was on display and contribute to the work of the hospital. The composer George Handel donated an organ to the hospital, which he christened with a special performance of his most famous work, *Messiah*.

More recently, the 1960s marked the early days of this latest boom in celanthropy. Following the assassination of Martin Luther King Jr., film star Marlon Brando, who had already raised money for UNICEF to help with famine relief, pledged 12 percent of his earnings to the Southern Christian Leadership Conference in support of civil rights. Around the same time, Arlo Guthrie performed benefit concerts for Chilean freedom fighters, and Brigitte Bardot campaigned to protect seals. In 1971, George Harrison of the Beatles organized the pioneering awareness and fundraising Concert for Bangladesh, then in the grip of famine. This was the precursor of the Live Aid concert in 1985, which raised over $140 million for the people of Ethiopia and inspired a whole generation of celebrity activists, not least Bono.

Today, the number of celanthropists, and the seriousness with which they approach their good work, is unprecedented. Angelina Jolie has scaled up her philanthropy over time, starting in 2001, when she gave $1 million to help Afghan refugees. Later she became a Goodwill Ambassador for the U.N. High Commission for Refugees, and in 2005 she provided $500,000 to fund a new American National Center for Refugee and Immigrant Children for its first two years. She is believed to give away one third of her income, through the Jolie-Pitt Foundation, which she formed with her fellow movie star in 2006. It has donated millions of dollars to organizations such as Global Action for Children and Doctors Without Borders. Pitt has become heavily involved in rebuilding New Orleans, helping to finance green buildings in one of the areas hardest hit by Hurricane Katrina.

Jolie's experience starting out is typical of many philanthrocapitalists. "I first used to respond to needs when I saw them," she recalls. "A school or a well needed to be built, so I just wrote a check. I was in the country, I could see that it was being done—I could call the engineers, see the school or the well." However, the lack of focus and strategy started to get her down. "I got really sad, really angry, really hopeless. Everyone goes through these stages, when you don't know what to invest in, what to devote time to. So I started to focus on a specific plan." She formed her foundation and developed a strategy, initially focused on Cambodia and refugees.

Oprah Winfrey, the daytime TV goddess and chief executive of Harpo Productions, had a fortune estimated by *Forbes* at $2.5 billion in 2008; she is thought to be the richest ever African American. The magazine also ranked her as America's most powerful celebrity. In 1998, she launched Oprah's Angel Network, a charity to encourage people around the world to help the underprivileged. In 2005, *Business Week* ranked her the thirty-second-most-generous American philanthropist, reporting that she had given away $303 million. She donated $10 million to support relief work after Hurricane Katrina. In 2004, she visited South Africa and donated gifts, schoolbooks, and uniforms to fifty thousand children, and in January 2007, the Oprah Winfrey Leadership Academy for Girls opened near Johannesburg, financed with a $40 million gift from Winfrey.

Winfrey has never been content to merely write checks and throw them at the needy. She favors a hands-on approach to philanthropy; she personally interviewed many of the thousands of candidates who applied for 150 places at the Leadership Academy, for example. She is following the classic philanthrocapitalist strategy of creating leverage, covering all the administrative costs of Oprah's Angel Network so that every penny donated by others goes to good causes, and using her television magnetism to attract viewers to *The Big Give*, a reality show in which ten people are presented with huge sums of money and compete to find the "most powerful, sensational, emotional and dramatic ways to give to others."

Among the sports stars joining the philanthropic throng, Lance Armstrong, testicular cancer survivor and seven-time winner of the Tour de France, has so far contributed $55 million to cancer research—not least by raising over $10 million through sales of yellow rubber "Livestrong" bracelets. In 2007, in an attempt to leverage their collective expertise and name recognition, a dozen sports stars, including Armstrong, Andre

Agassi, and Muhammad Ali launched Athletes for Hope, an organization designed to help their sporting colleagues become philanthropists by providing a sort of clearinghouse to connect them to charities. Between them, the twelve had already given and raised around $500 million for their respective foundations.

Comic Relief was the brainchild of Richard Curtis, who went on to direct hit movies such as *Four Weddings and a Funeral*, *Notting Hill*, and *Love Actually*. Its centerpiece is "Red Nose Day," held every second year and culminating with a telethon on BBC television featuring comedy acts by top celebrities, which has raised over £300 million over the last twenty years. In 2007, Curtis was instrumental in creating a special fundraising edition of the hugely popular show *American Idol*, called *Idol Gives Back*, to support good causes in America and Africa with the assistance of celebrities ranging from Tom Cruise to Miss Piggy. The show raised $70 million and, reflecting this charitable theme, no contestant was eliminated that week. Even the show's impresario, and supposedly nastiest judge, Simon Cowell, emoted about the importance of charity. He has since pledged to give away (eventually) the bulk of his fortune, already estimated at more than $400 million.

Leverage through partnership with business was taken to a new level for *Idol Gives Back*. NewsCorp pledged to donate ten cents for every vote cast during the show, for the first fifty million calls (i.e., up to $5 million). MySpace created a special profile page for the event in order to spread the word. Regular show sponsors and special contributors also donated funds, including Coca-Cola, Ford, AT&T, Allstate, and ExxonMobil.

The pop star Shakira, whom wags have described as Colombia's "leading legal export," started her Fundación Pies Descalzos, named after her breakthrough third album, in 1997, to help refugee children. She began her philanthropy two years earlier, at age eighteen, in response to the violence in her native Colombia, but soon realized she needed to set up an organization in order to be effective. She hired María Emma Mejía, a former foreign minister of Colombia, to head the foundation. As of 2005, it looked after 2,630 children in five schools. About 40 percent of the money came from Shakira, the rest from other donors. Among other businesslike initiatives, the singer struck a partnership between Pies Descalzos (which means "bare feet") and sports-shoe maker Reebok. According to Shakira, they made a "great joint venture, because Reebok had a human rights organization. I was trying to solidify my foundation.

Reebok donated fifty thousand pairs of shoes. We had so much in common, I realized we could achieve a lot together."

She also became a Goodwill Ambassador for UNICEF, and in 2006, with writer Gabriel García Márquez and various other artists and businesspeople, she launched a new foundation to fight poverty called Latin America in Solidarity Action, whose Spanish acronym is ALAS, or "wings." This aimed to further leverage her brand and philanthropic expertise and share it with newer celanthropists such as Puerto Rican pop star Ricky Martin. One of its program provides health and nutritional aid to expectant mothers and children under two years old. Another encourages exploited and homeless children to enroll in school. In 2008, ALAS formed a partnership with a foundation created by Mexican billionaire Carlos Slim Helú, then the third-richest man in the world.

CELANTHROPISTS GIVE MORE THAN money. They also bring brand credibility, access, and insight. This is particularly true of a significant new sort of celanthropist: former world leaders who set up philanthropic foundations, not least Bill Clinton and Nelson Mandela. Although they rarely bring much of their own money to the table, they do have another hugely valuable asset: convening power—like Jolie's, their phone calls are invariably taken. This asset can be monetized, and Clinton and Mandela have raised large sums of money for the foundations that bear their names.

The William J. Clinton Foundation, the parent organization of the Clinton Global Initiative (CGI), is also focused on programs to promote education and fight HIV/AIDS, poverty, and climate change. Since it was established in 1997, it has raised hundreds of millions of dollars, largely by making the former president's brand available to help lesser-known philanthropists achieve greater impact.

In 2007, Clinton collaborated with Frank Giustra, a Canadian mining tycoon, and others to help poor miners in Latin America. Giustra is "an amazing person," says Clinton. "He started helping me on AIDS. Then said I will give you a hundred million dollars plus half of whatever else I make in future. He told his friend, who also gave a hundred million. Carlos Slim Helú was so excited that he put up a hundred million, as no one had ever done anything like this for Latin America." By summer 2007, twenty-four mining companies had expressed an interest in signing up to what was by now the Clinton Giustra Mining Initiative. "This could get very big in a hurry. If we do this right, we could have a significant sustainable development initiative. This ought to be a multibillion-dollar effort," Clinton says.

The Clinton Foundation learned a lot from the example of Jimmy Carter, the most active former president until Clinton, who, among other things, has helped find a cure for river blindness, has been involved in peace negotiations and election monitoring, and is now a member of Richard Branson's group, the Elders. (Using the phone call test, Branson, though a businessman, also qualifies as a celebrity, as does Bill Gates.) "Carter has been a model organizationally on how to set up a structure for a former president to go out and do things," says Bruce R. Lindsay, the Clinton Foundation's chief executive. Lately, Carter has been successful in starting to build an endowment for his foundation. "I hope we will soon start to do the same," says Lindsay.

After he stepped down as president of South Africa, Mandela lent his name to several foundations, which by some accounts resulted in the dilution of his brand, as people were not clear which foundation was closest to his heart. The biggest, the Nelson Mandela Foundation, was established in 1999 to build on his humanitarian legacy, particularly in HIV/AIDS and education. Mandela was also intimately involved with Branson's creation of the Elders. In 2008, British former prime minister Tony Blair continued the trend by launching a foundation to promote peace between religious faiths.

Another rapidly evolving category of celanthropist is the working royal. As royals have moved on from ruling towards having to justify their continuing place at the top of society, a growing number are figuring out how to use their public brand and connections to achieve significant impact for the philanthropic causes they support. The leading pioneers in this branch of philanthrocapitalism have been two British royals, with two sharply contrasting approaches to celanthropy (and, some might say, pretty much everything else). The late Princess Diana became highly skilled at using her global brand to generate publicity for a cause, and her former husband, Prince Charles, has proved a surprisingly effective social entrepreneur.

The Prince's Trust was set up by Prince Charles in 1976 to help disadvantaged young people overcome barriers in their lives. It has raised many millions of pounds and claims to have helped over half a million people and led to sixty-six thousand businesses being started. The prince has also played a key role through his influential International Business Leaders Forum in encouraging companies to become more involved in solving society's problems, first in the 1980s in Britain and now globally. He has also created a profitable business selling organic food and has been an outspoken campaigner on green and architectural issues.

Princess Diana raised the profile of many charities during her life, including those focused on HIV/AIDS and on land mines. Prime Minister Tony Blair was reportedly considering appointing her as a special ambassador when she was killed in a car crash in Paris in 1997. She lives on through the Diana, Princess of Wales Memorial Fund, which was established shortly after her death, with £19 million from her will and sales of the Elton John tribute song "Candle in the Wind." Fundraising brought in a further £80 million. After a tricky start, in which it blew at least £3.4 million in a lawsuit with the Franklin Mint over the use of Diana's image, the fund accelerated its giving to victims of land mines, the terminally ill (especially those with AIDS) in Africa, and disadvantaged children in Britain. Though the Diana brand remains as strong as ever, this embarrassing incident led to the decision to spend her foundation out of existence as fast as possible.

Meanwhile, Diana's philanthropic tiara has been inherited by Queen Rania of Jordan, who shares Diana's beauty and empathetic nature, particularly when dealing with the marginalized and disadvantaged. Among other things, she actively supports microfinance, the protection of children from violence, the promotion of early-childhood development, and getting technology into schools.

The presence of royalty, including Queen Rania, and a growing number of other celebrities at the World Economic Forum's annual gathering in Davos is perhaps the strongest proof that celanthropy should be taken seriously. Yet the WEF has not found the inclusion of celebrities to be particularly easy—perhaps because it is still trying to figure out which celanthropists are up to snuff. Royals are seldom a problem. Bono, too, is always welcome in the Swiss Alps, as is Richard Gere, a supporter of the Dalai Lama. On the other hand, although she reportedly raised $1 million in five minutes, the actress Sharon Stone seems to have breached Davos etiquette in 2005 when she stood up at a discussion on Africa, pledged $10,000 to buy antimalarial bed nets, and implored others to do likewise.

Jolie is well regarded by Davosians, and was an impressive participant in both 2005 and 2006. However, problems arose in the second year, when she turned up with Pitt as the two-headed superstar Brangelina. The couple was not at fault, but in their presence, everyone from chief executives to WEF staff started to behave like love-struck teenagers, mobbing them and disrupting proceedings. It seems that the couple was reluctantly not invited back in 2007, though they wanted to come.

"UNBOUND BY POLITICAL constraints," celebrities can "bring new perspectives which expand the range of ideas represented in our national dialogue," argues Darrell West, a political scientist at Brown University, in the 2007 article "Angelina, Mia and Bono: Celebrities and International Development." (Actress Mia Farrow has become a spokesperson for activists campaigning against the genocide in Darfur.) Several changes in society have increasingly produced cultures that "glorify fame and fortune," West writes, including highly competitive news and marketing industries, which recognize that few sources provide better copy than actors, athletes, and entertainers, and a lack of trust in conventional politicians and experts.

The decline of trust in other institutions has created a corresponding surge in demand for celebrity activists from politicians, businesses, and others who hope to gain trust by association, argues West, by forming partnerships with "people who have greater public credibility." The growing cost of advocacy fuels this, as celebrities can raise lots of money as well as offer a cheap means of attracting publicity.

There can be no doubting the massive exposure that a cause can gain by having a spokesperson such as Bono, Jolie, or Jay-Z (who has teamed up with MTV and the United Nations to raise awareness about water shortages around the world).

In their Brookings paper, Brainard and Chollett note that some "worry about the proliferation of actors and the oversimplification of messages such as Make Poverty History." They point to some evidence that "advocacy networks have proven far more effective in instances of humanitarian crisis . . . where the face of human suffering is a powerful motivator for grassroots engagement, than on trade liberalization or dismantling agricultural subsidies, where domestic opposition is strong and the connection to poverty not as clear." In short, they write, advocacy, including that done by celanthropists, "lends itself to sim⁻ˡ sometimes simplistic messaging but is far less amenable to telling a complicated story." (Likewise, in his acclaimed book *The Bottom Billion*, Paul Collier says that the "development buzz" generated by celebrities is "at times a headless heart.")

There may also be a question of attention span, they suggest. "Can a campaign achieve success where there is no Hollywood storyline—no heroes and villains and conclusive triumphs, only the slow struggle of well-meaning people to overcome the vagaries of nature and set the stage for future generations to lead modestly better lives?"

Yet Patty Stonesifer, the longtime chief executive of the Gates Foundation, became a believer after initial skepticism about the value of celebrities. That, after all, is why the foundation seeded DATA. "One of our most important partners is Bono. If you had told me that ten years ago, I would probably have said no."

One reason for this growing enthusiasm has been the realization that to achieve its goals, the Gates Foundation could not rely on technological solutions but needed to influence public opinion and thereby shape the right policy context. "I did not realize how much advocacy we would have to do," says Stonesifer.

Bono had a tough time when he first tried to convince Gates of the need for advocacy. "Bill wasn't really about advocacy. We had to tell the most successful businessman on earth that there was more value in getting governments to prioritize these interventions than doing it himself," Bono recalls. "It can be very hard to convince someone with such deep pockets that he can't do everything himself."


ONE SIGN OF the seriousness of some celanthropists is the growing institutionalization of their philanthropy, including the establishment of foundations and hiring of professional philanthropic advisers. But by far the most businesslike example of celanthropic organization building is the formation of DATA. Its roots extend back to the Band Aid record of 1984 and Live Aid concert of 1985, organized by Irish rock musician Bob Geldof and featuring Bono. As well as raising lots of money, these had generated massive publicity about the problems of developing countries and turned a generation into activists. A newly elected backbench MP called Tony Blair founded the Band Aid cross-party Parliamentary committee.

Eventually, encouraged by British activist Jamie Drumond, Bono and Geldof became involved in another campaign, Jubilee 2000, built on the fact that the interest owed by Ethiopia each year on its debt dwarfed the money raised by Live Aid—and that many other poor countries were in a similar position. To help Ethiopia and other highly indebted countries, the campaigners believed that they had to move beyond an approach based on charity—epitomized by Geldof's Live Aid appeal to TV viewers to "give us the money now"—to focus instead on achieving structural change.

Jubilee 2000 is widely regarded as a success, not least for getting international agreement to a G8 program of debt forgiveness known as the Heavily Indebted Poor Countries (HIPC) initiative. Indeed, Jubilee 2000 has been described by Nancy Birdsall and John Williamson of the Center for Global Development as "by far the most successful industrial-country movement aimed at combating world poverty for many years, perhaps in all recorded history."

Energized by this success, and facing the fresh challenge of needing to win the backing of new American president George Bush, Bono, Drumond, his colleague Lucy Matthew, and their close friend Bobby Shriver—a member of the Kennedy political dynasty in America— decided to create a properly funded organization to take their campaigning to the next level. Geldof later joined them in a "half in, half out" role.

Bono had long been a friend of President Clinton and had found it easy to pitch to him directly about the need for debt cancellation. But, the rock star recalls, when Bush took office, "it was clear he didn't want to meet me. Why would he? We saw the need to formalize our organization, because he is very formal. We needed to make sure our backroom operation was world-class—in fact better than USAID, DFID [Department for International Development]. We needed to professionalize our research, our lobbyists, hire the best and the brightest."

They named the organization DATA—which stands for both Debt, Aid, Trade, Africa and for Democracy, Accountability, Transparency, Africa—and set about raising money to put its activities on a sound footing. (Geldof came up with the name after a meeting with Nelson Mandela who had urged him to build on the debt campaign with work on trade, AIDS, and governance.) McKinsey, the blue-chip management consultancy, worked closely with DATA from the start, helping to develop its strategy.

According to Shriver, DATA was a "classic start-up," not least because the founders had a hard time raising any money at first and initially had to rely on gifts from Shriver's mother, an office borrowed from Universal Music, and the charity Oxfam, which contributed money toward Drumond's salary. Many letters were sent, and meetings held, but to no avail. Then Bono met Gates and got his $1 million plus two matching donations. Another boost came in 2005, when leading Silicon Valley venture capitalist and philanthropist John Doerr saw Bono give a speech, via a hologram, at the annual Technology, Entertainment, Design conference in Monterey, California. He was introduced to Bono by Roger McNamee, the rock star's business partner in Elevation Partners, a private-equity firm. Doerr offered to make a $10 million donation over five years—$2 million a year—provided DATA could leverage his gift with other similar pledges. This it did, thereby ensuring it had adequate funding until 2010, and so could concentrate fully on campaigning rather than shaking a tin can.

Asked why he did not simply fund DATA himself, Bono says that as a philanthropist he is "not in that league." He also regarded his ability to raise the funds from others as a test of whether it was a good idea—a classically philanthrocapitalistic way of thinking. "There is a sort of discipline you learn as an artist. If it is any good, it will get money. It's like, you don't finance your own movie, or it will be a vanity project."

Once funded, DATA set about raising public awareness in G8 countries about the case for a big package of debt cancellation, additional aid, and trade reform at the G8 meeting coming up in 2005. In the United States, it fathered the One campaign. In the U.K. and Ireland, it played an important role in the equivalent Make Poverty History campaign—though there is some controversy about the respective contributions to that campaign made by DATA and leading charities such as Oxfam. Strikingly, in Britain, in contrast to America, after that G8 meeting, Make Poverty History was soon itself history, though DATA is more active than ever, with a staff of nearly one hundred people in London and Washington, D.C. By 2008, the One campaign was reckoned to be the second-biggest pressure group in America (behind the National Rifle Association), with 2.5 million supporters in its database.

In America, DATA's influence has been enormous. Through a complex network of introductions, Bono became involved in devising the Millennium Challenge Corporation, President Bush's vehicle for supporting developing countries that demonstrate through their actions a commitment to good government. "We worked with the Bush administration on Millennium Challenge—we were in Condi's office at the time it came out," he recalls. "The administration had a mood of wanting to help, but that they were not in the mood for building presidential palaces. They wanted to know if they could find a way to fast-track those countries that were getting to grips with their problems." DATA also played a key role in securing funds from the Bush administration for tackling HIV/AIDS under PEPFAR, among other achievements.

By 2007, Bono was working so closely with the Bush administration, especially Secretary of State Condoleezza Rice, that some Democrats privately started to lose their enthusiasm for working with him—though, crucially, never Bill Clinton.

In 2006, Bono (with Shriver) launched a different sort of initiative, combining his activism with a new form of corporate philanthrocapitalism. In collaboration with several leading companies, such as American Express, Nike, Gap, Motorola, and Apple, he launched a brand, Product (RED). This for-profit venture channels a proportion of revenues from sales of (RED)-branded credit cards, mobile phones, T-shirts, computers and so on to the Global Fund to Fight AIDS, Tuberculosis and Malaria. In its first year or so, (RED) benefited the Global Fund to the tune of $45 million, says Bono.

The idea came out of conversations that Bono had with the former U.S. treasury secretary Robert Rubin, who "suggested that to solve a lot of these problems I was talking about people needed to understand we had achievable goals, not misty-eyed bleeding-heart stuff. He really struck a chord with me. I realized we needed to market these ideas in the way a sports shoe company or, dare I say it, a cigarette company does," recalls Bono. He began to think about "how to get the same kind of marketing budgets as those companies, and how we could get into using the marketing of the corporate world, these creative minds and their money." The idea was to create a brand that could "piggyback on the corporate world" by actually generating new customers for its business partners, a classic win-win. With an upside from the brand, companies would start backing it with their marketing budgets, not their far-smaller philanthropic funds.

Bono believed that the use of brand (RED) would deepen customer loyalty to its partner companies. "(RED) can't make a crap company into a bright light. But if you take two equal firms, (RED) can help one shine brighter," he says. "The brand concept is very simple: if you buy a (RED) product, you are buying antiretroviral drugs for people who can't afford it." But he also wanted the brand to have "a certain sex appeal, smartness, that doesn't talk down or attempt to guilt-trip people. Somewhere between desire and virtue is our place. People can buy nice things but at the same time have an impact on the biggest health crisis in six hundred years."

The goal was to tap into what Bono calls "conscious consumerism." Increasingly, customers realize they have a lot of power when they are spending, and they have an appetite to know as much as possible about the companies they buy from. But it was also to spread the word about the problems of the developing world, and increase the pressure on governments to solve them. "That ultimately is why we are doing (RED)," says Bono, "to create more heat on politicians in America."

In March 2007, *Ad Age*, an advertising industry trade paper, claimed that up to $100 million had been spent on building the (RED) brand but it had, at that point, raised only $18 million for the Global Fund. This was furiously denied by (RED), which pointed out that $25 million had been raised and that the brand's alleged spending was not only exaggerated but also included mostly money that the partner companies would have used for other marketing if not for (RED). "The *Ad Age* criticism was not well thought-out," says Bono. "The claim that we had used fifty million dollars in ad budgets misses the point, as the money was going to be spent anyway, and it was our goal to change what it was spent on. Then they calculated the value of my TV appearances on *Oprah*, CNN, and so on, and added that as a cost. Wow. That is like throwing stones at a fire engine when it is going to put out a fire. Bilious."

In the long run, the proof will be in the pudding. If (RED) generates additional profits for the companies involved, then they will continue on with it. If not, sooner or later they will stop. Worryingly for Bono, American Express proved reluctant to extend its use of the (RED) brand outside the U.K., where it was launched in early 2006. Apparently, it was so popular that it started to cannibalize existing customers, who switched from their old AmEx card to a (RED) one, thereby reducing the company's take. (It had to pay 1 percent to the Global Fund of all the money spent by the customer using the card.) On the other hand, insists Bono, "Everyone else is flying. Steve Jobs is really thrilled. Gap has had its bestselling new line in twenty years."

Wish him well. The *New York Times* has christened these various organizations the "Bono activism conglomerate." Could there be a more businesslike approach to philanthropy?

ON THE SUPPLY side, activism often provides an economic benefit to celebrities, points out political scientist West, allowing them to "stay in the news even when they have no new movie or CD to promote." Yet the fact that celebrities have their own agendas, ranging from managing their own brand to their own impulses, can make them a high-risk partner in philanthropy.

As celanthropists increase their role, however, they are likely to be subject to the same scrutiny and pressures for accountability and transparency as any other philanthrocapitalist. There have already been some unfortunate examples. Basketball legend Michael Jordan, arguably the wealthiest American former sportsman, not least through his close business relationship with Nike, established the Michael Jordan Foundation in 1989. Among other things, this supported the Special Olympics and Ronald McDonald's Children's Charities. However, he abandoned the foundation in 1996, following public criticism for maladministration.

Another danger is that people buying into a celanthropist's brand may seek some sort of quid pro quo, with the potential to damage the brand or at least impose an unacceptable burden. This was a risk that DATA sought to minimize during its fundraising. Many would-be donors with whom DATA met gave the impression that they believed their gift meant "Bono might do something for them," says Shriver.

Another danger is that ill-informed celebrities will use their influence to lead public opinion (and charitable donations) towards superficial or ill-conceived solutions to complex problems like poverty and war. Some critics of celanthropy fear that public debate will become dominated by superficial appeals from celebs, excluding traditional politicians and civic leaders and further "dumbing down" public debate. If politics "becomes mere entertainment, the danger is that society loses its ability to solve pressing social problems" warns West.

Even if the public were as dumb as these doomsayers would have us believe, one encouraging sign is that some celanthropists, at least, have been willing to admit to a gap in knowledge and to work hard at acquiring expertise. They are not all content to continually do their philanthropy, well, like a virgin. Bono can hold his own with any expert on aid or development. Perhaps more surprisingly, so too can Jolie, at least on her chosen issues.

"I was very fortunate—raised in L.A. and New York, I didn't know quite a lot," confesses Jolie. "In my work, by chance I visited many countries, saw a whole world I knew nothing about, and should have known about." This seems to have created both a desire to do something and a realization that she had much to learn, having long believed, she says, that "you need to earn the right to speak." People "shouldn't listen to someone, agree with them, because you like them in another field. I'm an actress, so I am certainly not an authority on many things." So when she approached the U.N. High Commission for Refugees (UNHCR) about becoming a Goodwill Ambassador she decided—not least in order to reassure the U.N.—not to tell the press until she felt she knew what she was talking about. "I spent a year before joining UNHCR just trying to learn, opening my eyes. I became a genuine supporter of the staff on the ground. I got angry about how little people know about refugees."

Since then, she has focused more energy on advocacy in Washington. In 2003, she started working with refugee centers, and found that children had no legal status if they were trafficked into America and that they would struggle to get a lawyer to represent them. "It seemed inhumane, so I started a center for pro bono lawyers for kids." She is now regarded as something as an expert on refugees when she lobbies the politicians in Washington, having, she says, "been in the field with refugees more than some of the senators I have spoken to."


JOLIE HAS ALSO worked closely with Jeffrey Sachs, whom she met, inevitably, in Davos. The charismatic Sachs may be the closest the world has seen to a celebrity economist (though the bisexual John Maynard Keynes, with his Russian ballerina wife, might rival him for the title). As well as making a documentary with Jolie, and having Bono write the introduction to his bestselling antipoverty book, *The End of Poverty*, Sachs has persuaded Madonna and several other celanthropists to finance his Millennium Village project.

Indeed, Madonna's notorious orphan-adopting visit to Malawi in 2006 was intended to inform her about Millennium Villages. Sachs's goal in launching the project is to show how bottom-up policies focused at the village level can achieve the U.N.'s Millennium Development Goals—a strategy not obviously advanced by Madonna's policy of one child not left behind. But the furor over the adoption was not the only controversy arising from her involvement. Her cofounder in Raising Malawi, her nonprofit organization, is Michael Berg, the head of the Kabbalah center in Los Angeles and one of the driving forces behind the practice's growing popularity. She had reportedly planned to build a care center in a village in Malawi—a day camp for orphans whose relatives take them in but struggle to feed them—where she had hoped to offer courses based on Spirituality for Kids, Kabbalah's children's program. According to some reports, UNICEF turned down the chance to partner with Raising Malawi because of its links with Kabbalah.

Sachs was not bothered, however. "In the very noisy and complicated world that we have, people that reach large numbers of people, like Madonna does, have an extraordinarily important role to play," he told *Time*. "When they're devoting their time, their money, their name, a lot of effort, a lot of organization skill to all of this, it makes a huge difference. The cynics are just wrong. They don't get it." Madonna has promised to raise at least $3 million to fund programs that would mostly help orphans in Malawi. She is reportedly supporting Millennium Villages to the tune of at least $1.5 million.

Perhaps Millennium Villages will prove to be the unfortunate modern equivalent of Mrs. Jellyby's adopted village of Borrioboola-Gha. The conventional wisdom is that anyone can make one developing-country village work by bringing in enough experts and throwing enough money at the problem, but that creating a few model villages does not scale up to a solution to the problems of many villages, let alone a country. Indian social entrepreneur Bunker Roy may be right when he claims that "for the cost of one U.N. Millennium Village, 100,000 families living below the starvation line could receive two square meals a day in 50 villages. When that sort of money is available, it is foolish and absurd to spend it on one village."

And yet, Sachs has put his reputation, and his donors' money, on the line. He knows he will only be judged a success if he can demonstrate that his answers can work on a large scale. Indeed, in 2007 he started to raise funds to create Millennium Districts that he hoped would show that the Millennium development goals could be achieved through bottom-up policies in an area of five hundred thousand people, not merely a village of fifty thousand.

Likewise, Winfrey has been criticized for the allegedly elitist nature of her Oprah Winfrey Leadership Academy. Writing in the online magazine Black Agenda Report, Reverend Irene Monroe asks, "Why would she spend $40 million on one school when she could have spent $1 million on 40 schools—if her objective is to improve and democratize education for girls throughout South Africa?" Yet Winfrey has been clear about the strategy behind the school, which is based on leverage. The aim, she says, is to develop leaders, with the ability to guide Africa in a better direction. "When you educate a girl, you begin to change the face of a nation," she explained when she opened the school. The conventional wisdom may doubt it, yet Winfrey may be right, and her philanthropy means we will get to find out. And, as has been noted earlier, one of the potential strengths of philanthropists is their ability to pursue strategies that run counter to the prevailing wisdom.

As for Bono's views on poverty and development, Theroux is scoring cheap points by bringing celebrity into it. Clearly, there is a lively debate going on among experts about the proper role of aid, debt relief, and trade. Theroux happens to be in the opposite camp to Bono. Either way, Bono's celebrity status surely has nothing to do with it. As Theroux himself notes, Bono's views are shared by Bill Gates, who is certainly no empty-headed celebrity.

As with the rest of philanthrocapitalism, the impact and effectiveness of celanthropy will often be a subject for debate, especially when it comes to the bigger, bolder initiatives. For instance, did that initial $1 million investment by the Gates Foundation in DATA really deliver all those billions of dollars in aid and debt relief promised at the G8? Leverage is a somewhat fuzzy concept, particularly when it comes to clearly demonstrating causality and attributing credit. There were many steps and many partners between the original $1 million of seed capital and the G8 agreement. Perhaps those billions would have been promised anyway, even if DATA had not existed?

And despite those promises, have the dollars actually been secured in reality? As Bono commented, in textbook philanthrocapitalistic lingo, after the 2007 G8 failed to follow through to his satisfaction on the 2005 commitments, "Do they think we can't read or count? We are looking for accountable language and accountable numbers. We didn't get them today." Yet he also points out that "in the seventeen nonoil countries in Africa that got debt cancellation, there has since been average growth of 5.5 percent a year. Amazing. The OECD [Organisation for Economic Co-operation and Development] says 1 percent of that is directly attributable to debt cancellation. But it says there are also twenty million additional children going to school."

Shriver, for one, believes it was the indisputable evidence of Bono's ability to deliver results that enabled DATA to raise funds from its philanthrocapitalistic backers. Bono had been clearly responsible for raising $435 million from the U.S. Congress for the HIPC program during the Clinton administration. "The thing we used to sell DATA to American philanthropists was this American success," says Shriver, insisting that there is "zero doubt it was our success," and our investors saw a result that was measurable and specific: "The thing that got us financed was the four hundred and thirty-five million dollars success, not the celebrity." If that was indeed so, how encouraging. For celanthropists, as for all philanthrocapitalists, it should be the results that count in the end.

## CHAPTER 12

# Virtue's Middlemen

"I LOVE YOU, AND I'LL BE GLAD TO give you dinner at my home anytime you want to eat, but you can't come to my meeting," says Bill Clinton, recalling how he told a friend who had been "a big supporter of mine when I was president" that he was not welcome at the Clinton Global Initiative (CGI). His friend's crime? Failing to honor a pledge he had made, with appropriate fanfare, at the previous year's CGI meeting.

Clinton is no big hitter in terms of giving money away, for obvious reasons. "I entered the White House with the lowest net worth of any president in the twentieth century," he says, "and I left it ten million or twelve million dollars in debt." Speaking and consulting fees have since taken him back into the black, but not yet by enough to make him a significant philanthropist in his own right. Instead, he has become a force in the business of giving by leveraging his personal brand. He has raised millions for his William J. Clinton Foundation by working with other philanthropists who can see ways to get more bang for their buck by teaming up with the former president. But his masterstroke has been to raise billions of dollars by creating the CGI through his foundation.

The CGI has turned Clinton into arguably the leading dealmaker in global philanthropy by institutionalizing his ability to convene and his ability to affirm—or in the case of that friend, to not affirm. Each September since 2005, at his invitation, more than a thousand business leaders and other movers and shakers have gathered in a hotel in midtown Manhattan to pledge to do good in exchange for Clinton's approval.

The manner in which this approval is delivered is pure showbiz. Clinton enters the crowded hotel ballroom to rousing music and presides over the event like an older, more earnest version of Oscars host Jon Stewart. He begins the closing session by listing the grand total of pledges—in 2006, "three days, two hundred and fifteen commitments, 7.3 billion dollars." Big screens show pictures of the powerful audience clapping. There are Hillary and Chelsea, the Google guys, Barbra Streisand. Then several rapporteurs stand and tell Clinton about the themes of the discussions and name-check the most important donors, who are called forward.

The environment report-back, for example, starts with the naming and acclaiming of Richard Branson, who at the 2006 CGI meeting had made his pledge to invest ten years of his profits in technologies to combat climate change. Next up is a new pledge by Wal-Mart to introduce environmentally friendly packaging. The retailer's boss, Lee Scott, is called onstage by Clinton to sign a huge pledge certificate, which is held up by the two men for a photo. Another commitment is to fund a CGI effort to persuade the world's forty leading cities to go "carbon neutral." This is a great achievement, says Clinton, because "I have actually managed to get Barbra Streisand and Rupert Murdoch to agree on something." Streisand donated the first $1 million; Murdoch, the next $500,000. Clinton hugs his old showbiz friend, and as she is signing the pledge certificate, he confides that Streisand has just said that Murdoch is much richer than her so he should be giving more—"some politics at last," Clinton jokes. And so on, as the coffers fill.

For Clinton, who says he has endured enough hot air at conferences to last him several lifetimes, the goal of the CGI is to deliver action. From the start, the aim has been to "give people of means and people who need funding a chance to come together in a forum where, instead of just talking about things, we would figure out what ought to be done, and everybody who came would have to make a commitment to do something."

In terms of pledges, its success rate has been astonishing. By 2007, some six hundred pledges had been made, involving more than a thousand organizations in over one hundred countries, with the potential to improve over one hundred million lives, according to Clinton.

The challenge is to ensure that these pledges are meaningful. It is easy enough to make headlines by promising millions or billions; but pledging is not the same thing as actually putting up the money, let alone guaranteeing it is used to good effect. The CGI attracts its share of chancers and self-publicists, so its credibility depends on ensuring that those who make pledges are held to account if they do not deliver. The amount of time spent by CGI staff working with potential donors to devise and monitor pledges has increased sharply since 2005. Despite the fact that monitoring still relies too much on self-reporting, the CGI says that at least fourteen invitations to the meeting have been withdrawn over the years because of a failure to honor a pledge.

The task of monitoring and enforcement is made harder, yet more important, by the central role played by CGI's founder. What gives the CGI its power is Clinton; yet the personality, connections, and reputation of the former president in some ways pose a big risk to CGI's credibility. Many of those attending the annual event are "friends of Bill" (FOB), either from political days or, more recently, from business, leading critics to question whether he will be tough enough on those who do not honor their pledges—hence Clinton's story about that conversation with his errant friend. Each year, the costs of the CGI gathering have been underwritten by business services tycoon Tom Golisano, so at least one of the several billionaire businessmen FOB's is honoring his pledge.

Some critics have suggested that the line between Clinton's involvement in philanthropic and business activities is sometimes too blurry. For example, the *New York Times* has reported that, in September 2005, days before the first CGI gathering, Clinton visited Kazakhstan with mining tycoon Frank Giustra, where they enjoyed a "sumptuous midnight banquet" with the country's dictatorial president, Nursultan Nazarbayev. Two days later, Giustra announced a lucrative deal to invest in three uranium projects run by Kazakhstan's state-owned uranium agency. Giustra has since become a regular participant at the CGI and one of the biggest donors to the Clinton Foundation.

Clinton sings from the hymn sheet of philanthrocapitalism, enthusiastically espousing a businesslike approach to giving money. He calls the new generation of business-minded philanthropists "bleeding-heart cheapskates," saying that they are "not naive, they don't want to waste a lot of money, they like low administrative overhead, they measure pretty ruthlessly for return." It is this mind-set, he says, that has led him to include companies in the CGI, even to the extent that he has affirmed pledges by corporate bosses, such as Wal-Mart's Scott, that stand to make the firm bigger profits. This, too, has attracted considerable criticism. Skeptics dismiss the CGI as a beauty pageant for lipstick-wearing pigs. After all, to a chief executive under fire, such as Scott, a photo with the charismatic Clinton at CGI has obvious PR attractions that may have nothing to do with saving the planet. Even Clinton's former secretary of labor, Robert B. Reich, attacked the CGI in his 2007 book, *Supercapitalism*.

Clinton insists that he sets the bar particularly high when it comes to championing a for-profit pledge at the CGI. He says he will only acknowledge such a pledge if it will have "a significant impact on the public good. Let's just take Wal-Mart for example. If Wal-Mart really does sell one hundred million compact fluorescent bulbs and people buy them, and screw them in, and use them, it will have the $CO_2$ impact of taking seven hundred thousand cars off the road. That is a significant public good." The CGI says it has been particularly tough in monitoring companies that make pledges, not least Wal-Mart, which according to John Needham, a former chief executive of CGI, has "followed through on its commitment in a very measurable way."

But its relationship with business has not been the only source of controversy for the CGI. From its launch, perceptions of the CGI were colored by the possibility of Hillary Clinton becoming president, returning her husband to the center of world politics. In 2007, the potential First Spouse insisted that he would continue his philanthropic work even if his wife were in the White House, though he conceded that some things would have to change. In particular, his foundation would have to be more transparent. Some critics argued that his continuing political role gave the CGI much of its power and it remains to be seen whether the CGI's role will change, now that Hillary's presidential ambitions have been thwarted, at least this time round.

Some who attend the CGI meeting think that the World Economic Forum in Davos is a more neutral and serious venue for bringing together philanthropists, business leaders, politicians, and social entrepreneurs to address society's big challenges—though the WEF does not attempt to generate the sort of specific action pledges that the CGI does. For his part, Clinton insists that Davos and the CGI are complementary, not alternatives, and that his goal is to expand the role of the CGI. In September 2007, he launched the CGI University to spread the philanthropic message to students. He is also taking it global through a CGI

Asia in Hong Kong, financed in part by billionaire Ukrainian philanthropist Victor Pinchuk.

"THE CGI IS a marketplace, a sort of eBay for giving," says Needham, the initiative's former chief executive. Clinton himself is the market maker in chief, who gets deals done in the CGI marketplace. The former president has created a new role for himself as a sort of today's philanthropic intermediary, trying to increase the efficiency of giving. In this, he is not alone: indeed, one of the more significant aspects of today's philanthrocapitalism is the emergence of a wide variety of intermediaries and professional advisers whose goal is to raise the performance of today's philanthropy by improving how those with the resources interact with those who need them. These intermediaries and advisers may turn out to deserve much of the credit for this latest golden age of philanthropy—if philanthropy does indeed mirror the world of business.

One of the most striking features of capitalism in the past couple of decades has been the growing importance of professional advisers, intermediaries, and other service providers, and of a market-based system that seems designed to let them thrive. Some of today's most admired global companies are Goldman Sachs, an investment bank; Fidelity Investments, a fund management firm; and McKinsey, a management consultancy. In essence, what each of them does is apply professional expertise and focus to helping those with money and those with ideas work together more effectively. This includes applying cutting-edge business practices and management theories, rigorously analyzing performance data, and making better use of the increasingly large global capital markets in shares, bonds, and derivatives.

Critics of capitalism often regard intermediaries, advisers, and markets as parasites—unproductive Mr. Ten Percents who live off the work and talents of others. The inevitable mistakes made by a Goldman (selling securities that perform badly, say) or a McKinsey (providing consultancy to a firm that later goes bust) are cited as evidence of their pernicious influence. Certainly, markets seem prone to bubbles and meltdowns, fund managers sometimes lose money, investment banks have done some disastrous deals, and consultants have given bad advice. Overall, however, these downsides are far exceeded by the benefits of professional interme-

diation and support; if not, demand for it would not continue to grow. Indeed, it is not too great a stretch to argue that the emergence of specialist
providers of investment banking, money management, and consulting
has been one of the main drivers of greater efficiency and wealth creation
in the business world during the past few decades.

The transparency of financial markets, and the way in which they
allow firms and investors to manage risk with far greater precision,
has created an intense pressure to perform and a demand for specialist
expertise, on everything from deal making to corporate strategy, which
would have been unimaginable a generation ago.

Whilst some people are skeptical about the invasion of MBA-enabled
executives in suits into the Birkenstock world of charity, many philanthrocapitalists believe that the world of giving could benefit at least as
much as business has done from a bigger role for professional intermediaries and advisers, and from the sort of transparency and accountability that exists in financial markets.

Like philanthropy itself, there is nothing new about the idea of professionals advising and intermediating giving. When Lady Spencer,
Margaret Georgiana, one of Britain's major donors in the eighteenth
century, was inundated with letters begging for funds she hired investi-
gators to test the truth of claims made by her correspondents. In the
1770s, this process was formalized within the Ladies' Charitable Society.
In the mid-nineteenth century, Charles Dickens worked as an adviser to
one of the major philanthropists of his day, also picking up a lot of material for his novels. In 1881, Sir Henry Burdett, the son of a clergyman,
published *Burdett's Official Intelligence*, the definitive guide to British
and American securities, followed in 1893 by the equally definitive, but
probably less read, *Hospitals and Asylums of the World*. By building a reputation for thorough research, and through some well-targeted flattery,
Burdett was adopted by the Prince of Wales, the future Edward VII, as
his philanthropic adviser. Under his influence, the prince lent his support to a range of charities, mainly linked to hospitals, and set up what is
now known as the King's Fund, probably the most respected independent voice on health care issues in the U.K.

Later, in America, J. D. Rockefeller had the Reverend Frederick T. Gates
to advise him, and many a tycoon since has turned to his priest, private
banker, or tax adviser for guidance on giving. The emergence of foundations with paid staff was part of the same process of professionalization,

though not of independent specialization. In the past few decades, private banks in particular have become increasingly adept at providing philanthropic advisory services, and even offering special courses to educate the children of the wealthy in how to become effective philanthropists. However, these services have often been limited in their effectiveness by the goals of the provider, which are more focused on keeping the client happy and most of his money in the bank than on maximizing the effectiveness of his philanthropy. This is why the emergence of innovative new specialist intermediaries and advisers, whilst still in its early days, is such a potentially exciting feature of philanthrocapitalism.

Goldman Sachs, McKinsey, and Fidelity and their peers are themselves becoming more involved in philanthropy. Beyond them, there is a flowering of new organizations, the equivalents of investment banks, money managers, consultancies, and so forth, that aspire to transform the efficiency and effectiveness of philanthropy. Many of these have been started by people who made their money as a professional intermediary or adviser, including several alumni of Goldman Sachs.

"IN FINANCIAL MARKETS in the late 1990s there was an enormous industry dedicated to putting capital to use where it gets the highest returns. So why couldn't the same be true of philanthropy?" Gavyn Davies says, recalling a question that came up in a conversation with his colleague Peter Wheeler in the cafeteria of Goldman Sachs's London headquarters. The two men were trying to work out how best to give away some of the millions they had earned as partners in the world's leading investment bank. They soon found themselves focusing on one of the biggest challenges facing philanthrocapitalism.

In investment banking, it is taken for granted that decisions about how to use capital are based on rigorous research into the performance of firms, industries, economies, and markets. So it was only natural that Davies, a highly respected British economist who is close to Prime Minister Gordon Brown, and Wheeler would look for someone to advise them how to invest their philanthropic capital. "We found there wasn't enough information produced in a hardheaded, independent, high-quality way," says Davies. So they decided to fill the void. Inspired by the idea of creating an organization that could guide donors on where to get the best returns on their gifts, in 2002 they launched the nonprofit New

Philanthropy Capital (NPC) to do investment-banking-style research and analysis for the world of philanthropy.

Involvement in philanthropy is par for the course at Goldman Sachs, which has long been the most philanthropically minded of the financial powerhouses at the heart of capitalism (see "The Goldman Standard of Giving" box on pages 223–24). Funding a new entity that would provide valuable information to many other philanthropists had an additional attraction to Davies and Wheeler: leverage. "We wanted our own charitable donations to be the foundation of a much bigger edifice. This was an investment designed to have a levered effect on other people's giving," says Davies. "We wanted to increase giving by enabling donors to be more confident that they were having an impact on people's lives." But this is not easy. "When you come into this world from Goldman, you realize how screwed up it is," says Martin Brookes, who joined NPC from Goldman to head its research effort and in 2008 became its chief executive. "We are trying to fix the plumbing."

By 2007 NPC had built up a staff of around fifty professionals and was producing a steady stream of research reports on, say, charities catering to the elderly, or organizations addressing at-risk youth. These reports had many similarities to Goldman's reports on, say, the steel or advertising industry, including recommending specific organizations to "invest" in.

The challenge for NPC has been exactly how to analyze charitable sectors and which to focus on. The lack of good data in the philanthropic world is a huge problem. Some organizations that do gather data, such as America's Center for Effective Philanthropy, are reluctant to publish their findings; CEP, for instance, wants to remain on good terms with the foundations that pay for it to produce its Grantee Perception Reports. Most data typically comes from tax returns and voluntary annual reports by foundations, though even this data is published far more slowly than comparable data in the business world.

At least what data there is can now be viewed relatively easily using the GuideStar Web site, a sort of "Bloomberg screen" for philanthropy. Launched in America in 1994 by entrepreneur Buzz Schmidt, and since rolled out in several other countries, GuideStar publishes raw data from tax returns, covering more than 1.7 million nonprofits in America alone. Yet this data is often too limited to provide an accurate assessment of performance. Hence the need for research firms such as NPC.

At its best, NPC provides the sort of performance metrics that new philanthropists love. It does such things as calculate the rate of return on supporting a charity that gets a persistent truant to attend school regularly (1,160 percent, it turns out). In a similar spirit, Geneva Global, an American firm founded in 2000 that focuses on effective giving to developing countries, measures the performance of donations using units of what it calls Life Change. As well as providing research, it manages funds for donors, sending potential donors a monthly catalog with a choice of evaluated projects and later providing feedback on what their money has achieved. In 2008, Geneva Global expects the donations it has advised on to "measurably improve" the lives of at least 2,323,557 people in developing countries.

NPC believes its analysis has already helped change the funding strategies of donors in the U.K., where it has initially been focused. NPC says its research has levered an extra £3 million to a group of small and medium-size charities focused on truancy, to pick one example.

As well as providing much of its research free to the public, NPC works as an adviser to individual philanthropists and foundations. A typical client is Ramez Sousou of TowerBrook, a London-based private-equity firm, who has dealt with NPC on behalf of his firm's corporate foundation and also the Private Equity Foundation, which represents thirty U.K. private-equity firms. Sousou says that NPC "can't tell you what you care about, but they helped us figure out our values, agree on our strategy, evaluate our options, do our due diligence, and monitor the impact of our money."

NPC has won many fans among the new generation of philanthrocapitalists in Europe, not least by helping them scale up their giving at a faster pace. As one client explains, "I wanted to start making strategic grants very quickly without having to get up the learning curve fast myself or to hire my own staff to do it. Using NPC enabled the foundation to double the size of its giving in the U.K."

The combination of giving away much of its research whilst charging clients for customized work has proved a challenging business model for NPC. Indeed, one of the big uncertainties about the new "professional services" sector of philanthropy is whether there will be enough money in it to be sustainable. With a budget of around £2.5 million in 2007, NPC does not expect to become self-sufficient until 2010 at the earliest. In 2007, around 25 percent of its budget came from client fees, another 25 percent from foundation grants, and the other half from its core funders, including Davies and Wheeler.

NPC says its choice to give away its research is a deliberate one. The company, says Brookes, is "trying to change the system, to create a wider debate about what is performance in the charitable sector and how it is evidenced." Thus NPC presents itself as simultaneously a service (for donors) and a cause (for everyone).

Not everyone loves NPC's approach though. Some in the voluntary sector have complained that its focus on hard, quantitative measures of performance may be inappropriate for the intangible, people-centered issues that are at the core of the voluntary sector; they say it may be too obsessed with finding what is measurable. On the other hand, some of NPC's clients wish that it showed more the courage of its convictions, by criticizing poorly performing charities as well as celebrating winners. Its unwillingness to criticize may be borrowing too closely from the Wall Street model of research, which has traditionally issued many more "buy" recommendations than ones to "sell."

Measuring and comparing the work of charities is complex, however; more so than analyzing businesses. As a result, NPC began by focusing on smaller, relatively uncomplicated charities. "I'm not underestimating the difficulty of analyzing, say, Unilever, but no one has ever done it for a big nonprofit," says Brookes, who nonetheless expects eventually to start publishing "nuanced" reports on some of the larger charities. "Intellectually, we should be able to measure their role in the market, management capacity, funding, ability to deliver, impact," he says.

Since nonprofits can combine very different activities, from lobbying to delivering services on the ground, Brookes says, "the quality variation within a large nonprofit is breathtaking." Barnardo's, a venerable British children's charity, "does over two hundred different things, reflecting a randomness about how they grew up responding to different pots of money. To analyze a company like Apple, you essentially need to understand two things; to analyze Barnardo's, you need to understand many more things."

NPC also wants to play a leading role in developing performance measures for philanthropy that are as robust as profit is in the business world. For Brookes, this means figuring out the effect that the philanthropic activity has on the sense of well-being of the beneficiary. In 2007, NPC conducted a pilot questionnaire for adolescents before and after an Outward Bound course designed to develop character and boost self-esteem, which it benchmarked against UNICEF data to produce

## THE GOLDMAN STANDARD OF GIVING

Goldman Sachs has earned its reputation as one of the most consistently successful institutions of capitalism. But the investment bank, founded in New York in 1869, has long been a leading practitioner of philanthrocapitalism too, with a corporate culture that encourages, even expects, its leaders to give back to society both through philanthropy and public service.

In the early twentieth century, Henry Goldman, son of the firm's founder and its senior partner for many years, gave substantial sums of money to help develop the science of physics, backing Albert Einstein with research money (and even giving him a yacht for his fiftieth birthday). As a patron of the arts, he funded the training of violinist Yehudi Menuhin, to whom he gave a Stradivarius.

Two other early Goldman Sachs leaders played an influential role in the development of the civil rights movement in America. Walter Sachs was a strong supporter of the National Association for the Advancement of Colored People (NAACP) and was its first treasurer. His brother, Paul, was credited by an important client of the bank, Sears Roebuck owner Julius Rosenwald, with inspiring him to be a philanthropist. Rosenwald gave much of his fortune to support African American causes.

Reflecting the firm's public service ethos, Treasury Secretary Hank

what Brookes calls "sensible results." The plan is to scale this up across a range of philanthropic activities.

IN 2006, AFTER twenty-three years at Goldman Sachs (and a seven-year spell trying to make it as a rock guitarist), Chuck Harris cofounded SeaChange Capital Partners to create a new sort of investment bank for the nonprofit sector. (Soon after, Robert Steel, the other cofounder, left to become an undersecretary of the U.S. Treasury.)

Harris had long donated his spare time to nonprofits, particularly those involved in education, and had concluded that in the nonprofit sector, in sharp contrast to the business world, it was often easier for new start-ups to raise money than for established organizations. In the business world, a proven company has a myriad of options to get money to fund its growth plans. It can borrow from a bank; raise debt in the

Paulson was among several Bush administration recruits from Goldman Sachs. Paulson, who was previously the company's boss, has pledged to give away the bulk of his fortune, estimated at $800 million, to support environmental conservation through his Bobolink Foundation.

John Whitehead and John Weinberg, company coheads in the 1970s and 1980s, established an expectation that all of the firm's partners would be philanthropists. Whitehead (who served as deputy secretary of state in the Reagan administration) also endowed the first university course taught on social enterprise, at Harvard Business School. After the terrorist attacks of September 11, 2001, he chaired the committee tasked with redeveloping the devastated parts of lower Manhattan. He has also mentored many of the firm's partners in their philanthropy.

In November 2007, Goldman Sachs launched a philanthropic fund, GS Gives, to which it expects each of its 350 partners to contribute a fixed percentage of their annual pay. "We know we make a lot of money, and we know that we live in this world and we have a responsibility to give something back," said Lloyd Blankfein, Goldman's boss, announcing the fund. "It is in the long-term interest of this firm to do good things and not just dress up as if we are doing it. And we are really doing it."

bond market; and sell shares privately to investors (private placements) or in the public stock markets through an initial public offering, or once it is publicly listed, a secondary offering.

Not so the established, ready-to-grow nonprofit, which typically has to spend a vast amount of time and effort raising money, whether through applying for grants from foundations or government or appealing directly to the public. Gather two or three voluntary sector leaders together and they will complain about the time and expense of raising money. And they are right—it costs $22 to $43 for a nonprofit to raise $100 in the United States, according to the *Stanford Social Innovation Review*. Compare that with the 7 percent fee that an investment bank such as Goldman Sachs charges for organizing an IPO.

John Whitehead, Goldman's eminence grise of giving, had often discussed with Harris and Steel his belief that the philanthropic sector needed its own "investment bank." Taking Whitehead's advice to "start small, so your mistakes are small," Harris and Steel formed SeaChange and set out to raise an initial $15 million of start-up capital, with the goal of reaching $100 million in three years, half from outside donors and the rest from the founders. Goldman Sachs stumped up $5 million of the initial funding and said this would increase if SeaChange reached various milestones.

To maximize its leverage, SeaChange is building a network of wealthy individuals and family foundations that will receive details of opportunities to invest in selected nonprofits and be invited to meet their management and hear their growth plans at "road shows" similar to those held by investment banks. SeaChange's typical nonprofit client will have a demonstrable record of success, revenues of between $2 million and $75 million, and ambition. SeaChange will cover its own costs by taking a small portion of the funds it raises.

Harris was also influenced by the time he spent working in the development department of College Summit, a nonprofit dedicated to increasing the number of low-income students who go to college that was founded by dynamic social entrepreneur J. B. Schramm. Harris saw a need to finance College Summit in the same way he would a corporation at the same stage of its development. So a twelve-page placement memorandum was drawn up and circulated among potential donors, raising a total of $15 million of equity capital from ten donors within six months.

This was money for the organization to use as it pleased—not restricted, in the typical grant-making way, to a specific project. With that money in the bank, raising additional funds was much easier. "People want to invest in well-capitalized organizations," says Harris, pointing out that College Summit's senior executive team is now "able to focus more on strategy than on fundraising." SeaChange has also helped raise $60 million for Teach for America, as well as continuing to work with College Summit.

This investment-banking approach has not been an easy sell. "It is really hard," Harris says. "In the absence of financial returns, one of the big paybacks for folks who are active philanthropically is a sense of ownership and connection to a great project. And I think that drives both individual philanthropists and foundations to want their own projects. It's the exact opposite of the co-investment model that's popular in the business sector. What we need to do is to get people, at least some of the time, to think about doing things differently."


"IF WE CAN unleash a new entrepreneurial, collaborative kind of philanthropy, we can create new patterns that will help reshape the entire system—combining the innovation of the business world, the passion and humanity of the nonprofit world, and the inclusive, networked culture of the digital world to generate transformative change," argued Steve Case, a philanthropist who made his fortune as cofounder of Internet giant AOL, in a speech to fellow donors in 2006. His last point is important. In the for-profit world, networking is hot, online and off-line. Increasingly, the same is true in philanthropy, as some philanthrocapitalists—Bill Clinton first among them—even believe they can have a greater impact by leveraging their personal networks of contacts for good than by the money they give. This is certainly not your father's idea of the old boy network.

The big, high-profile off-line networking events are the CGI and the World Economic Forum in Davos. But many philanthropists are joining one or more of the growing number of smaller networking organizations that champion giving, allow givers to share experiences and lessons, and generally seek to spread best practice. Though they do not have the in-your-face, deal-oriented networking that takes place at the CGI, they are no less serious for being lower key.

In 2001, David Rockefeller (a grandson of the Rockefeller Foundation founder and a mentor to Bill Gates) and his daughter Peggy Dulany launched one such organization: the hugely influential Global Philanthropists Circle, of which Dulany has become de facto chief mentor. Described by *Business Week* as "the most elite club in the world," it "brings together many of the most respected individuals and families from every part of the globe who are committed to using their time, influence and resources to address some of the world's most significant problems." In 2007, its members represented sixty-eight wealthy families from twenty-two countries. In 2003, a junior version of the Circle was created, the Next Generation Group, to encourage younger people, from their teens to early thirties, to be involved in philanthropy.

A notch below this "elite club" are the increasing number of networking organizations that are simply for the exchange of information between philanthropists; others go one step further and help donors jointly fund projects through giving circles as well as network, such as SV2 in Silicon Valley. In Britain, the Funding Network aims "to make giving both fun and a learning experience." It is modeled on an influential recent innovation in the business world, the gatherings of "angel" investors, such as those organized by First Tuesday, which meets on the first Tuesday of every month to hear about start-up investment opportunities. In America, the Wealth and Giving Forum, founded in 2003, is an exclusive, invitation-only club where the rich can meet in private "to reflect with their peers on how best to allocate their wealth."

As well as the new networking organizations, the traditional American trade associations for philanthropists are starting to compete to embrace the spirit of philanthrocapitalism. In 2008, the biggest such association, the Council on Foundations, gathered three thousand philanthropic leaders from around the world to explore new approaches to giving at its first global philanthropy Leadership Summit. It is also sponsoring an inquiry into how to make philanthropy more effective. It is getting its act together not least in response to the vitality of the California-based Global Philanthropy Forum, launched in 2002, and of trade group rivals such as Independent Sector, which includes foundations and nonprofits; the conservative Philanthropy Roundtable; and the liberal National Committee for Responsive Philanthropy.

Likewise, new trade associations and events are flowering in other countries where philanthropy is on the rise. In the U.K. there has been a recent surge in interest in promoting giving as a cause and helping individual philanthropists. To do this more effectively, the Institute for Philanthropy was established in 2000 by Lady Hilary Browne-Wilkinson, a City lawyer, with funding from one of Britain's most innovative philanthropists, Joel Joffe. In 2006 the institute hired as its chief executive Salvatore LaSpada from the Rockefeller Foundation, who launched a program to educate "young inheritors" aged eighteen through twenty-eight about why and how to give and brought with him a program of global philanthropy workshops, to train donors.

The Forum for Active Philanthropy was created in 2006, the product of work by the Rockefeller Foundation and the Bertelsmann Foundation to build on existing programs to encourage donors, principally in Germany. The philanthropy networking body Worldwide Initiatives for

Grantmaker Support, created in 2000, is based at the Asia Pacific Philanthropy Consortium in the Philippines, which has members from China, India, Japan, the United States, Australia, and New Zealand, among other countries. The consortium's remit includes promoting the quantity and quality of gifts and lobbying governments to make giving easier.

Also spreading the trend to emerging markets is one of the world's oldest intermediary organizations. The Charities Aid Foundation (CAF) traces its origins to 1924, when the umbrella body for the nonprofit sector in Britain (now called the National Council for Voluntary Organisations) started promoting giving and helping charities to develop. CAF has a long track record of innovation, and in the 1990s it began to support a network of independent national CAFs in India, Russia, and several other countries. Its most recent innovation is CAF Global Trustees, which provides direct advice to the rich on how to give their money away (if you have less than $10 million to donate, don't bother asking). Its clients include the new rich of several emerging economies, including, it is said, several Russian oligarchs.

For those who really want their philanthropy done new-economy style, Internet connectivity presents an abundance of opportunities and experiments for both the superrich and those with only a few dollars to give away. The low marginal costs of the Internet mean that there is the potential to create many new opportunities for effective giving and for monitoring how the money is used.

One promising innovation is GlobalGiving.com. Founded in 2000 by Mari Kuraishi and Dennis Whittle, two former executives at the World Bank, GlobalGiving is an online "marketplace for goodness." The Web site lists information about causes that need money, provides an easy way of donating—in amounts as small as $10—and reports back regularly on how the money is being spent. GlobalGiving retains 10 percent of each gift to cover its operating costs. In 2007, GlobalGiving and another online giving site, Network for Good, partnered with the Jean and Steve Case Foundation to launch America's Giving Challenge—an attempt to increase donations made online. Facebook, a social networking Web site, is also exploring ways it can help people to support good causes.

The Internet is also making possible direct interactions between those with the money and those who need it. For example, Kiva allows people in rich countries to provide micro-loans direct to needy borrowers in developing countries. It remains to be seen which online models will prove viable in the long run, but already there is an impressive amount of innovation. Even for big donors who want a high level of engagement in their philanthropy, the Internet is likely to playing a growing role, even if only as part of a broader philanthropic strategy.

ANOTHER OF THE boom industries of the past few decades is fund management—a classic profession of intermediation. Firms such as Boston-based Fidelity Investments have generated huge profits by investing trillions of dollars of other people's money. Fund managers have provided specialist investment skills for the wealthy as well as low-cost ways for people who are not wealthy to have a stake in the world's leading firms. As a result of growth and innovation, there is now a huge variety of specialist fund managers, ranging from mutual fund companies like Fidelity to company or public sector pension funds, hedge funds, and private-equity firms. Even governments have been getting in on the act by creating specialist "sovereign wealth funds." In each case, the aim of fund management—not always delivered—is to invest capital where it will have the greatest impact (i.e., the highest return) by using professional expertise that the owner of the money does not have.

In philanthropy, too, the specialist fund manager is on the rise (and not just Bill Gates working for Warren Buffett). Among those offering professional giving management is Fidelity itself. With assets of over $5 billion, the Fidelity Charitable Gift Fund, founded in 1991, gave $1.17 billion through 287,000 grants to needy organizations in 2007, up by 24 percent from $950 million in 2006. This made it the fourth-largest public charity in America. It is what is known as a donor-advised fund—similar versions of which are now offered by many of Fidelity's competitors, such as Vanguard Investments and Charles Schwab. These work by the philanthropist making an irrevocable donation to a fund, which is then managed on his or her behalf by a fund manager. Fidelity charges a fee of 0.6 percent of the assets under management, relatively modest, especially in comparison with what it typically charges to manage mutual funds.

The sums going to donor-advised funds in America have soared in the past few years. In some cases, little of the money has been paid out to good causes, prompting criticism in Congress, though Fidelity says it pays out each year around one quarter of the money coming in. Fidelity boasts that "donors can maximize both their charitable impact and individual tax benefits as they make giving part of their personal and financial plans." Technically, the donor gives up sovereignty over the money to the donor-advised fund, retaining only an advisory role in how it is used. But wise firms such as Fidelity understand that to keep its customers happy, that advice ought to be heeded.

In Britain, New Philanthropy Capital and the Charities Aid Foundation have collaborated to launch mutual-fund-like "cause-related funds" that allocate money to a carefully selected portfolio of charities, monitor its impact, and keep donors informed about progress. The first two funds—launched in 2006 with the slogan "Know the cause, don't know the charity?"—concentrated on charities in particular sectors, as their names suggest: the Engaging Young Lives Fund and the Fulfilling Older Lives Fund.

One of the most admired of the new philanthropic investment vehicles is the Acumen Fund. Created in 2001 by Jacqueline Novogratz, a former employee of the Rockefeller Foundation, Acumen invests philanthropists' money in firms that offer the potential to create jobs in poorer parts of the world. Many of these investments are in the form of an equity stake in a for-profit enterprise, and Novogratz is a strong advocate of harnassing market forces and the profit motive to achieve economic development. "Markets are undoubtedly our best listening device, and they can help us identify the level of smart-subsidy needed to make goods and services available to low-income people so that they can solve their own problems," she says.

By 2008, Acumen had invested in companies that provide clean water at affordable prices, health clinics for poor districts in India, and a pioneering factory that sells affordable bed nets for use in the fight against malaria. It had built a $20 million investment portfolio, which it hoped to grow fivefold within five years. One of its biggest early supporters was Google, which invested $5 million in October 2005.

The investors in Acumen have no prospect of getting their money back. If Acumen's investments are successful, any profits to Acumen will be reinvested. Other than that, it will remain dependent on further philanthropic dollars. The question is, will this limit Acumen's ability to grow to a scale where the firms in which it invests have a dramatic impact in terms of economic development?

Novogratz aims to have $100 million under management by 2012. By contrast, one of her brothers, Michael Novogratz, was a partner at the hedge fund company Fortress and became an instant centimillionaire when it went public with a market capitalization of $14 billion in February 2007, at which point it was managing assets of around $30 billion. Nonetheless, whilst such sums are beyond their wildest dreams, as a force for good, Jacqueline Novogratz and her fellow philanthropic fund managers may have far more impact.

IN THE SAME way that Goldman Sachs and Fidelity epitomize one of the major developments in capitalism, the rise of the financial intermediary, so McKinsey is the best-known company in the management revolution that has transformed business and is now reaching to philanthropy. McKinsey has built up a powerful portfolio of consulting clients, including two thirds of the Fortune 100 companies, as well as many governments. While often ridiculed by disgruntled middle managers, who complain about young, arrogant McKinsey consultants, fresh out of Harvard Business School, stating the obvious in fluent PowerPoint, management consulting has grown into a multibillion-dollar industry that helps businesses grow and adapt. The talent of firms such as McKinsey has been to apply the fast-growing academic discipline of management to the challenges facing particular companies.

Now, as philanthrocapitalists attempt to increase the efficiency of doing good, there is a boom in consulting firms, including McKinsey, offering services both to philanthropists and nonprofits. This, in part, reflects a growing interest in philanthropy and nonprofits by management gurus following the lead of the late Peter Drucker, including Michael Porter, Mark Kramer, Jim Collins, and Greg Dees. The *Harvard Business Review* increasingly features articles about big philanthropy and nonprofit management. In 2003, Stanford University launched the *Stanford Social Innovation Review* as a dedicated management and policy journal for the social sector.

As with much in today's philanthrocapitalism, professional consultants are not entirely new to the business of giving. In 1919, Harvard University launched a fundraising campaign and hired John Price Jones to help. With George Brakeley, Price Jones went on to build a for-profit business that provides advice to organizations needing to raise funds.

Catering mostly to universities and arts institutions, Brakeley Briscoe is one of the leading American fundraising consultants. Though Brakeley Briscoe works only with those who need money, not those who have it to give, it has benefited from the rise of the new breed of philanthropist. "Organizations needing money have had to improve their pitch to deal with philanthropists who are behaving as investors," says John Kelly, head of Brakeley's international business. Happily for him, that means they have a greater need of professional advice. "Convincing people you have a clearly defined vision and a need is what unlocks big gifts of money by exciting the donor." The downside of all such highly motivated donations can be that they come with strings attached, says Kelly. "The challenge is not to take money from people who want to do things the organization doesn't. But some organizations find it difficult to say 'thanks, but no thanks.'" Presumably, Brakeley Briscoe can provide helpful advice on this too.

Another venerable organization selling philanthropy advice is Rockefeller Philanthropy Advisors. In 2002 the family spun off the philanthropic office of Rockefeller Financial Services, a firm that helped manage the financial affairs of family members. It is now arguably the largest advisory firm focused only on philanthropy. By 2008, it boasted a full-time staff of thirty-five who "facilitated" gifts totaling $200 million a year in more than fifty countries by some 150 clients.

Since 1999, McKinsey has grown rapidly its business advising the nonprofit sector. Its Social Sector Office typically charges half the (substantial) fees that the firm usually extracts from business clients to make this advice affordable (with further discounts, and even pro bono work, available on application to particularly deserving causes). It has three main focuses: philanthropy, global public health and economic development, and opportunity creation. Notable McKinsey clients include the Gates Foundation and Bono's campaigning organization, DATA.

While McKinsey has chosen to cross-subsidize its work with philanthropists and nonprofits within its mainstream business, two other leading management consultancies have adopted more innovative structures to serve the business of giving. In 2000, Bain helped launch a separate business, Bridgespan, under the leadership of Thomas Tierney, a former head of Bain. The new firm was also seed-funded by several foundations that wanted a better consultancy for the sector, including the Atlantic Philanthropies and the Gates Foundation.

Tierney is a firm believer in the virtues of intermediaries. "Think about where business was post World War Two, in the fifties and sixties," he says. "One of the major differences between then and now is the evolution of the intermediaries, such as search firms, consulting firms, investment banks, human resources firms, intermediaries that provide business-to-business services." In the philanthropic and non-profit world at the end of the 1990s, there were plenty of specialist consultancies, but none of a significant scale. "We found three thousand or more boutique consulting firms addressing these sectors, but there was no established firm with more than about ten people," he recalls.

One challenge was to figure out which of the core skills of a management consultancy such as Bain would be relevant to nonprofits. "Whilst we recognized that there are significant differences between for-profit and nonprofit sectors, we believed that there is great power in data-driven results-oriented analysis in the nonprofit sector," says Tierney. "We saw potential to do both consulting and executive search for non-profits, particularly those in the three-million- to ten-million-dollar budget range."

Tierney says that the demand from philanthropists and nonprofits has been enormous and that so far Bridgespan has only been able to meet a small fraction of it. In 2006, Bridgespan was able to serve only 10 percent of its demand and, Tierney says, had to turn down "the vast majority of approaches from serious clients." Bridgespan has also created a specialist executive-development organization, Bridgestar, devoted to recruiting and building effective leadership teams for its nonprofit clients.

Bridgespan hires its own staff on lower salaries than Bain, which means it can charge lower fees than McKinsey typically does. Bridgespan works closely with Bain, which allows some of its staff to work for the nonprofit consultancy on secondment. Like McKinsey, Bain finds that offering the chance to work in the philanthropic and nonprofit world helps recruit today's increasingly idealistic MBAs—though a downside for the client is that the low (or sometimes nonexistent) fees mean that they will often have relatively junior consultants working for them.

Since 1998, there has been a thriving partnership between Monitor Group—a management consultancy created by several Harvard Business School professors, including Michael Porter—and venture philanthropy fund New Profit Inc. Founded by social entrepreneur Vanessa

Kirsch, New Profit has nurtured a portfolio of innovative young non-profits that it believes can achieve "transformative social impact." These have included Teach for America, College Summit, and the Freelancers Union, a fast-growing new trade union for the sort of workers that traditional unions tend to ignore. Monitor provides funding to New Profit, as well as in-kind support including strategy consulting and executive coaching for the social entrepreneurs in its portfolio.

New Profit is notable for using a management tool known as the "balanced scorecard," popularized by Harvard Business School professor Robert Kaplan. This tool, which has been hugely popular in the business world, helps companies to measure progress towards their strategic goals in a broader, richer way than simply focusing on profit or cash flow. Instead, the balanced scorecard translates the strategy into several measurable indicators of performance.

Kirsch pretended to be a student in order to get a meeting with Kaplan, whom she then convinced to adapt the balanced scorecard for nonprofits. Kaplan is now one of the philanthropists backing New Profit. The top measure in a business's balanced scorecard is financial impact; in New Profit's scorecard, it is social impact. She says this has been crucial in helping its portfolio organizations to grow, and to figure out how best to use the expertise available from Monitor.

THE DREAM OF many philanthrocapitalists is that one day there will be, in the words of former eBay chief executive Jeff Skoll, a "social stock market" to bring together philanthropists and socially driven organizations, just as the mainstream stock market brings together investors and companies.

It is easy to understand the appeal of this idea, for the stock market is arguably the ultimate capitalist intermediary. It makes it easy for entrepreneurs with good business ideas to raise the capital they need and provides real-time performance ratings of the firms whose shares are traded in it, which is why investors demand and will pay well for good data and research analysis about those firms. A falling share price can force a poor manager from his job and signal to investors that they would do better to put their money elsewhere, or it can trigger a takeover bid from a rival firm that believes it could do a better job of running it.

Compared with the power of the stock market, the sort of marketplaces provided to philanthropy by, say, the CGI or Web sites like GlobalGiving are decidedly second best. But is a social stock exchange ever likely to be created? And would it really be valuable?

So far, the most promising moves in this direction have involved identifying socially virtuous companies on the mainstream stock market. Several indices of "good companies" have been created by the existing stock exchanges, so that socially oriented investors can separate the sheep from the goats among for-profit businesses that are already publicly traded. For example, the London Stock Exchange now has a FTSE4Good index, which includes the fifty biggest firms traded on the exchange that achieve the necessary level of performance on the environment, relations with stakeholders, and human rights. A rival Dow Jones Sustainability World Index tracks the performance of over three hundred of what it regards as the "world's leading sustainability companies."

This reflects, in part, the growing popularity of socially responsible or mission-related investing. This popularity is due in part to some investors being willing to give up some of the likely profits on an investment so that a company can use the money to behave in ways that have a greater social impact. But it is also due to the growing belief that socially driven firms can earn higher returns than other companies—a belief popularized by investment firms such as Generation, formed in 2004 by former American vice president Al Gore and David Blood (a former partner of, inevitably, Goldman Sachs). The firm, nicknamed "Blood and Gore," buy shares in firms it believes are environmentally sustainable because these companies, by better understanding their social context and risks, will "deliver superior long-term results."

Yet whilst Generation is betting that there can be a social win-win whereby being good equals better financial returns, it also recognizes that sometimes that will not happen. It has established its own corporate philanthropy, the Generation Foundation, which has as a senior fellow Jed Emerson, who is the leading advocate of "blended value," a measure that evaluates organizations by not just their financial returns but also their overall social impact. By this model, the ideal for socially oriented firms is to maximize their "triple-bottom line": financial results, impact on the environment, and benefit to society.

For those firms that generate profits but are willing to give up some profitability in return for social and environmental impact, a social stock market that protects them from being acquired by investors driven only by profit—those who might buy the company and abandon its costly so-cial and environmental goals—might have some appeal. Designing such a market is not easily done, though. For one thing, it is hard to dis-tinguish between when a firm is less profitable than it could be because it is pursuing greater social and environmental impact and when it is less profitable because it is inefficiently run. Presumably, the social stock market should allow shareholders to replace management in the latter case but not the former—but how to create the rules for that? It would be easier if there was agreement on how to measure social and environ-mental impact, but there is not. In the traditional stock market, there is broad agreement on what is meant by profit and how to measure it. A social stock market is unlikely to thrive until the same is true of an orga-nization's triple-bottom line or blended value.

That assumes the organizations listed on the social stock market make at least some profit, or have a reasonable expectation of doing so. But could a social stock market ever exist for the many organizations backed by philanthropy that are never going to make a profit?

It would be great to have a trading-based system that puts an objective "price" on different nonprofits based on their social-impact performance prospects, so that philanthrocapitalists could decide which to invest in and which not to. Such a social stock market might put pressure on these nonprofits to perform better and perhaps even drive a much-needed wave of mergers in the nonprofit world. Yet the price of shares on a tra-ditional stock market is determined by the opportunity to acquire a slice of a limited pool of future profits. Without the prospect of profits to di-vide, why would a philanthropist ever buy a share in such an organiza-tion from another philanthropist when he could simply give the money directly to the organization itself?

A genuine social stock market that allows philanthropists to give more efficiently to every sort of nonprofit may prove to be a step too far for phi-lanthrocapitalism. That possibility is conceded by Wheeler, the NPC cofounder, in an article in *Alliance* magazine, "Towards a Social Stock Exchange—Barking Up the Wrong Tree?" Instead of focusing on design-ing a social stock exchange, he argues, it would be better to address sev-eral other questions, including how to develop standards of transparency and reporting for organizations that focus on social returns; why "after so many years of talking about it, have we made so little progress in reduc-ing transaction costs for those looking to raise capital? Are we missing a trick?"; and what role competition should play among providers of capital and the social organizations seeking it.

Make some real progress on addressing these questions, concludes Wheeler, and "we may decide we don't even need a social stock exchange—that we have been barking up the wrong tree all along. But if we still want one, we will be a lot closer for having the initial conditions for success in place."

## CHAPTER 13

# The Age of Plutocracy?

"I INDULGE IN POLITICAL PHILANTHROPY," says George Soros. "I try to use my money to influence how governments spend money." He has given away billions of dollars to support causes ranging from democracy in the former Soviet Union to decriminalization of recreational drug use in America. Though plenty of people regard his efforts as laudable, the political nature of many of his causes has earned Soros a diverse and impressive range of enemies. As well as christening him "public enemy number one," American right-wing commentators delight in calling him names, such as "Soros the Beastman." Russian leader Vladimir Putin apparently resents him for having sparked populist revolutions that ousted Moscow-friendly governments in Serbia, Ukraine, and Georgia. Even radical lefty philosopher Slavoj Žižek, whom one might think would approve of Soros's championing of democracy, has branded him an "enemy of every true progressive struggle."

To have given so much money away—an estimated $6 billion so far, and counting—and yet to be so widely reviled is a testament to the deep-seated fears that many people have about the mixing of money and politics. *Plutocracy*, derived from the Greek words for wealth (*ploutos*) and to rule (*kratien*), is not usually a term of approval.

For much of the twentieth century, public worries about plutocracy were largely restricted to America—and even there they ebbed and flowed. In the rest of the world, rather than trying to curb and regulate the powers of the rich, progressives often sought simply to do away with them altogether, whether through taxes, confiscation, or worse. Even when these policies were implemented ineffectively, as was often the case, they tended to carry enough force to convince the wealthy that discretion was the better part of valor, and that they had best not draw attention to themselves, including by engaging in philanthropy.

In America, the explosion of superwealth in the late nineteenth century certainly got the public's attention in what had been a relatively equal society. But the absence of popular enthusiasm for Socialism or Communism, unlike in Europe, also meant that there was little interest in abolishing the rich through the radical policies of class war. Now, with the demise of Communism and the rise of global superwealth, the politics of plutocracy is enjoying a revival even outside the United States.

Soros is a role model for many of today's philanthrocapitalists, and a partner to some of the most significant of them—including Bill Gates and Michael Bloomberg—typically when pursuing their social goals requires changes in government policy, as increasingly it does. A growing number of philanthrocapitalists are realizing that one of the most effective ways to leverage their money to change the world is to use it to shape how political power is exercised.

This prompts all sorts of difficult questions, not least for those who understand how necessary it is for philanthrocapitalism to achieve its potential. Should we worry about the growing ambition and ability of the rich to influence political decisions? Will this coming golden age of philanthropy also be an age of plutocracy—and if so, can anything be done to make this prospect less worrying for the public?

GEORGE SOROS BECAME famous around the world in September 1992, when his Quantum hedge fund bet that the British pound would fall out of the European Union's exchange-rate mechanism. The events of "Black Wednesday" won him notoriety as the "man who broke the Bank of England." He could measure the success of his trading strategy easily enough, simply by looking at his bank balance, which reportedly swelled by a cool $1 billion as the pound plunged. Soros refuses to apologize for building his fortune this way. "I don't feel any sense of guilt about having made money, as I made it according to the rules that prevail. I am aware of the inadequacy of the rules, but I am advocating changing them. If I wasn't playing by those rules, I'd be less well positioned to change them."

His commitment to philanthropy began long before Black Wednesday, in the 1970s. Successful investments had swelled his personal fortune to $30 million, which seemed "more than sufficient for me and my family." This realization, which for others might induce a profound sense of relaxation, instead sparked what Soros calls a midlife crisis. He resolved the crisis by launching his first Open Society Institute, with a name and an inherently political mission that reflected his commitment to democracy. Inspired above all by the philosopher Karl Popper, Soros wanted his giving to open up closed societies, make open societies more viable, and to "promote a critical mode of thinking."

"At first the foundation developed very slowly," Soros admits. "It was amateur hour as we figured out what works." But philanthropy Soros-style was first seen to good effect when he supported dissident groups in Eastern Europe, including Charter 77 in Czechoslovakia, Solidarity in Poland, and Jewish refuseniks in the Soviet Union. He then opened a foundation in his native Hungary that gave small grants to support civil society, with the hope of leveraging substantial change. This foundation, he says, carefully calibrated its activities so that the programs that would be considered constructive by the government outweighed those that would be regarded with suspicion by the authorities in charge of ideology. "The idea was to break the monopoly of the party-state," he says, claiming that the Hungarian foundation did so and proved great value for money.

There is no way of measuring the contribution that Soros's philanthropy made to the collapse of the Soviet Union in 1991, though by that time he had already earned a reputation within it as a smart operator, willing to take risks. He immediately dove into the complex business of helping countries recover from decades of Communism. His annual expenditure in the region jumped from $3 million to over $300 million in three years. "Other Western foundations moved so slowly that it took them years to overcome the legal obstacles," recalls Soros, which meant that "we had the field to ourselves." He established foundations in Estonia, Lithuania, and Ukraine even before they became independent. The Central European University, which was meant to serve as an intellectual resource for his foundation network, started offering graduate courses even before it was accredited. The first students received their degrees retroactively.

Soros is adamant that the rapid growth of the Open Society network in

Eastern Europe "would not have been possible if we had operated in a more conventional manner." This is typical of his approach to business and philanthropy. Soros invariably attributes decisions to his complex, Popper-influenced theory of how the world works, which he calls "reflexivity." The result, in both spheres, is that he takes big risks, moves fast, pursues lots of different strategies at once, and takes controversial positions. He regards as a strength the ability of his foundations to "proceed by way of trial and error." He says he is "ready to accept errors and to abandon projects when they fail. This gives us a comparative advantage. Bureaucracies find it difficult to admit failure; this makes them risk averse. We can tolerate risks; therefore we can reap greater rewards."

Sometimes Soros gives money to campaigns that he expects to fail simply to send a message by taking a stand. Unlike most traditional foundations, he does not shy away from taking on causes that will win him no friends. "In the social sphere, I take positions because I believe in them, whether I succeed or not. That is the difference between financial markets, which are not governed by moral considerations, and the social sphere, where morality ought to play a role," he says.

Among Soros's admitted failures is his work in China in the 1980s, where he went into partnership with an institute that was promoting economic reform by providing scholarships for Chinese to study abroad. When Soros discovered that the foundation was "effectively run by the political police," he closed it, just before the Tiananmen Square massacre. He also owns up to having got out of South Africa too early because he overestimated the strength of the apartheid system.

Soros now funds a network of over twenty foundations that he has built across the globe. The list of countries changes all the time, sometimes by his own choice (he has proved unsentimental when he feels that his foundations are ineffective) and sometimes because of government hostility. For example, his freedom of action was dramatically curtailed in Russia with the rise of the authoritarian government of Putin. Soros wound down his Russia operations, in his view, "just in time to avoid persecution" (see "Soccer, Philanthropy, and Politics" box on pages 244–45).

"Soros became a kind of spook for people who hate any kind of democracy," says Mikhail Saakashvili, the president of Georgia, when asked about Putin's claims that Soros paid for the "Rose Revolution" of 2003 that had swept him to power. "Apparently, George loved it."

Soros won't admit to reveling in the Kremlin's disapproval. "I'm not in favor of revolutions," he says. "Yet we do support forces that sometimes find expression in revolution, when evolutionary change is obstructed by government." He also dismisses Putin's attempts to blame the Rose Revolution on outside interference. "For Putin, it is easier to blame an external, nefarious conspiratorial force than to admit that the people are fed up," he says. Saakashvili agrees, although Putin would probably cite that as evidence of a conspiracy. "Soros has done good things, in terms of encouraging hope," Saakashvili says. "But the main forces of change come from within society. Some support from abroad is nice. But nobody can come in from abroad and do your own job."

For Soros there is also the risk of getting into bed with individual politicians or parties. He protests that he is sticking to his original mission in Georgia, the fight against corruption, which led to his falling out with the main casualty of the Rose Revolution, former president Eduard Shevardnadze and has since caused a cooling of his relationship with Saakashvili.

It is not just autocratic leaders in the former Soviet Union who are suspicious of Soros's philanthropy. His American Open Society Institute, which is run by a former head of the American Civil Liberties Union, Aryeh Neier, has dared to campaign for a relaxation of prohibitions on recreational drugs. Even Soros was surprised by the hostility his stand provoked. His Project on Death in America, devoted to reducing the pain associated with dying, also created controversy over claims that it advocated euthanasia—although Soros insists that it did not, but in fact advocated better end-of-life care.

Soros's involvement in the 2004 U.S. presidential campaign was his most controversial venture into party politics. "I do not feel comfortable about engaging in partisan politics," he writes in his 2006 book, *Age of Fallibility*, especially "since the Democratic Party does not stand for the policies I advocate; indeed, if it did, it could not be elected." But in the end he felt he had no choice. "I believed that Bush was too extreme," he explains, "and had gone beyond what was acceptable in an open society."

As well as voicing his own criticisms of Bush, Soros also funded grassroots voter-mobilization efforts and tried to bring in other donors. In the end he failed to unseat President Bush but he remains unapologetic. "Having exerted myself in promoting the ideas of open society abroad," he writes, "I felt honor bound to do the same at home."

Soros also thinks that a lot of the criticism against him is exaggerated. In 2007, he was widely reported to be behind a political ad that labeled the U.S. military commander in Iraq, General David Petraeus, as "General Betray Us." The ad was produced by the organization MoveOn.org, which had campaigned against Bush in the presidential election with support from Soros. But he insists that he has given MoveOn.org no money since 2004 and has no control over its campaigns.

Soros is not some latter-day Garibaldi leading an army of grant makers to stir up revolutions across the former Soviet Union and on to the United States. His foundations have invested large amounts in education and have played a leading role in the fight against HIV/AIDS in Eastern Europe.

## SOCCER, PHILANTHROPY, AND POLITICS

In the early 1990s, a fire sale of government assets in the former Soviet Union opened the door for some imaginative and aggressive young men to amass considerable fortunes. For a while, these so-called oligarchs seemed set to become the political leaders and power brokers in Russia and Ukraine. Now they are more interested in soccer and philanthropy, following the example of Roman Abramovich, who has spent millions of his own money buying success for London soccer team Chelsea and providing social services for the fifty thousand souls who inhabit the remote Russian province of Chukhotka, from whence much of his oil wealth comes.

In his eight years in the Kremlin, President Vladimir Putin showed the oligarchs that it was not the tycoons but the state that ran Russia. In 2005, he humbled the richest man in Russia—Mikhail Khodorkovsky, owner of then oil giant Yukos—by having him charged with tax fraud. Khodorkovosky attracted the ire of the Kremlin because of the political edge to his philanthropy. It wasn't just that the name of his Open Russia Foundation echoed that of the loathed Soros's Open Society Institute. Khodorkovsky was spending big ($200 million a year) on issues such as civil and human rights that were deemed too political. And he had drafted heavy-hitting foreigners, including Henry Kissinger and Lord Rothschild, to sit on its board.

Khodorkovsky remains in jail and his foundation has fallen silent. So too have the other oligarchs. Personal philanthropy is acceptable to, even encouraged by, the Kremlin, as long as it is limited to buying artistic treasures to bring home to the motherland, supporting museums, or sponsoring

One of his most significant achievements has been focused on corporations rather than governments—or, rather, on reducing the corruption of governments by corporations. He funded the Publish What You Pay campaign, supported by several NGOs including Global Witness, to persuade oil and mining companies to disclose all the payments they make to the governments of the countries where they operate. The aim was to generate leverage by enabling the citizens of those countries to hold their governments accountable for where the money goes.

But since companies listed on major stock exchanges could not be compelled to publish country-by-country accounts, Soros switched the

academic excellence. Corporate social responsibility is positively encouraged because the Kremlin expects companies to give back to the Russian public.

While the Russian oligarchs initially set out to pull the levers of political power from behind the scenes (until Putin yanked that rug from under them), to the west, in Ukraine, their peers sought public office as members of parliament. In contrast to the atrophied political debate in Russia, Ukraine has become a freer, more open place since the Orange Revolution of 2004 (in which Putin also saw the hand of Soros), when forces unknown failed to assassinate the anti-Kremlin candidate and then botched rigging the elections.

Now, the Ukrainian oligarchs are increasingly turning to political philanthropy (as well as buying soccer clubs). Leading the pack is billionaire Victor Pinchuk, who has become something of a mover and shaker in Davos and the Clinton Global Initiative. His eponymous foundation is promoting European Union membership through a group called the Yalta European Strategy (YES). Now joining him is the richest man in Ukraine, Rinat Akhmetov, who has recently started using his philanthropy to create policy think tanks including the Foundation for Effective Governance, which includes several eminent foreigners on its board to demonstrate its integrity. For both men, the growth of their interest in philanthropy has coincided with a loss of interest in party politics—Pinchuk stepped down from parliament in 2006, and Akhmetov was expected to soon follow suit. How long before Russia's "silent oligarchs" rediscover the courage to engage in the sort of politically sensitive philanthropy that can tackle the big issues facing their country?

campaign's attention from companies to governments. The British government, the World Bank, and the International Monetary Fund all came on board, and with their help the Extractive Industries Transparency Initiative (EITI) was born in late 2002. Corporations, governments, and civil society were brought together to develop disclosure standards for companies and governments in oil-, gas-, and mining-dependent countries. Soros's foundation network is still deeply involved in this effort and has set up Revenue Watch groups in several countries to track payments to governments. So far, the EITI has already recovered a billion dollars in Nigeria alone. "As I like to put it," says Soros, "we have hit pay dirt."


OF ALL THE philanthrocapitalists, Soros has the most impressive track record on using giving to lever political change. But he is not the only one trying to do so. Recall that Soros provided start-up capital for DATA, Bono's campaigning organization, with software tycoon Ed Scott and the Gates Foundation—which as well as funding new initiatives in the public education system also joined with Eli Broad to put education reform on the presidential election agenda through the campaign Ed in '08.

Richard Branson, Jeff Skoll, and others are directly funding a gaggle of (technically former, but still hugely influential) world leaders through the Elders. Having financed Al Gore's *An Inconvenient Truth*, among other movies with a message, Skoll is now looking to further increase the impact of his philanthropy on policy, particularly towards climate change. Marion and Herbert Sandler, who made their fortune from banking, are trying to influence the battle of ideas by improving the quality of journalism (see "Up to a Point, Mr. and Mrs. Sandler" box on pages 248–49). Google.org and Omidyar Network are philanthropic organizations that have deliberately given up tax advantages available to traditional foundations so that they can engage in political campaigning in order to achieve their goals.

In 1993, controversially, Chuck Feeney became involved in the Northern Ireland peace process. The billionaire philanthropist was one of a group of American-based Irish-American businessmen who became "amateur envoys" with a mission to help promote a dialogue among the governments of the U.S., Britain, and Ireland, and all the parties in Northern Ireland. In 1994, Feeney agreed to pay $20,000 for thirty-six months to Sinn Fein to run a political office in Washington, D.C. This was made as a personal donation, not a gift from Atlantic Philanthropies, and Feeney was insistent from the start that the money was for a democratic process only, and not to fund violence (though such a clear line is inevitably hard to draw). All his payments were reported to America's Department of Justice. Nonetheless, several newspaper reports suggested that the payments meant that Feeney was a supporter of the Irish Republican Army, which he adamantly denies. (Indeed, in pursuit of peace, he gave money to both sides, including $200,000 to Gary McMichael, a representative of loyalist paramilitary group the Ulster Defence Association.)

After the ceasefire became permanent, Feeney directed $30 million through Atlantic to projects in Northern Ireland, including $2.5 million to help Loyalist and Republican ex-prisoners move into "positive politics." Gerry Adams, the veteran Irish Republican leader, has claimed that the intervention of the American business people, including Feeney, brought the ceasefire forward by about a year and that scores of lives were saved as a result. According to Adams, "the Irish peace process is the most successful U.S. foreign policy issue and those in at the birth of that have been validated and vindicated, and Chuck more so in that he put up hard cash, he put money where his mouth is. The investment he made to the peace process was pivotal. It was a brilliant investment." But one that might easily have gone wrong.

(Less happily, one could even look at Osama bin Laden as a kind of political "philanthropist": he is believed to have used some of his family's business fortune to fund al-Qaeda terrorism with the goal of leveraging political change.)

While Soros and some of his fellow philanthrocapitalists are figuring out how to be effective political philanthropists, some critics are questioning whether they should be involved in politics at all. For instance, in his 2007 book, *Foundations of Betrayal: How the Liberal Super-Rich Undermine America*, Phil Kent attacks the Open Society Institute and several other big foundations, arguing that "the anti-freedom and even anti-American agenda many pursue should make patriotic Americans angry."

Soros, whom he calls "Dr. Evil," is only second on Kent's hit list. Pole position is still held by the Ford Foundation, "the activist leader among thousands of wealthy foundations that fund hard-core leftist and anti-American organizations and projects." As Kent sees it, the liberal foundations, which also include Rockefeller, Hewlett, MacArthur, and the Pew Charitable Trusts, are helping radical Muslims and even suicide bombers; backing radical environmentalists with huge grants; and working to undermine America's free enterprise system, traditional

---

### "UP TO A POINT, MR. AND MRS. SANDLER?"

Writing in *Slate* magazine in October 2007, Jack Shafer hailed the creation of an investigative journalism agency as the sign of the "third wave in American journalism [following the partisan press and the commercial press]—that of the *foundation press*." The agency, ProPublica, has been principally funded with a $10 million gift from billionaires Marion and Herbert Sandler, who made their money from Golden West Finance Corporations. ProPublica, which is led by a former managing editor of the *Wall Street Journal*, claims to be filling a gap created by intense competition in the commercial media. The aim is to produce original investigative journalism that "shines a light on exploitation of the weak by the strong and on the failures of those with power to vindicate the trust placed in them." Could philanthrocapitalism usher in a new era of high-quality, responsible journalism?

Money and the media have long been an explosive mixture, and press barons have long been Exhibit A for those who worry about plutocracy. Their dubious image can be traced back to long before Lord Copper, the fictional British newspaper proprietor of Evelyn Waugh's 1938 novel, *Scoop*—a man so opinionated and fearsome that his editor dare not say no to him. (The closest he gets to disagreeing with the boss is to say, "Up to a point, Lord Copper.")

The baddies of fiction are an amalgam of some extraordinary real-life characters who have made their money from the media, many of whom also dabbled in politics. William Randolph Hearst, who tub-thumped for the Spanish-American War of 1898 and was the inspiration for the Orson Welles movie *Citizen Kane*, served in Congress and ran unsuccessfully for the governorship of New York. Lord Beaverbrook, who made the *Daily Express* Britain's bestselling newspaper for many years, was a member of Parliament and later served in Winston Churchill's War Cabinet, notably boosting aircraft production. Robert Maxwell, whose *Daily Mirror* tried to offer a left-of-center challenge to Margaret Thatcher in the 1980s, had served as an MP too, although he later dedicated much of his energy to suing critics who, it turned out after his death, seem mostly to have been culture, and national sovereignty. And all are doing so under a cloak of secrecy.

telling the truth about the old rogue (although whether he really worked for Mossad is not proven).

Among the living, politicians both fear and revere one man above all: Rupert Murdoch, whose British newspapers were credited with almost single-handedly awarding John Major a surprise victory in the 1992 general election and whose Fox News channel seems designed to irritate American liberals. Murdoch has never sought political office, unlike his fellow media barons Michael Bloomberg and Silvio Berlusconi. Nor is he regarded as much of a philanthropist, though several of his papers consistently lose money, so are arguably a form of charity.

Governments have tried different ways to curtail the power of media barons, including setting limits on the size and scope of their business interests through competition legislation and, particularly in the U.K., by promoting public-service broadcasting as a state-subsidized alternative.

The Sandlers are not the first philanthropists to attempt to create a virtuous news organization. Britain's *Guardian* newspaper has had no proprietor since 1936. It is owned by a foundation, the Scott Trust, a creation of J. R. Scott, the son of the newspaper's great editor and owner, C. P. Scott. Faced with death taxes that could have forced him to sell the paper, J. R. Scott passed ownership to the charitable trust, thereby ensuring that the *Guardian* remained faithful to his father's maxim: "Comment is free, but facts are sacred . . . The voice of opponents no less than that of friends has a right to be heard." In 2006, there was speculation that a similar structure might be applied to the *Los Angeles Times* if the California philanthropist Eli Broad was to buy it. According to the *New York Times*, as proprietor, Broad would want "fewer stories on movies and more about the city's museums and classical arts"—which sounds rather dull.

One man's media baron is another man's champion of freedom, regardless of whether he is making a commercial investment or a philanthropic gift. It remains to be seen if ProPublica will produce investigative stories about the Democratic Party, to which the Sandlers have been substantial donors. Will it be a case of "up to a point, Mr. and Mrs. Sandler"?

Kent's concerns pale besides some of the plutocratic conspiracy theories that have spread over the years. One popular target is the Bilderberg Group, a gathering of CEOs and politicians who are supposedly conspiring to enforce global capitalism—or so it was believed by, among others, Saddam Hussein and Slobodan Milosevic. Another is the summer gathering at Bohemian Grove in a redwood forest north of San Francisco, attended by Warren Buffett, among other tycoons. Officially, the gathering is innocent, summer-camp fun—but it has been credited with the birth of the Manhattan Project and thus the atom bomb, and Bohemian Grove allegedly contains a campsite reserved for the Rockefeller family, where they are said to bed down with bankers, oil company executives, and heads of think tanks. (David Rockefeller was behind the creation of another target of conspiracy theorists, the Trilateral Commission—whose purpose is to foster better dialogue between the leaders of Asia, Europe, and America.)

Above all, conspiracy theorists are obsessed with the World Economic Forum held in Davos in the Swiss Alps. The annual meeting each January is a favorite target of antiglobalization protesters who think that inside the security ring, Davos Man (as Samuel Huntington christened its attendees) is busy taking all sorts of self-seeking plutocratic decisions. Whether or not as a direct response to these protests, and the creation of the rival World Social Forum, in recent years the agenda at Davos has broadened from economic growth and trade to address the big social challenges facing the world, such as development, poverty, and climate change.

Whilst Kent attacks philanthropic plutocrats from the political right, there are also plenty of left-wing critiques of the growing political power of the rich. Starting in the 1980s, there has been a "fusion of money and government" in America, writes Kevin Phillips in his 2003 book, *Wealth and Democracy: A Political History of the American Rich.* Phillips, who used to work in the Nixon administration but has since moved to the left, argues that a government-led economic boom has dramatically increased the wealth of the richest 1 percent of Americans, who were the main political supporters of the policies behind the boom—which Phillips says did not provide much benefit (if any) to the rest of the population.

Similar criticisms have been made in other countries, including Britain. "The new super-rich have the means through the financing of political parties, the funding of think tanks and the ownership of the media to shape government policies or to deter reform of a *status quo* that suits them," argues BBC business editor Robert Peston in his 2008 book, *Who Runs Britain? How the Super-Rich Are Changing Our Lives.*

This is the third period in American history of political dominance by the wealthy, writes Phillips, each of them "zeniths of corruption and excess," marked by little growth in median incomes whilst the tax code is twisted to the benefit of the rich. The first was the era of the "robber barons" in the nineteenth century: a period when industrial magnates exerted enormous political influence through their firms, described by American historian Arthur Schlesinger Sr. as a "government of the corporations, by the corporations and for the corporations."

The second was in the 1920s, as Republican tax cuts after 1921, designed to keep the economy going after the wartime boom, fueled the stock market bubble that burst spectacularly in 1929. A populist target during this period was Andrew Mellon, then one of the three wealthiest men in America. Having built his fortune in banking, Mellon was U.S. Treasury secretary throughout the 1920s, pushing down the rate of income tax and estate tax. He was vilified by Franklin D. Roosevelt, who spouted anti-Mellon rhetoric as he introduced a massive extension of state welfare in the New Deal.

While the primary targets of populists during these periods of plutocracy have been the fortunes of the wealthy and the ways they made their money, there has been plenty of controversy over the integrity of their philanthropic efforts. In the early twentieth century, as crusading journalist Ida Tarbell railed against all things Rockefeller, including his charity, foundations were criticized for their support for academic studies of the underlying causes of poverty and racism. In Congress, the Walsh Commission on Industrial Relations, fearful of Rockefeller's use of his own foundation to investigate the causes of the industrial dispute that in 1914 sparked the "Ludlow massacre" at one of his companies, recommended limits on the size of foundations for fear that otherwise they would "manipulate the economy and . . . influence public opinion."

Mellon spent his final years in the 1930s on trial for tax evasion, a charge that was widely seen as politically motivated. It has long been claimed that Mellon eventually struck a deal with FDR in which he made a huge philanthropic gesture, donating his art collection to the nation, in return for easier treatment on his taxes by the government, though the evidence suggests that the gift was planned far earlier.

In the McCarthyite 1950s, the big foundations were investigated by the Cox and Reese committees, which ultimately gave them the all clear on suspicions of un-American activities. By the 1960s it was widely felt, especially among Republicans, that the wishes of foundations' original donors were being neglected, and that both foundations and corporate donors alike had been captured by a liberal clique. However, the attack was led by a Democrat, Texas congressman Wright Patman, whose obsessions included a hatred of the civil rights movement and a suspicion of the rich (he had tried to impeach Mellon in 1932). The Ford Foundation drew particular criticism, not least when it abandoned all pretense of political neutrality and offered grants to the staff of Bobby Kennedy after his assassination.

J. D. Rockefeller III organized the foundations' defenses against this "gathering storm," forming the Peterson Commission to carry out a balancing investigation to Patman's. (This was chaired by Pete Peterson who, nearly forty years later, used much of the fortune he had made from selling shares in Blackstone, the private-equity firm he cofounded, to endow an eponymous foundation with a mission to improve the way America is governed.) It did not issue a report until 1970, by which time the 1969 Tax Reform Act had placed significant new restrictions on the work of foundations, including limiting their political activities and requiring them to pay out a minimum percentage of their assets each year. Nonetheless, Rockefeller was credited with saving them from more draconian regulation through his lobbying of Congress. Since then, politicians have occasionally attacked foundations, but mostly for their wastefulness, not their supposed political clout—although as other philanthrocapitalists join Soros in becoming politically active, that could change.

DESPITE THE PARTISAN bluster of some critics, over the years wealthy Americans have used their money to support political causes of both left and right. Even Phillips concedes that, whilst the overall impact of the political power of the rich has been negative for society, there is also a tradition of some wealthy people becoming progressive leaders in America—including Jefferson and both Roosevelts. Indeed, he says,

"Most of the successful political mobilizations against abusive elites, in short, have appealed to a reform-minded portion of rich Americans."

In response to criticisms that he is an overly powerful lefty, Soros points out that there is what he calls "a very large right-wing philanthropic machine" and "a whole cottage industry attacking me, mostly financed by Richard Mellon Scaife" (a billionaire heir to the Mellon banking fortune and an enthusiastic champion of right-wing causes, best known for hating Bill Clinton and for a messy divorce from his second wife). The right-wing political philanthropists "have not been attacked the way I have been attacked," says Soros, which he thinks "reflects that they already have more influence."

One of the achievements of the right-wing foundations that Soros cites is the creation of the discipline of "law and economics," which grew out of the University of Chicago in the 1970s. This movement, whose ranks include two winners of the Nobel Prize in Economics, Ronald Coase and Gary Becker, uses considerations of economic efficiency to help solve legal questions. As well as having a perceived free-market bias, law and economics is opposed by those, usually on the left, who believe that law should focus on absolutes of what is right, not engage in utilitarian calculations of economic benefits.

Law and economics was helped in getting established by the John M. Olin Foundation, whose story is told in a 2005 book, *A Gift of Freedom*, by John J. Miller. After an early period when it acted as a conduit for CIA money to various anti-Communist organizations, says Miller, the foundation, endowed by munitions tycoon and free marketer Olin, grew into a "venture capital fund for the conservative movement."

The Olin Foundation also provided early support for the conservative thinker Allan Bloom, author of the hugely influential *Closing of the American Mind*, and funded institutions such as the Heritage Foundation and Federalist Society, which provided much of the ideological rigor in the Reagan revolution. While focusing on the intellectual high ground, it was also opportunistic, supporting General William Westmoreland's lawsuit against CBS following criticism in a documentary on the Vietnam war, and funding the Lay Commission on Catholic Social Teaching to challenge liberal bishops in the church.

The vision behind the Olin Foundation came from William E. Simon, who had served as Treasury secretary under Nixon and believed that the left dominated the foundation world. In his 1978 book, *A Time for Truth*,

Simon called on the political right to build a counter-intelligentsia to take over the "intellectual superstructure" of America. Businesses and the rich who believed in capitalism should focus their funding of higher education only on those institutions that subscribe to pro-business teaching, Simon argued. They should channel funding only to those parts of the media that were pro-capitalist. And they should support pro-business philanthropic foundations. "Capitalism has no duty to subsidize its enemies," he concluded.

Less celebrated but in some ways even more successful than Olin was wealthy British chicken farmer Sir Anthony Fisher. On the advice of the great libertarian Friedrich Hayek, he was one of the major donors to the Institute of Economic Affairs, which had a huge influence on the policies of Margaret Thatcher's government. With some right-leaning American philanthropists, Fisher also funded the Manhattan Institute, which was to play a key part in New York City's escape from financial and social meltdown during the 1990s, by providing many of the policy ideas implemented by Rudy Giuliani when he was mayor.

Such has been the success of the right-wing foundations that the Rockefeller Foundation funded a 2005 study by Andrew Rich of Stanford University, "War of Ideas," which asked "why mainstream and liberal foundations and the think tanks they support are losing in the war of ideas in American politics." The right-wing foundations, Rich concluded, "are succeeding by aggressively promoting their ideas. By contrast, liberal and mainstream foundations back policy research that is of interest to liberals. But these funders remain reluctant to make explicit financial commitment to the war of ideas. And they do relatively little to support the marketing of liberal ideas." Until now, perhaps, thanks to Soros and some of his fellow liberal philanthrocapitalists.

THE TRADITIONAL AMERICAN solution to the perceived threat of plutocracy has been to curb the political power of the rich through a mixture of transparency and regulations while still allowing people the opportunity to become and remain wealthy. This, increasingly, is also the approach being taken elsewhere.

It reflects an understandable prejudice that the rich are fundamentally self-interested and therefore not to be trusted with political influence. But in the age of philanthrocapitalism, a more positive view of the engagement of the rich and their foundations in politics may be needed. Transparency should still be required, but as much to give the superrich the ability to be truly effective in their philanthropy as to rein them in.

As hyperagents, the superrich can do things to help solve the world's problems that the traditional power elites in and around government cannot. They are free from the usual pressures that bear down on politicians and activists and company bosses with shareholders to please. To Soros, it is a responsibility of the wealthy to take a stand on tough issues, such as decriminalizing drug use. "I have done so because I felt I was in a better position than most of the others who could have made themselves heard. I was not dependent on government or business contacts. I could afford to take the heat," he says.

In a similar spirit, Vinod Khosla, a legendary Silicon Valley venture capitalist, says he has used some of his fortune to pursue political change in part because the status quo is being maintained through massive spending by big oil companies whose motives are less benign than his own. In 1993, having made his fortune as a cofounder of Sun Microsystems, Khosla moved his family to India in an attempt to become a traditional philanthropist. He commuted in six-week stints between India and his work in Silicon Valley, but he quickly concluded that giving a few computers to schools was not the way to achieve fundamental change; a more structural approach was needed.

He became convinced that climate change is the biggest threat facing the planet and committed himself to fighting it, both by investing hundreds of millions of dollars in developing clean, carbon-free energy and by changing the law. In 2006, in partnership with other philanthropists, including Google's Larry Page and his former business partner in venture capital John Doerr, Khosla backed an attempt to introduce new legislation imposing higher costs on oil companies, known as Proposition 87, in a referendum in California.

Though Khosla claimed that his intent was to use his wealth to counter the "oil industry's massive PR machine," he instantly became a political target. As the *Wall Street Journal* reported, "Some oilmen fume that Prop 87's supporters have invested large sums in alternative fuels and stand to benefit from any public policy that fosters their growth. This conflict of interest, rather than an altruistic concern about global warming, explains venture-capitalist support for the measure, oil companies say." The proposition was defeated.

Khosla had dismissed claims that he was conflicted by promising that if the proposition passed, he would donate every penny he made on his clean-tech investments to charity. "It would have cost me a lot of money. I had no conflict of interest. I had a negative incentive to support the proposition. But I care about where the world is going."

But he found that his pledge to give away any money he would make on clean energy seldom got reported. Other philanthrocapitalists who pursue for-profit investments as part of their philanthropic strategy should take note: they may find themselves similarly misunderstood.

Still both Khosla and Soros make a good point. In some ways, their vast wealth may make them less conflicted when they pursue political change than most of the people they are fighting against, who may have to do the bidding of a paymaster. This belief is shared by a growing number of philanthropists, some of whom are putting it to the ultimate test by trying to get elected. Some, such as Michael Bloomberg, have even won.

In a way this is a reversion to the original sense of plutocracy, where the rich occupy the powerful positions in government, as they did in the city-states of ancient Greece and the Italian merchant republics. As late as 1895, it is estimated, nearly one third of the millionaires living in Britain were elected members of Parliament (to which should be added the titled millionaire landowners sitting in the House of Lords). The twentieth century was something of an exception as the rich retreated from an active role in politics. Yet in important and positive ways, the new wave of tycoons entering politics has the potential to be nothing like the plutocracy of old.

MICHAEL BLOOMBERG, WHO became mayor of New York City in 2001 soon after the September 11 terrorist attacks, makes no apology for being a billionaire politician. On the contrary, he claims that his riches liberate him from the conflicts that dog other politicians. One of his biggest advantages in office is that he doesn't need the job. He has no need to indulge in graft, with all the compromises that go with it, either to secure his personal finances or to repay debt to campaign funders. His wealth also means that he comes cheap: at his request, as mayor of New York he is paid only one dollar a year. "Most people in government are doing it for a living. For me, public service is public service," he says.

Bloomberg did not have to make promises to political interest groups to get nominated. He has been able to appeal directly to the electorate without needing to appeal to the narrow interests of party. He is, in the words of Harper Lee, "beholden to nobody and nothing."

The lure of politics for Bloomberg is the leverage he gets. "I can probably change the world more as mayor of New York than I can as a philanthropist," he argues. "The smoking ban is a good example. I have given a $125 million grant to fund research into stopping smoking a couple of years ago, and will probably repeat it. But nothing it achieves will be comparable with passing a small law in New York [to ban smoking in public places], that was first copied by neighboring states, then Europe." When it comes to spending a fortune, politics may give the best return on every philanthropic buck, according to Bloomberg. "I spent $75 million then $85 million on my election campaigns. I have always felt this was the best investment in helping the world I could have made. I couldn't have done as much without being mayor."

Not that Bloomberg rejects the normal sort of philanthropy—he still has big plans to give away most of his fortune to eliminate smoking worldwide and is working on a radical approach to malaria. "We are trying to build a better mosquito," says Bloomberg, who is spending $100 million through his foundation to develop a bug that won't carry the malaria virus but is strong and hardy enough to drive the malarial mosquitoes out of their environmental niche.

Bloomberg's political experience has also taught him that philanthropy can be far more innovative than government. "Innovation involves doing things when you don't know what the end result will look like, what color it will be, how to market it, what exactly it is going to do. You can't get public money for that," he says. Government finds it hard to innovate because the legislative process "requires horse trading and everybody has to get something." As mayor, he has used his own money and that of other philanthropists, including Gates, to get around this inertia to test ideas, some of which have then won public funding once they have been proven to work. This strategy has been used most prominently within the New York school system, but other examples include a $50 million conditional cash transfer fund that pays poor families that achieve performance targets in education, health, and training, and a scheme to encourage poor people to open bank accounts by matching their initial savings, up to $250 each.

This strategy relies on the public having confidence in the legitimacy of the superrich, especially given the risk that they may actually be pursuing self-interest in these areas. Bloomberg's opponents have accused him of using his philanthropic activities to help him get elected, and of using his political office to further his business interests. Bloomberg gives the first argument short shrift: "You don't get a lot of votes giving to a small museum in Harlem," he says, noting that he has covered himself on the latter charge at least by putting his business into a blind trust while mayor.

One reason why these charges have not stuck in the way that similar claims leveled at media tycoon Silvio Berlusconi have during his stints as prime minister of Italy is the system that America has put in place over the years to protect itself against plutocratic abuses. When the rich get involved in politics, they must do so transparently and are subject to intense scrutiny. There are clear rules governing conflicts of interest, such as favoring a personal business. The legal system is tough on those found to abuse their position. There are tough limits on media ownership. Alas, the same is not true in Italy. Bloomberg's media company operates in a competitive market; Beslusconi's media empire wields near-monopoly power. Bloomberg also has competence on his side—to say nothing of his freedom from allegations of having Mafia connections.

There is no question that Bloomberg earned his money fairly. Indeed, he believes his success in business increases his legitimacy as a politician—so much so that he pondered running for the White House in 2008. During his mayoral campaigns, he did "extensive polling" on whether voters minded a wealthy candidate. "The fact you were rich didn't matter at all. When you said, 'He made his own money,' it was one of the strongest positives. Americans don't want the other guy to fail—they want to succeed themselves. It is a difference in the American ethic," Bloomberg says. But who knows? One day, perhaps the rest of the world will think the same way.

## CHAPTER 14

# The Gospel of Wealth 2.0

It is October 25, 2025. In the library of Lord Branson's luxurious eco-friendly space mansion, beneath a hologram of Andrew Carnegie, Bill Gates is celebrating his birthday with his closest friends. The views are spectacular. From above, planet Earth has never looked better—and, Gates thinks to himself, back on the ground things are looking pretty good, too.

Nowadays, nobody gives much thought to the fact that Gates once ran Microsoft, a firm that had made something called software for long-forgotten gadgets called personal computers. Today, the headlines proclaim, LEADER OF THE PHILANTHROCAPITALISM REVOLUTION TURNS 70.

By giving away the bulk of his own $100 billion fortune, plus the other $100 billion handed to him by his old friend Warren Buffett, Gates has helped to save millions of lives and improved the quality of life for hundreds of millions more. He has also inspired many of the world's growing army of billionaires (there are now 3,500 of them, according to the 2025 *Forbes* list) to join him in giving their time and money to tackle some of the biggest problems facing humanity. And not just billionaires: a mass-affluent version of Gates's brand of "intelligent philanthropy" has become a passion of millions at the wealthier end of the world's ever more prosperous population.

Among the guests today are several of his fellow philanthrocapitalists, each of them, like Gates, now a member of the Elders group launched by Branson and Nelson Mandela all those years ago. They had last met at the United Nations special session to learn lessons from their greatest triumph; it was called "Darfur and the Elders: how the genocide was ended." Across the room, Gates sees Jeff Skoll, fresh from collecting an Oscar for his latest movie, *An Inconvenient Truth 7*, which caused quite a stir by denouncing the professional eco-warriors who continue to spread fear of climate change long after that threat has been tamed. He is chatting to two of the most successful Skoll Foundation social entrepreneurs. One, an Indian woman in her forties, has played a big part in beating climate change through her business selling solar-power systems to villages across the developing world. The other, a young Chinese man, had transformed his mobile-phone-based political networking organization into a lucrative for-profit business after it played a key role in pushing China to embrace democracy.

Oprah Winfrey is sitting next to one of the first graduates of her Leadership Academy, who has just been appointed South Africa's minister for education. Nearby, Mo Ibrahim is congratulating the final winner of his good governance prize (it is no longer necessary), the just-retired president of Zimbabwe. And there is Melinda, congratulating Angelina Jolie on the Nobel Peace Prize she has just won for her success in improving the lot of millions of refugees.

Any moment now, an even more special guest will arrive aboard SpaceForceOne. They were the fiercest of business rivals back in the day, but recently Gates has formed a supereffective partnership in the war on disease and poverty with his fellow philanthrocapitalist, the first billionaire to be elected president of the United States, Google cofounder Larry Page.

As he surveys the room, Gates feels justifiably proud of what he and his philanthrocapitalist friends have achieved. It has not been easy. As Buffett has reminded him many times, giving money away is a "tougher game" than making it. Smiling, Gates gazes at the shining planet before him and reflects on how dramatically things have changed since he started his philanthropy in the mid-1990s, and how much healthier the state of the world is now.

WELL, WE CAN dream. Yet philanthrocapitalism does have the potential to make the world a vastly better place, as the rich play a leading role in tackling some of the biggest challenges facing humanity today. The question is not can philanthrocapitalism achieve its extraordinary potential, but will it?

That will depend on many things, including, crucially, whether many of the wealthy people who have yet to get serious about philanthropy do so. Andrew Carnegie was right: those who benefit the most from economic prosperity have a duty to use their money and talents to make the world a better place. But many of today's rich have yet to rise to the challenge.

The need is all the greater because the world is now a far more complicated place than in Carnegie's day, many of the challenges facing humanity are new and extraordinarily difficult, and the traditional providers of solutions do not seem up to the task. Carnegie was thinking very much about the problems of the industrialized world of America and Europe; the world we live in today faces global problems, from climate change and the threat of pandemic disease to terrorism. Carnegie's world was one in which government was beginning to flex its muscles and people were increasingly looking to the rational state to resolve society's problems; today the state is in crisis, and in some respects big business seems better placed to expand its social role. Carnegie's gospel was a one-sided bargain, an appeal to the rich; but today the wealthy lack the power, and indeed the legitimacy, to act alone.

Some admirers of philanthropy think the answer is to turn back the clock, to the Carnegie era or even the Victorian era. Take, for example, the anti-state liberal Matt Ridley. In *The Origins of Virtue* he argues that the state needs to be chopped back further to make space for the voluntary sector, because of the corrosive effect of public provision. In Britain, for example, he writes that "the welfare state and the mixed-economy 'corpocracy' replaced thousands of effective community institutions—friendly societies, mutuals, hospital trusts and more, all based on reciprocity and gradually nurtured virtuous circles of trust—with giant, centralized Leviathans like the National Health Service, nationalized industries and government quangos, all based on condescension . . . Heavy government makes people more selfish, not less." Things did not go quite so far in America, but similar arguments are often heard.

Yet the past golden ages of philanthropy ran out of steam in part because charity has limits. It could not deal with the scale of poverty in Renaissance Europe, so the state increasingly stepped in to tax and provide welfare, such as through the English Poor Law of 1601. Coram's Found-ling Hospital in eighteenth-century London helped many children, but it had to turn away more children than it accepted, deciding a child's fate by drawing lots. All the generosity of the Victorian philanthropists could only scratch the surface of social deprivation; President Herbert Hoover's voluntarist response to the Great Depression was too little and poorly targeted.

What is needed instead is a compact, a new "social contract" between the rich and everyone else. Like any contract, this will have two sides. For the rich, there should be a clear set of rules, so that they know what they must do in order to win society's acceptance. Call this the "Good Billionaire Guide." For everyone else, there should be a clear under-standing of how society will behave towards the rich if they abide by these rules (perhaps even including the circumstances in which politi-cians will refrain from populist billionaire bashing) and a strong, trans-parent regulatory system so that we can hold them to account.

Such a social contract would provide a basis for figuring out what is the most effective division of labor in solving major world problems, so that philanthropists, business, governments, NGOs, and citizens can form partnerships in which each plays the role to which it is best suited, and stays away from activities where it lacks the requisite talents or in-centives. For instance, philanthropists at their best can take the sort of big risks, and pursue long-term strategies, that others typically cannot or will not. What Carl Schramm, head of the Ewing Marion Kauffman Foundation, writing in the *Harvard Journal of Law and Public Policy* in 2006, called the role of "institutional entrepreneur," challenging other social institutions. Equally, even the fortunes of multibillionaires like Gates are dwarfed by government and big-business budgets, and some of society's largest problems are likely to be impossible to solve without the support, and the active involvement, of the citizenry. Saving the world will require everyone to play a part; philanthropists, even if they perform to the best of their abilities, will not be able to do it on their own.

In short, it is time to update Carnegie's ideas for the twenty-first cen-tury: the gospel of wealth 2.0.

IN THE AGE of philanthrocapitalism, what should it take for a billionaire to win the approval of society? Judging by some of the criticisms leveled even at Gates, it may be easier for a camel to pass through the eye of a needle than for a rich man to win three unqualified cheers from the public in the twenty-first century. That needs to change.

In the December 17, 2006, issue of the *New York Times Magazine*, Peter Singer, one of today's leading moral philosophers, questions whether Gates is generous enough. Noting Gates's belief that "all lives—no matter where they are being led—have equal value," Singer asks whether any of us could walk past a child drowning in a pond when we could save the child at little cost to ourselves. His unsurprising conclusion: "Even though we did nothing to cause the child to fall into the pond, almost everyone agrees that if we can save the child at minimal inconvenience or trouble to ourselves, we ought to do so." From this, Singer argues that, as much as Gates has done for the poor already, there is still more that he could do—and that not doing so is the same as leaving the child, or lots of children, in the pond to drown.

"His 66,000-square-foot high-tech lakeside estate near Seattle is reportedly worth more than $100 million," Singer observes. "Among his possessions is the Leicester Codex, the only handwritten book by Leonardo da Vinci still in private hands, for which he paid $30.8 million in 1994 . . . Are there no more lives that could be saved by living more modestly and adding the money thus saved to the amount he has already given?"

Like Carnegie, who urged the wealthy to "set an example of modest, unostentatious living, shunning display or extravagance," Singer seems to have little tolerance for the lavish lifestyles of the rich, even of those like Gates who are anything but flashy. Yet, he is surely too harsh on Gates, who is giving as fast as he can find effective ways to put his money to work. Singer would do better to direct his challenge at the many other superrich people who have yet to embark seriously on philanthropy, who could afford to give away millions or even billions of dollars without reaching the point where they have to make any lifestyle choices.

Of course, as the leaders of both China and India have warned their newly rich tycoons, ostentatious displays of wealth in countries where hundreds of millions of people still live in poverty may increase the risk of serious social instability. Yet rather than scold them to refrain from pleasure, far better to encourage them to engage in helping poorer people in more constructive ways.

One tycoon who understands what is at stake is Nandan Nilekani, the cochairman of Indian software giant Infosys: "In a country with as much stark poverty and income disparity as India and which has just tentatively embraced free market ideology, it becomes all the more critical that the rich embrace philanthropy," he says. "It is not only the moral and ethical thing to do. It is also vital to making entrepreneurial capitalism acceptable to the people as the best form for the economy. The rapid rise of philanthropy amongst India's business leaders is the fork in the road between India becoming a modern equitable free market democracy or going back to a stultifying socialistic state."

A truly fair social contract might actually allow the rich who give generously more grace than their peers to indulge themselves free from criticism in their yachts, space flights, and Rod Stewart–serenaded birthday parties. Philanthrocapitalism need not go hand-in-hand with puritanism.

Singer also makes the case that the rich should give away most of their money on the grounds that most of the credit for their wealth-creation belongs to society. The tycoon who says, "I created this wealth, it is my property, therefore it is entirely up to me to decide how much of it, if any, to give away," is wrong, argues Singer. Gates and other wealthy people have been able to earn their vast fortunes only because they live in favorable social circumstances, with abundant "social capital" (including the rule of law, an education system, high levels of trust between individuals, and so on). As "they don't create those circumstances by themselves," says Singer, society has a strong claim on much of their fortune, especially if the estimate he cites by economist Herbert Simon is right, that at least 90 percent of what people earn in wealthy societies is a product of "social capital."

Warren Buffett provides some support for this way of thinking, crediting America (and the particular moment in time when he was born there) for much of his success. "If you stick me down in the middle of Bangladesh or Peru, you will find out how much this talent is going to produce in the wrong kind of soil," as he puts it. If only we could test this proposition, and discover if Simon's 90 percent is right, by transporting Buffett back in time to begin his life all over again in Dhaka or Lima.

The 90 percent estimate is certainly controversial. There is little agreement among economists on how to measure social capital, let alone figure out how much it contributed to the success of a particular businessperson. Nor is it clear that, even if the 90 percent number is right, it provides sensible grounds for judging or guiding philanthropy.

Besides, it can reasonably be argued that society has a long-established process of charging people for the use of its social capital: taxation. Nowadays, in contrast to the mid-twentieth century, nobody in government thinks that the tax rate for wealthy people should be anywhere near 90 percent. Admittedly, this change of heart may owe more to the practical impossibility of collecting high rates of tax from people who can afford the best accountants and bankers to move their money around the world to wherever tax rates are lowest, than to fresh thinking about what the tax rate should be in theory.

Tax complicates the Good Billionaire Guide. Even the saint of rock, Bono, received a volley of abuse from politicians, the church, and NGOs when it was revealed that he had moved part of his business from his native Ireland to the Netherlands in order to pay less tax. His fall can only have been greater because he had climbed into the saddle of a moral high horse to demand that the Irish government spend more public money through the government aid agency Ireland Aid. Yet he is unrepentant. "Ireland's prosperity is very much driven by tax creativity, inventiveness," he explains. "It is completely in the spirit and letter of the law for U2 to be tax innovative. It's the culture. So, bollocks to those critics."

Certainly, illegal tax evasion is unacceptable for a philanthropist (except in extreme circumstances when the state is itself acting illegally or unjustly to expropriate your assets). Yet the nooks and crannies of the global tax system allow for perfectly legal tax-avoidance strategies that can sharply reduce a wealthy person's (or rock band's) payments to the state. Judging the generosity of a philanthropist must involve taking into account how much tax he pays; someone who pays a lot of tax can legitimately argue that they need do less voluntary giving to good causes. Beyond that, however, there are tricky choices to be made about how the billionaire divides his resources between giving privately and paying tax. Among the factors to be taken into account is how well the money would be used by the government compared with what would be done with it philanthropically.

Some critics go further than Singer. The trendy Slovenian Marxist psychoanalyst and philosopher. Slavoj Žižek, writing in the *London Review of Books*, has denounced even Gates's philanthropy as simply "a humanitarian mask hiding the underlying economic exploitation."

Admittedly, whatever Gates did in business, Žižek would see him as an exploiter—that's Marxism—but there is a more subtle argument here as well. Microsoft has had run-ins with the antitrust authorities in America and Europe. Has Gates earned his money through hard work or by exploiting monopoly power?

This question has been asked of many billionaires, including the world's first: Rockefeller's Standard Oil Company monopoly was eventually broken up by trustbusters. Yet the antitrust laws put in place to stop the likes of Rockefeller are Exhibit A in Gates's defense: the legal mechanisms to deal with anticompetitive practices have investigated Microsoft and imposed penalties, so Gates can argue that he has paid his dues.

More fundamentally, the success of Microsoft has clearly been primarily based on entrepreneurial creativity, and certainly not the monopolization of scarce preexisting assets, such as oil. Gates has not exploited his workers—many of whom have become millionaires—let alone put their lives in peril. While Microsoft may have enjoyed some monopoly power, it has always been exposed to dynamic competitors, from Apple to Google, which meant it had to keep innovating, reducing prices, and generally seeking to please its customers.

The rise of the knowledge economy means that a growing number of the new rich can plausibly claim to have made their fortunes without exploiting anyone—the Google guys being perhaps the example par excellence. In principle, that ought to make it easier for society to applaud them and any philanthropy they do. However, not all of today's new rich can brush off Žižek's critique so easily.

Hernando de Soto, the Peruvian economist whose bestseller *The Mystery of Capital* is a powerful call for capitalism to be redesigned to better include the poor, contrasts the form of capitalism in which Gates thrived with what passes for capitalism in many poor or badly run countries. "At the end of the day, the argument Bill Gates can use against anybody in the U.S. is 'you could have done it, too.' In America, there is equality of opportunity. But there is none in the developing world, where the rich have surrounded themselves with high walls," says de Soto. He argues that many of the rich in the developing world use power and patronage to make money, not productivity and efficiency.

Some of the wealthy oligarchs of the former Soviet Union, whom many critics believe in effect stole their businesses from the public during the mass privatizations of the early 1990s, seem to fall into this category. That makes it harder for society to judge their growing interest in philanthropy. All the giving in the world cannot wash away their sins. Yet perhaps some encouragement through the prospect of social redemption is in order, as it is surely better that they give the money to the needy than use it to further inflate the bank balances of already wealthy soccer stars.

ALTHOUGH HIS ARGUMENTS point to a more extreme conclusion, Singer ultimately recommends that the richest 0.01 percent of Americans (with an average income of $12.8 million a year) should give away one third of their income (presumably similar logic applies to their total wealth), with the proportion declining incrementally for less-well-off people. (The top 0.1 percent would give away 25 percent of their annual income; the top 1 percent would give 15 percent, and so on.) This is on the grounds that, he believes, it would generate enough money to eliminate world poverty. That is a bold claim, to say the least, and one that fails to address the need for money to solve a myriad of other problems besides poverty. Nonetheless, urging tycoons to give away one third of their fortunes seems a good rule of thumb for now; achievable enough for today's best philanthropists (Gates, Buffett, Soros) to pass with flying colors, but tough enough to provide a serious challenge to the great majority of other billionaires who have yet to seriously embrace philanthropy.

Yet not everyone is convinced that society should be encouraging its leading businesspeople to become philanthropists. Robert Barro, an economist at Harvard University, criticized Gates in the *Wall Street Journal*, accusing him of failing to appreciate properly the positive contribution that he had already made to human well-being, and arguing that his philanthropy will probably be a waste of money. Gates has no need to "give back," not least because he has already given so much by creating Microsoft, which, according to Barro's calculations, has already benefited humanity to the tune of "about one trillion dollars—or more than ten times his planned donations." Barro concludes, "By any reasonable calculation, Microsoft has been a boon for society and the value of its software greatly exceeds the likely value of Mr. Gates's philanthropic efforts."

Barro fears that Gates "may not understand the vital role wealth creation plays in society." Yet, as every good philanthrocapitalist should be,

Gates is into his capitalism just as much as his philanthropy: he simply believes there is a win-win to be had, doing good in creating wealth that can then be put to good use by giving it away. In his 2008 speech at Davos advocating "creative capitalism," he explained that "the genius of capitalism lies in its ability to make self-interest serve the wider interest. The potential of a big financial return for innovation unleashes a broad set of talented people in pursuit of many different discoveries. This system driven by self-interest is responsible for the great innovations that have improved the lives of billions." In other words, "It is not from the benevolence of the butcher, the brewer, or the baker that we expect our dinner, but from their regard to their own interest," as the great eighteenth-century economist Adam Smith put it in *The Wealth of Nations*.

Indeed, one of the insights that the newly rich philanthropists are bringing to their giving is an appreciation of the virtues of business. People such as Tom Hunter and organizations such as the Shell Foundation understand that job-creating economic growth is a far better way to help the majority of poor people than aid handouts. Pierre Omidyar and Jeff Skoll understand that finding a profitable way to tackle a social problem will often mean that the solution is scaled up far more quickly than when it is dependent on grants or changing government policy. Gates, Wal-Mart's Lee Scott, and G.E.'s Jeffrey Immelt, among others, also recognize that, in the past, business leaders have often failed to understand the role their firms play by meeting important social needs, and this lack of understanding has over the years meant that firms have missed many profitable opportunities to "do well by doing good."

Gates is surely right to argue for more effort to be made, by governments and business to create even more incentives—whether financial or in terms of positive public recognition of good behavior—to find market-based solutions to big problems. Yet, what Gates recognizes, and Barro apparently does not, is that for all its virtues, business cannot meet all society's needs. There is also a need and a responsibility to give, and the benefits for society from well-executed philanthropy are potentially huge.

Yet every successful businessman has a tricky decision to make as he considers becoming an active philanthropist; it is not just about when to stop accumulating money and start putting it to work, but whether the social good that results from spending his days focused on business is more or less than the good that would flow from instead spending the time focused on giving. One reason Gates felt comfortable about leaving Microsoft in 2008 to go full time at his foundation was that he believed his usefulness at the firm was declining fast and that "it was inevitable that at some point you would want younger people setting the technology of a software company . . . [So I am] creating an opportunity at Microsoft for other people to step in while I get to put more into what is sort of a new frontier."

The striking thing about many of today's booming "winner-take-all" industries, from software to finance to sport, is that people get to the top faster and careers at the top tend to be relatively short-lived. That is why a growing number of wealthy people are able to become philanthropists at a far younger age than in the past, and why they are probably right to devote much of their time to giving rather than trying to make more money.

Asked whether he thinks he will ultimately do more good for the world through Microsoft or his philanthropy, Gates says, "There isn't any clear math for these things." The personal computer certainly had a massive impact, but if Microsoft "hadn't come along, how much longer would it have been before someone else in the software industry did?" He now expects through his philanthropy to be part of something that will have an "unbelievably great" impact. "I don't think there is any measure which allows the two things to be compared. But I do think it shows how lucky I am to have been involved in two such phenomenal things."

IF GATES IS truly determined to give away his fortune, says Barro, instead of sticking to his current philanthropic plans he would do better to "cut a $300 check to everyone in the U.S., or donate the money to the U.S. Treasury with the aim of reducing the national debt." As for which appeals most to the economist; "Frankly, I would have preferred to get the $300 per person 'Gates Grants.' "

By assuming that Gates will inevitably squander his fortune through his philanthropy, Barro is drawing the wrong conclusion. Yet in highlighting those two alternative uses for Gates's money, Barro has thrown down a challenge to Gates and every other philanthrocapitalist. Can they do more good with the money than the government or the public at large? The case for philanthrocapitalism is that, yes, they can.

There are two conceptual problems, at least, with those $300 Gates Grants. First, if they were distributed without restrictions on how they were used, much of the money might simply be spent, not given to charity. Despite all the benefits that result from for-profit firms serving consumers, believe it or not, there are big problems that will not be solved just by marginally increasing American consumer spending—problems such as poverty in the developing world or one million deaths a year from malaria that Gates is addressing through his foundation.

What if people were required, instead, to give their Gates Grants to a charity? This might at least address a need that the market cannot solve. Yet the second problem, dispersing his money widely, would deprive Gates of his "hyperagency." Having a well-endowed foundation, and his other assets of celebrity and powerful connections, gives Gates the power to shape the problem-solving agenda in ways that small gifts cannot. There would not now be a global effort to eradicate malaria if Gates had not chosen to make that a goal of his foundation.

Is that hyperagency all it is cracked up to be? Can philanthropists really make better use of the money than government? The fact that many donors benefit from large tax breaks for giving means that this is the minimum acceptable level of performance by philanthropists, and that there is a direct public interest in ensuring that the money is well spent. In America in 2003, for example, foundations gave away $30 billion, but also collected $5 billion from tax breaks on the gifts they received and $15 billion through tax relief on their investment income.

Ultimately, Barro's criticism of Gates boils down to a belief that his philanthropic efforts to reduce poverty and eradicate diseases are unlikely to outperform previous government-led efforts: "Although Mr. Gates is probably smarter and more motivated than the typical World Bank bureaucrat, he likely won't do much better."

Yet this is prejudging a marathon at the end of the first mile. There is no a priori reason to assume that philanthropists will not be able to use their money to greater effect than governments. On the contrary, philanthropy has achieved many great things in the past—not least the billion-life-saving green revolution that Gates is now trying to reinvent in Africa—and armed with the leading exponents and cutting-edge methods of modern capitalism, there is every reason to think it can perform wonders again.

One way to ensure that it does is to change how society ranks philanthropists, away from a simplistic focus on how much they give. "I was appalled," wrote journalist Arianna Huffington in 1999, "to find the Slate 60 [ranking of top donors] citation that winemaker Robert G. Mondavi had dropped $20 million on the American Center for Wine, Food and the Arts in his hometown of Napa, Calif., only a click away from the news that Ron Burkle, Ted Forstmann, and John Walton gave $30 million to the Children's Scholarship Fund for low-income children." Huffington's response was to create a "Virtue Remix" of the Slate rankings, by awarding plus points for giving to poverty-related causes, giving time as well as money, and so on, and negative points for paying for buildings, having those buildings named after you, giving to privileged institutions, giving only in old age, and so on. While there is room to quibble with some of the assumptions behind Huffington's remix, she does have a point.

Ultimately, though, there is a need for rankings based on what philanthropists actually achieve with their giving. Among other things, that will require much greater transparency about what money is given to and how it is used, combined with serious impact analysis and public debate. Without such transparency, it will be no surprise if the public becomes increasingly skeptical about philanthropy's effectiveness and starts to demand tighter regulation, such as limits on foundation size, tighter rules on which activities are eligible for tax-exempt status, representation by beneficiary groups on foundation boards, and so on. That would not necessarily be a good thing: giving a greater role to legislators and bureaucrats is only likely to inhibit the imagination, innovation, and risk-taking that lie behind the best philanthropy. And tighter regulation is only likely to diminish the willingness of the wealthy to give. Striking the right balance between transparency, regulation, and freedom for philanthropists will be one of the trickier parts of the new social contract.

WHILE ONE KEY ingredient of philanthrocapitalism is the responsibility and willingness of economic winners to give on a large scale, another is that they apply to their giving the same talents, knowledge, and intellectual vigor that made them rich in the first place. Philanthrocapitalism is about being a businesslike giver.

Yet what it means to be businesslike is easily misunderstood. As management guru Jim Collins has written, "We must reject the idea—well intentioned, but dead wrong—that the primary path to greatness in the social sectors is to become more like a business." Being a businesslike giver does not mean trying to make NGOs and other organizations serving the public more like companies; it describes the way of thinking that a philanthrocapitalist should bring to solving society's biggest problems.

Whilst hopefully some of these problems will be solved using for-profit business models, many will not. But that does not mean they cannot be addressed in a businesslike way, in the sense of a serious focus on results; understanding where to use scarce resources to have the greatest impact through leverage; a determination to quickly scale up solutions that work and a toughness in shutting down those that do not; backing entrepreneurial, innovative approaches to problems; forming partnerships with whoever will get the job done soonest and best; and taking big risks in the hope of achieving outsize impact.

Mistakenly confusing being businesslike with becoming more like a business can cause people to worry unnecessarily about philanthrocapitalism, as is clear from *Just Another Emperor? The Myths and Realities of Philanthrocapitalism*, a book published in March 2008 by Michael Edwards, a veteran philanthrocrat at the Ford Foundation. Stressing that he was writing in a personal capacity, Edwards claims that "the philanthrocapitalists are drinking from a heady and seductive cocktail, one part 'irrational exuberance,' two parts believing that success in business equips them to make a similar impact on social change, a dash or two of the excitement that accompanies any new solution, and an extra degree of fizz from the oxygen of publicity that has been created by the Gates-Buffett marriage and the initiatives of ex-President Clinton."

Philanthrocapitalism, he concludes, is "in part a symptom of a profoundly unequal world. It hasn't yet demonstrated that it is the cure"; the "hype surrounding philanthrocapitalism runs far ahead of its ability to deliver real results"; and the "use of business thinking can damage civil society, which is the crucible of democratic politics and social transformation. It's time to differentiate the two and re-assert the independence of global citizen action."

Edwards makes several important points. He stresses the need for philanthrocapitalists to learn from people with experience in tackling society's big problems, echoing Mario Morino's concerns about top businesspeople failing to make the transition to successful philanthropist because of their arrogance and not-invented-here syndrome. He rightly notes the importance of understanding how social change takes place. He recognizes the need for philanthrocapitalists to be accountable to the public and for their activities to be transparent.

Yet Edwards wrongly asserts that philanthrocapitalism is "in danger of passing itself off as the whole solution, downgrading the costs and trade-offs of extending business and market principles into social transformation." One of the striking things about the leading philanthrocapitalists from Gates on down is that they do not see themselves as the whole solution, and are constantly looking to partner with governments, social entrepreneurs, NGOs, businesses, and mass movements to make change happen.

Largely because Edwards is fixated on an overly narrow definition of what it means for a philanthropist to be businesslike, he fails to grasp the potential of philanthrocapitalism, not least through these partnerships, and claims that the use of business and market thinking can "damage civil society." How does he square that with the businesslike efforts of George Soros to promote democracy around the world, or of Jeff Skoll to energize public opinion through his movies with a message, or of Richard Branson to add an innovative new institution, the Elders, to the global governance system?

The real worry about philanthrocapitalism is not that the new generation of big givers will be too businesslike, but that they will not be businesslike enough. If philanthrocapitalism is to succeed, it will be because these philanthropists take impact seriously and apply their business talents just as rigorously as they did when they made their money. That is easier said than done, not least because philanthropy lacks many of the market forces that keep businesspeople disciplined, focused on success, and willing to make the tough decisions necessary to survive and prosper.

It is easy to talk the philanthrocapitalistic talk, but incredibly hard to walk the walk. There are no barriers to calling yourself a venture philanthropist, for example, if you have some money to give and some spare time to spend "mentoring" your favorite charity executives. Yet, so far, few venture philanthropists have delivered the sort of results that would justify the comparison to venture capital: where is the venture philanthropy success to equal Google or dozens of other firms grown to massive scale by venture capital?

Perhaps that is the wrong definition of success in the philanthropic world, where the widespread adoption of an idea, rather than the creation of a large organization, may be reward enough. Yet where is the venture philanthropist who is truly trying to build a dominant global organization, paying top dollar for top talent (even if that means depriving other worthy organizations of essential staff), or trying to drive inefficient rivals out of the market? These traits are some of the key sources of success in venture capital.

Likewise, every philanthrocapitalist talks about the importance of leverage, and rightly so. For all their billions, their fortunes are dwarfed by those of their potential partners in government, businesses, and even sometimes large NGOs. The high hopes for philanthrocapitalism are based on the belief that the wealthy can be hyperagents, able to achieve impact far greater than their relative financial resources would suggest by targeting their dollars at tipping points or bottlenecks in the system to achieve maximum change. Partnership with government, business, or NGOs will be essential—but so will ensuring that any partnership is built on a sophisticated understanding of what each party is bringing to the alliance.

When it comes to the division of labor between philanthropists and the rest of society, there is no universal right answer or blueprint to turn to. For example, as Bill Clinton has pointed out, "How big a breach there is for philanthropy to fill depends on how effective public policy is at addressing the big problems facing us." That varies considerably from one government to the next.

And what potential partners want from philanthropists may not be the things that philanthropists can do best. In the penultimate episode of *The West Wing*, a favorite TV show of policy wonks, a multibillionaire Gates-like character tries to headhunt White House chief of staff C. J. Cregg to run his foundation. She initially declines, but urges him to build roads in Africa. There is plenty of evidence that roads and railways are good for an economy and good for poor people, but C. J.'s advice was wrong. Infrastructure is hugely expensive to build and costs a lot to maintain, as the English philanthropists in the Renaissance found out. All the philanthropic capital in the world could not build enough roads to make a real difference in Africa—and within five years they would be falling apart with no one to maintain them. Public and for-profit private capital should build roads.

To achieve leverage, philanthropists should not be competing with or substituting for government money; they should be trying to improve the way it is spent. Likewise, companies and NGOs will be only too happy to take a philanthropist's money, but they may be far less keen on the more valuable things the philanthropist can offer: insight and advice.

Nor is leverage just about resources. The state is better placed, for reasons of legal power and accountability, to do some things, like creating welfare systems that provide universal coverage with consistent standards and without discriminating against particular individual groups. By taking responsibility for the whole system, governments can also minimize bad incentives—for example, by ironing out poverty traps. Governments tend to be hopeless at risky innovation, on the other hand. Likewise, public companies are good at taking an idea that works and growing it fast to a massive scale, but they are less good at investing in ideas that have an uncertain or long-term payback.

Politicians have elections to worry about, company bosses their shareholders, and most NGOs are in constant fundraising mode. Philanthropists have no one to answer to but themselves (as Schramm says, they are "all assets and no liabilities"), and no time constraint other than the hopefully far-off moment of their death. As a result, they are more free than governments, public companies or NGOs to take big risks, to go against conventional wisdom, and to pursue strategies that will only ever pay off in the long-term.

This gives them huge opportunities, if they can get the details right. They can pilot risky projects that, once proven, governments can scale up—as has happened in New York under Mayor Michael Bloomberg. Indeed, other philanthrocapitalists might do well to follow in Bloomberg's footsteps by getting elected and then masterminding philanthropic leveraging of government from within. (Provided, like him, they can develop a thick skin.) Encouragingly, some reform-minded American mayors have started to follow Bloomberg's lead, even when they are not billionaires themselves. In impoverished Newark, for example, Mayor Cory Booker is getting philanthropists to pay for everything from better equipment for the police to new parks and charter schools. He has even recruited a philanthropy coordinator for City Hall.

Investing in activities that will not have a payback for many years is another huge opportunity, such as neglected areas in science and other research. It remains to be seen how many philanthrocapitalists will have what it takes to stay the course: just because they can take a longer-term perspective does not mean they will have the necessary discipline and determination. Another opportunity is to build up the social capital needed to generate jobs in poor countries, the payback on which has little appeal to politicians, being too diffuse compared with big announcements on government-to-government aid or debt reductions.

Creating market incentives for companies to do good—as Gates and the Children's Investment Fund Foundation, among others, have done with Big Pharma—is another opportunity that is only now being tapped. So, too, is investing in transforming activities that have traditionally been nonprofit into for-profit businesses that can grow much faster and reach many more people. Again, a thick skin may be required, as the nonprofit sector rarely appreciates having its old ways disrupted, as Pierre Omidyar found when his efforts to promote for-profit microfinance earned him a sniffy article in the *New Yorker* in which the world's most famous social entrepreneur and winner of the Nobel Peace Prize accused him of sucking the flesh and blood of the poor.

There are also big opportunities for philanthropists to step in to rectify government failures. American philanthropists giving to the developing world may be the best hope for restoring their country's battered international reputation, for example: in effect the privatization of soft power and public diplomacy. Philanthropists may be able to help more directly in international diplomacy too, including the effort to defeat international terrorism, not least by funding the sort of gatherings where political enemies can meet and talk that would cause a political storm were they organized by the government.

And, as both Richard Branson and Ted Turner have noticed, there may be huge opportunities for philanthropists in the current failings of the institutions of global governance—the solving of which is shockingly low on the agenda of the world's governments. To encourage them, the public should support formal roles being given to philanthropists in global governance, along the lines of the Gates Foundation seat on the board of the Global Fund to Fight AIDS, Tuberculosis and Malaria.

And, of course, there is the battle of ideas to be won. Philanthropists can provide a vital check and balance to often erroneous or ill-informed conventional wisdom by funding think tanks and even movements for social change, as Soros and Gates did with Bono's campaigning organization, DATA. Skoll's backing of films like Al Gore's *An Inconvenient Truth*, and Google's focus on Darfur, for example, have helped put neglected issues on society's agenda. This is where celanthropists have a particular edge: brand credibility. With the expansion of the global media, the causes that the world's leading celebrities support will have a growing reach. Yet again, though, as Soros has found—and other philanthrocapitalists no doubt will—taking a controversial position on a politically sensitive issue can expose you to an unpleasant amount of heat.

Will the new generation of philanthrocapitalists have the determination, persistence, and thick skin they need to make the most of these huge opportunities? After all, unlike back when the philanthropist was just an ambitious young business executive looking to make money, the incentives to do the hard stuff in philanthropy are incredibly weak. Philanthropists do not have to give their money away; their lifestyle will not suffer—it might even improve—if they keep their cash. And frankly, such is the way of the world that, if you are giving away money, there will always be plenty of people willing to don a black tie and tux in your honor, regardless of whether your money is achieving anything genuinely worthwhile.

Much will depend on whether the new philanthropic intermediaries, from New Philanthropy Capital to Bridgespan, succeed in making the world of giving more transparent and serious about measuring and debating impact. That in turn will depend on whether philanthropists are willing to volunteer accurate information about their performance, and especially their failures, when it is easier simply to talk about how much they have given and accept the plaudits.

In turn, the media, politicians, and civil society should engage constructively in the debate about the proper role and the impact of philanthropy—and if they are wise, philanthropists should encourage and lead that debate, rather than wait until something (presumably bad) makes them the subject of it. Philanthrocapitalists are destined be increasingly important public figures; so they had better get used to it.

The bottom line is that philanthrocapitalists have a remarkable opportunity to play a leading role in solving the biggest problems facing our world. That, and the constructive support and engagement with them of society, ought to be enough to motivate many of the richest people on the planet to put their money and talents at the service of the public and to do the businesslike hard work that will be needed to ensure their giving achieves its massive potential.

FAR ABOVE THE earth, Paul Hewson, the secretary general of the United Nations formerly known as Bono, is entertaining the crowd with a few of his old tunes. "I still haven't found what I'm looking for," he croons. "I have," Gates thinks, as he raises a glass of champagne. He has big news to share of the latest success of the philanthrocapitalism revolution. "I am proud to tell you that this year's World Development Report will confirm that malaria has been eradicated from the planet," he tells his guests. He pauses. "So, what shall we tackle next?"

# Acknowledgments

When we began to write this book, we had no idea what we had taken on. That we have completed it is the result of the help and encouragement of many people. We are grateful to them all, especially those who we have forgotten to list here and, no doubt, have been embarrassed to remember just after printing began.

We would like to thank in particular John Micklethwait, the editor in chief of the *Economist*; Joel Fleishman and the staff of the Terry Sanford Institute at Duke University; and the Department for International Development, for making it possible for us to write this book, and our colleagues, friends, and family for all their patience and encouragement. All errors are entirely our own.

John Turner, Joel Fleishman, Nick Lea, Holly Finn, Charles Handy, Alvaro Rodriguez Arregui, Victoria Penfield, Alice Jacobs, Tom Easton, Andrew Cave, Paul Innes, Karen Ford, Laurie Joshua, and Michael Borowitz have read drafts of some or all of the book, and made helpful comments. Nick Trautwein of Bloomsbury Press was a terrific editor. So was Barbara Beck, who encouraged and edited the *Economist* special report "The Business of Giving"—the foundation on which this book is built. Our agent, Daniel Mandel, was a constant source of good advice and positive thinking. Rosemarie Ward and Rebecca Feinberg provided invaluable research support.

John Lotherington and the 21st Century Trust held a particularly useful conference on the new philanthropy in April 2007. Events and seminars such as those on philanthropy at the World Economic Forum, the UBS Philanthropy Forum, the Skoll World Forum on Social Entrepreneurship, the Schwab Foundation annual summits, the annual meetings of the Association of Charitable Trusts and the Council on Foundations, the Brookings Blum Roundtable and the Global Philanthropy Forum provided many insights. So did conferences organized by students at Columbia Business School and Harvard Business School.

We would also like to thank, in no particular order, Sylvia McLain, Dambisa Moyo, Nick Cull, Martina Gmur, Owen Barder, Alison Staples, members of the Forum of Young Global Leaders, Julia Chandler, Nosheen Hashemi, Elizabeth Lawrence, Louise Katsiaouni, Christopher McNall, Diana Glassman, Justin Hendrix, Edward Carr, Iain Carson, John Smutniak, Daniel Franklin, Clive Crook, Jane Sautter and her colleagues at GTZ, Kim Samuel Johnson, Christina Barrineau, Mark Campanale, Elmira Bayrasli, Mike Battcock, David and Jenny Warbrick, Jennifer Robinson, Krista Parris, Myles Wickstead, Charlotte Morgan, Sir Gordon Conway, Musa Okwunga, Olga Alexeeva, Amar Bhide, Katherine Tran, Liesl Schillinger, Frances Burns, Ellen Gonda, Graham Kings, Melynn Glusman, Barry Varela, and, last but by no means least, Michelle Savage.

Finally, thanks to Yo! Sushi in Victoria Station, the British Library, and Charlie's Bar, Durham, North Carolina.

# Source Notes

This book would not have been possible without interviews and conversations, on and off the record, over many years with practicing philanthropists, including in no particular order: Bill Gates, Ted Turner, Bill Clinton, George Soros, Bono, Pierre Omidyar, Jeff Skoll, Sir Richard Branson, Angelina Jolie, Michael Bloomberg, David Rockefeller, Sir Evelyn de Rothschild, Lady Lynn Forester de Rothschild, Peggy Dulany, Jamie Cooper-Hohn, Howard Buffett, Nandan Nilekani, Mario Morino, Gavyn Davies, Lord Joel Joffe, Stephen Dawson, Noosheen Hashemi, Laurene Powell Jobs, Sir Tom Hunter, Stephanie Shirley, James Martin, Laura Arrillaga-Andreessen, Louise Blouin MacBain, Eli Broad, Peggy Dulany, Azim Premji, Mark Benioff, Arpad Busson, Kim Samuel Johnson, John Studzinski, Martin Varsavsky, Shakira, Steven Hilton, Douglas Miller, Fred Matser, Mo Ibrahim, D. K. Matai, Jack Hidary, Ray Chambers, Amy Robbins, Ramez Sousou, Alan Hassenfeld, Stanley Fink, Steve Schwarzman, Roger Hertog, Sir Ronald Cohen, Jon Corzine, Charly Kleissner, Sir Nicholas Ferguson, Nigel Morris, Barry Appleton, Jim O'Neill, Cherie Nursalim, Vinod Khosla, Victor Pinchuk, John Doerr, Ken Fisher, John Whitehead, Carlos Slim Helú, Peter Diamandis, Alberto Vilar, and Uday Khemka.

We have also spoken with many people who work with, study, or comment on the philanthropists. Although the list is too long to include everyone who has given us their valuable time and insights, it includes Patty Stonesifer, Larry Brilliant, Kurt Hoffman, Mary Robinson, Joel Klein, David Blood, Muhammad Yunus, Tom Vander Ark, Bobby Shriver, Steve Gunderson, Judith Rodin, Trevor Nielson, Jamie Drummond, Melissa Berman, Doug Bauer, Diana Aviv, Andrew Hind, Adam Meyerson, Jeffrey Sachs, Amir Dossal, Peter Singer, Linda Rottenberg, Peter Kellner, Hernando de Soto, Diana Leat, Phil Buchanan, Carlos Danel, Bill Drayton, William Zabel, Paul Schervish, Lester Salomon, Joan Di Furia, Vartan Gregorian, Luc Tayart de Borms, Sam Jonah, Volker Then, David Green, David Carrington, Pamela Hartigan, John Elkington, Geoff Mulgan, Rowena Young, Larry Mone, Lael Brainerd, Alex Nicholls, Rob John, Fritz Mayer, Robert

Dufton, Carl Schramm, Etienne Eichenberger, Felicitas von Peter, Charles Mac-
Cormack, Thomas Tierney, Bruce Lindsay, Michael E. Porter, Mark Kramer,
Katherine Fulton, John Bryant, Charles Handy, Teresa Lloyd, Andras Szanto, Ma-
bel van Oranje, Caroline Casey, Karim Kawar, Greg Dees, Bunker Roy, Ira Maga-
ziner, Rick Beckett, John Needham, Brizio Biondi Morra, Jane Wales, Sally
Osberg, Thomas Eymond-Laritaz, Jacqueline Novogratz, Vanessa Kirsch, George
Overholser, Clara Miller, Jeroo Billimoria, Nick Moon, Martin Fisher, Nancy
Lublin, Bruce McNamer, John Wood, Martin Brookes, Maximilian Martin, Nigel
Harris, Ian Davis, Lynn Taliento, and Mikhail Saakashvili.

The *Chronicle of Philanthropy* is the only dedicated journal in this field, al-
though the expanding literature on the nongovernmental sector as a whole is
increasingly focused on philanthropy, particularly the *Stanford Social Innovation
Review, Alliance* magazine, *Innovations* magazine, and the *Harvard Business Re-
view.* We have also drawn on articles from the *Economist,* the *New York Times,
Slate, Time,* the *Wall Street Journal,* the *London Review of Books,* the *Financial
Times, Foreign Affairs,* the *Los Angeles Times,* the *Independent,* the *Guardian,* the
*Observer,* the *Daily Telegraph, Fortune, Portfolio, Business Week,* the *Lancet, Foreign
Affairs,* and *Forbes.* We also drew on Charlie Rose's conversations with Bill Gates
and Warren Buffett on PBS's *Charlie Rose Show.*

We have also drawn on the following:

Archer, I. W. *The Pursuit of Stability: Social Relations in Elizabethan London.*
    Cambridge, UK: Cambridge University Press, 2003.
Association of Chief Executives of Voluntary Organisations. *Surer Funding,* 2004.
Atkinson, A. B., and W. Salverda. "Top Incomes in the Netherlands and the
    United Kingdom Over the Twentieth Century." *Journal of the European
    Economic Association* 3, no. 4:883–913.
Badgett, M. V. Lee, and N. Cunningham, "Gay Philanthropy: Giving and Volun-
    teering by Gay, Lesbian, Bisexual, and Transgender People." *The Policy Jour-
    nal of the Institute for Gay and Lesbian Strategic Studies* 3, no. 1 (May 1998).
Baumol, William J., Robert E. Litan, and Carl J. Schramm. *Good Capitalism, Bad
    Capitalism and the Economics of Growth and Prosperity.* New Haven, CT:
    Yale University Press, 2007.
Baumol, William J., and W. G. Bowen. "Performing Arts—the Economic
    Dilemma." *International Review of the Aesthetics and Sociology of Music* 4,
    no. 1 (June 1973): 137–39
Benioff, M., with Karen Southwick. *Compassionate Capitalism: How Corporations
    Can Make Doing Good an Integral Part of Doing Well.* Franklin Lakes, NJ:
    Career Press, 2004.
Benioff, M., with Carlyle Adler. *The Business of Changing the World.* New York:
    McGraw-Hill, 2006.

Bernstein, P. L. *Capital Ideas: the Improbable Origins of Modern Wall Street*. New York: The Free Press, 1993.

Bernstein, P. W., and A. Swan. *All the Money in the World: How the Forbes 400 Make—and Spend—Their Fortunes*. New York: Knopf, 2007.

Beveridge, William. *Voluntary Action: A Report on Methods of Social Advance*, 1948.

Bishop, M. "The New Wealth of Nations." *Economist*, June 2001.

———. "The Business of Giving." *Economist*, February 2006.

Bornstein, David. *How to Change the World*. New York: Oxford University Press, 2007.

Bourdillon, A. F. C. *Voluntary Social Services: Their Place in the Modern State*. London: Methuen, 1945.

Brainard, Lael, and Derek Chollet. *Global Development 2.0: Can Philanthropists, the Public, and the Poor Make Poverty History?* Washington, D.C.: Brookings Institution Press, 2008.

Breeze, Beth. *Investment Matters: In Search of Better Charity Asset Management*. Institute for Philanthropy, 2008.

Bremner, Robert H. *American Philanthropy (The Chicago History of American Civilization)*. Chicago: The University of Chicago Press, 1988.

Bremner, Robert H. *Giving: Charity and Philanthropy in History*. Edison, NJ: Transaction Publishers, 1994.

Brewer, J., and S. Staves, *Early Modern Conceptions of Property*. New York: Routledge, 1996.

Brooks, A. *Who Really Cares?: The Surprising Truth About Compassionate Conservatism*. New York: Basic Books, 2006.

Brown, E. R. *Rockefeller Medicine Men: Medicine and Capitalism in America*. Berkeley, CA: University of California Press, 1981.

Burlingame, O. F., ed. *The Responsibilities of Wealth*. Bloomington, IA: Indiana University Press, 1992.

Cannadine, David. *Mellon: An American Life*. New York: Vintage, 2008.

Carnegie, Andrew. *The Gospel of Wealth*. Bedford, MA: Applewood Books, 1998.

Carroll, C. D. "Why do the rich save so much?" in *Does Atlas Shrug? The Economic Consequences of Taxing the Rich*. J. B. Slemrod. Cambridge, MA: Harvard University Press, 2000.

Charities Aid Foundation. *International Comparisons of Charitable Giving*, November 2006.

Checkland, O. "Philanthropy in Victorian Scotland: Social Welfare and the Voluntary Principle," *Journal of Social History*, 40, no. 2, Winter 2006.

Chernow, R. *Titan: The Life of John D. Rockefeller, Sr.* New York: Vintage Books, 1999.

Clark, G. *A Farewell to Alms: A Brief Economic History of the World*. Princeton, NJ: Princeton University Press, 2007.

Clinton, William J. *Giving: How Each of Us Can Change the World.* New York: Knopf, 2007.

Cohen, R. *The Second Bounce of the Ball: Turning Risk into Opportunity.* London: Weidenfeld and Nicolson, 2007.

Collier, P. *The Bottom Billion: Why the Poorest Countries are Failing and What Can Be Done About It.* New York: Oxford University Press, 2007.

Collins, Jim. *Good to Great in the Social Sectors.* New York: HarperCollins, 2005.

Cooch, S., and M. Kramer. *Compounding Impact: Mission Investing by US Foundations.* FSG Social Advisors, 2007.

Cowen, T. *Good and Plenty: The Creative Successes of American Arts Funding.* Princeton, NJ: Princeton University Press, 2006.

Critchlow, D. K., and C. H. Parker, eds. *With Us Always: A History of Private Charity and Public Welfare.* Rowman & Littlefield, 1998.

Crook, C. "The Good Company," *Economist,* January 2005.

Crossen, C. *The Rich and How They Got That Way.* London: Nicholas Brealey Publishing, 2001.

Crutchfield, Leslie, and Heather McLeod Grant. *Forces for Good: The Six Practices of High-Impact Nonprofits.* San Francisco, CA: Jossey-Bass, 2008.

Cunningham, H., and J. Innes. *Charity, Philanthropy and Reform from the 1690s to 1850.* New York: Palgrave Macmillan, 1998.

Damon, W., and S. Verducci. *Taking Philanthropy Seriously: Beyond Noble Intentions to Responsible Giving.* Bloomington, IN: Indiana University Press, 2006.

Davies, J. K. *Wealth and the Power of Wealth in Classical Athens.* New York: Beaufort Books, 1981.

Derrida, Jacques. *Given Time: I. Counterfeit Money.* Chicago: University of Chicago Press, 1992.

Domhoff, G. William. *Who Rules America? Power, Politics, & Social Change.* New York: McGraw-Hill, 2002.

Donnachie, I. *Robert Owen: Social Visionary.* Edinburgh: John Donald Publishers, 2005.

Easterly, W. *The White Man's Burden.* New York: Oxford University Press, 2006.

Edwards, L. *A Bit Rich? What the Wealthy Think About Giving.* London: Institute for Public Policy Research, 2002.

Edwards, Michael. *Just Another Emperor? The Myths and Realities of Philanthrocapitalism.* London: Demos, 2008.

Elkington, J., and P. Hartigan. *The Power of Unreasonable People: How Social Entrepreneurs Create Markets that Change the World.* Cambridge, MA: Harvard Business School Press, 2008.

Faux, J. *The Global Class War: How America's Bipartisan Elite Lost Our Future— and What It Will Take to Win It Back.* Hoboken, NJ: Wiley, 2006.

Feng, B., and J. Krehely. *The Waltons and Wal-Mart: Self-interested Philanthropy.*

Fleishman, Joel. *The Foundation: A Great American Secret.* Cambridge, MA: Perseus Books Group, 2007.

Foundation Center, *Foundation Giving Trends 2008: Update on Funding Priorities,* February 2008.

Frank, Robert. *Richistan.* New York: Three Rivers Press, 2008.

Frank, Robert F., and Philip Cook. *The Winner-Take-All Society.* New York: Penguin Books, 1995.

Franklin, D. "Just Good Business." *Economist,* January 2008.

Friedmen, L. J., and M. D. McGarvie, eds. *Charity, Philanthropy and Civility in American History.* Cambridge, UK: Cambridge University Press, 2003.

Frumkin, Peter. *Strategic Giving: The Art and Science of Philanthropy.* Chicago: University of Chicago Press, 2006.

Fulton, K., with A. Blau, *Looking Out for the Future: An Orientation for Twenty-first-Century Philanthropists.* Monitor Group, March 2005.

Gaudiani, C. *The Greater Good: How Philanthropy Drives the American Economy and Can Save Capitalism.* New York: Henry Holt, 2003.

Geremek, Bronislaw. *Poverty: a History,* trans. by Agnieszka Kolakowska. Oxford: Blackwell, 1994.

Gray, B. Kirkman. *A History of English Philanthropy: From the Dissolution of the Monasteries to the Taking of the First Census.* Whitefish, MT: Kessinger Publishing, 2007.

Gray, B. Kirkman. *Philanthropy and the State, or Social Politics.* London: P. S. King, 1908.

Griffin, C. S. *Their Brothers' Keepers: Moral Stewardship in the United States, 1800–65.* New Brunswick, NJ: Rutgers University Press, 1960.

Hamer, John H. *America, Philanthropy and the Moral Order.* Lewistown, NY: Edwin Mellen Press, 2002.

Hands, A. R. *Charities and Social Aid in Greece and Rome: Aspects of Greek and Roman Life.* Ithaca, NY: Cornell University Press, 1968.

Handy, Charles and Elizabeth. *The New Philanthropists.* London: Random House UK, 2006.

Harris, J. *Unemployment and Politics: A Study in English Social Policy 1886–1914.* New York: Oxford University Press, 1984.

Hill, Christopher. *Society and Puritanism in Pre-Revolutionary England.* New York: St. Martin's Press, 1997.

Himmelfarb, Gertrude. *The Roads to Modernity: The British, French and American Enlightenments.* New York: Vintage, 2005.

HM Treasury. *The Future Role of the Third Sector in Social and Economic Regeneration: Final Report.* December 2006.

Hudson Institute. *Index of Global Philanthropy 2007.*

Ilchman, W. F., S. N. Katz, and E. L. Queen. *Philanthropy in the World's Traditions*. Bloomington, IN: Indiana University Press, 1998.

John, R., R. Davies, and L. Mitchell, *Give and Let Give: Building a Culture of Philanthropy in the Financial Services Industry*. London: Policy Exchange, 2007.

Jordan, W. K. *Philanthropy in England 1480–1660: A Study of the Changing Pattern of English Social Aspirations*. London: George Allen and Unwin, 1959.

Jutte, R. *Poverty and Deviance in Early Modern Europe*. Cambridge, UK: Cambridge University Press, 1994.

Kennedy, C. *The Merchant Princes*. London: Hutchinson, 2000.

Kent, Phil. *Foundations of Betrayal: How the Liberal Super-Rich Elite Undermine America*. Winston Salem, NC: Zoe Publications, 2007.

Landes, David. *Dynasties: Fortunes and Misfortunes of the World's Great Family Businesses*. New York: Viking, 2006.

Lansley, S. *Rich Britain*. Hampshire, U.K.: Politicos, 2006.

Lewis, H. *Are the Rich Necessary? Great Economic Arguments and How They Reflect Our Personal Values*. Mount Jackson, VA: Axios Press, 2007.

Little, Lester K. *Religious Poverty and the Profit Economy in Medieval Europe*. Ithaca, NY: Cornell University Press, 1978.

Lloyd, Theresa. *Why Rich People Give*. Association of Charitable Foundations, 2004.

Lundberg, F. *The Rich and the Super Rich: A Study in the Power of Money Today*. New York: Lyle Stuart, 1998.

Malone, Mike. *Bill & Dave: How Hewlett and Packard Built the World's Greatest Company*. Portfolio Hardcover, 2007.

Martin, M., and R. John, *Venture Philanthropy in Europe: Landscape and Driving Principles*. Oxford, U.K.: Saïd Business School, 2006.

Menning, Carol B. *Charity and State in Late Renaissance Italy: The Monte di Pieta of Florence*. Ithaca, NY: Cornell University Press, 1993.

Miller, G. *The Mating Mind: How Sexual Choices Shaped the Evolution of Human Nature*. New York: Anchor Books, 2001.

Miller, John J. *A Gift of Freedom: How the John M. Olin Foundation Changed America*. San Francisco, CA: Encounter Books, 2006.

Miskimin, H. A. *The Economy of Later Renaissance Europe 1460–1600*. Cambridge, UK: Cambridge University Press, 1977.

Mulgan, Geoff, and Charles Landry. *The Other Invisible Hand: Remaking Charity for the 21st Century*. London: Demos, 1995.

Murphy, Cullen. *Are We Rome?* New York: Mariner Books, 2007.

Nasaw, David. *Andrew Carnegie*. New York: The Penguin Press, 2006.

Nicholls, Alex, ed. *Social Entrepreneurship: New Models of Sustainable Social Change*. New York: Oxford University Press, 2006.

O'Clery, Conor. *The Billionaire Who Wasn't: How Chuck Feeney Secretly Made and Gave Away a Fortune*. New York: PublicAffairs, 2007.

O'Reilly, Bill. *Culture Warrior*. New York: Broadway Books, 2007.

Odendahl, T. *Charity Begins At Home: Generosity and Self-interest Among the Philanthropic Elite*. New York: Basic Books, 2001.

Orton, M., and K. Rowlingson. *Public Attitudes to Economic Inequality*. York, U.K.: Joseph Rowntree Foundation, 2007.

Ostrower, Francie. *Why the Wealthy Give*. Princeton, NJ: Princeton University Press, 1997.

Owen, David, *English Philanthropy 1660–1960*. Cambridge, MA: Harvard University Press, 1964.

*Oxford Dictionary of National Biography*. New York: Oxford University Press, 2004.

Peston, Robert. *Who Runs Britain? How the Super-Rich Are Changing Our Lives*. London Hodder and Stoughton, 2008.

Phillips, Kevin. *Wealth and Democracy: A Political History of the American Rich*. New York: Broadway Books, 2002.

Picard, Liza. *Elizabeth's London*. New York: St. Martin's Press, 2005.

———. *Doctor Johnson's London*. New York: St. Martin's Press, 2002.

———. *Victorian London*. New York: St. Martin's Press, 2007.

Piketty, Thomas, and Emmanuel Saez. *The Evolution of Top Incomes: A Historical and International Perspective*. Cambridge, MA: National Bureau of Economic Research Working Paper 11955, 2006.

Poynter, J. R. *Society and Pauperism*. Melbourne University Press, 1969.

Prochaska, Frank, *The Voluntary Impulse: Philanthropy in Modern Britain*. London: Faber, 1988.

Reich, Robert. *Supercapitalism: The Transformation of Business, Democracy, and Everyday Life*. New York: Knopf, 2007.

Ridley, Matthew. *The Origins of Virtue*. London: Penguin Books Ltd, 1996.

Rosenthal, J. T. *The Purchase of Paradise: Gift Giving and the Aristocracy 1307–1485*. London: Routledge and Keegan Paul, 1972.

Rothkopf, David. *Superclass: The Global Power Elite and the World They Are Making*. New York: Farrar, Straus and Giroux, 2008.

Rubinstein, William D. *Men of Property: The Very Wealthy in Britain Since the Industrial Revolution*. New Brunswick, NJ: Rutgers University Press, 1981.

Sachs, Jeffrey D. *The End of Poverty: Economic Possibilities for Our Time*. New York: Penguin Press, 2005.

Sala-i-Martin, X. "The World Distribution of Income (estimated from individual country distributions)," NBER Working Paper No. W8933, 2002.

Salomon, L. M., S. W. Sokolowski, and R. List. *Global Civil Society: An Overview*. Baltimore, MD: Johns Hopkins University, Centre for Civil Society Studies, 2003.

Sampson, Anthony. *Who Runs This Place?: The Anatomy of Britain in the 21st Century*. London: John Murray, 2005.

Schneewind, J. B, ed. *Giving: Western Ideas of Philanthropy.* Bloomington, IN: Indiana University Press, 1996.

Schramm, Carl J. "Law Outside the Market: the Social Utility of the Private Foundation." *Harvard Journal of Law and Public Policy,* Fall 2006.

Schwab, K. "Global Corporate Citizenship: Working with Governments and Civil Society," *Foreign Affairs,* Jan/Feb. 2008.

Simey, M. *Charity Rediscovered: A Study of Philanthropic Effort in Nineteenth-Century Liverpool.* Liverpool, U.K.: Liverpool University Press, 1992.

Simon, William E. *A Time for Truth.* Reader's Digest Association. 1978.

Slack, P. *Poverty and Policy in Tudor and Stuart England.* London: Longman, 1988.

Smith, A. *An Inquiry into the Nature and Causes of the Wealth of Nations* 1776. A facsimile of the first edition with an introduction by Edwin Connor, Chicago: University of Chicago Press, 1977.

Smith, A. *The Theory of Moral Sentiments.* Amherst, NY: Prometheus Books, 2000.

Sobel, Dava. *Longitude: The True Story of a Lone Genius Who Solved the Greatest Scientific Problem of His Time.* New York: Walker and Company, 2005.

Soros, George. *The Age of Fallibility: Consequences of the War on Terror.* New York: PublicAffairs, 2006.

Tayart de Borms, L. *Foundations: Creating Impact in a Globalised World.* Cornwall, U.K.: Wiley, 2005.

Tayart de Borms, L. and N. McDonald. *Philanthropy in Europe: A Rich Past, a Promising Future.* London: Alliance Publishing Trust, 2008.

Titmuss, Richard. *The Gift Relationship: From Human Blood to Social Policy.* New York: New Press, 1997.

Traub, J. *The Best Intentions: Kofi Annan and the UN in the Era of American World Power.* New York: Picador, 2006.

Weaver, W. *U.S. Philanthropic Foundations.* New York: Harper & Row, 1967.

Weill, S., with J. Kraushaar, *The Real Deal: My Life in Business and Philanthropy.* New York: Warner Business Books, 2006.

West, D. *Angelina, Mia and Bono: Celebrities and International Development.* Washington, D.C.: The Brookings Institution, 2007.

Wolff, E. *Top Heavy: The Increasing Inequality of Wealth in America and What Can Be Done About It.* New York: New Press, 2002.

Woolf, S. *The Poor in Western Europe in the Eighteenth and Nineteenth Centuries.* London: Routledge, 1986.

Wooster, M. M. *The Great Philanthropists and the Problem of "Donor Intent"* Washington, D.C.: Capital Research center, 2007.

Wooster, M. M. *Great Philanthropic Mistakes.* Washington, D.C.: Hudson Institute, 2006.

Wood, J. *Leaving Microsoft to Change the World: An Entrepreneur's Odyssey to Educate the World's Children.* New York: HarperCollins, 2007.

# Index